THE CHALLENGE OF
HONG KONG'S
REINTEGRATION
WITH CHINA

香港回歸中國之挑戰

THE CHALLENGE OF HONG KONG'S REINTEGRATION WITH CHINA

香港回歸中國之挑戰

edited by Ming K. Chan

陳明錄　編著

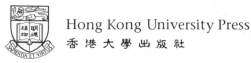

Hong Kong University Press
香港大學出版社

Hong Kong University Press
The University of Hong Kong
Pokfulam Road, Hong Kong

© Hong Kong University Press 1997

ISBN 962 209 441 4

Printed in Hong Kong by Kings Time Printing Press Ltd.

Contents

Contributors

John P. BURNS is Chair Professor of Politics and Public Administration, the University of Hong Kong. Recent publications include *Asian Civil Service Systems: Improving Efficiency and Productivity* (editor, 1994).

Ming K. CHAN is a member of the History Department, the University of Hong Kong. Concurrently, he is executive coordinator of the Hong Kong Documentary Archives, Hoover Institution, Stanford University. His recent books include *The Hong Kong Basic Law: Blueprint for "Stability and Prosperity" under Chinese Sovereignty?* (co-editor, 1991), *Precarious Balance: Hong Kong Between China and Britain, 1842–1992* (editor, 1994), *The Hong Kong Reader: Passage to Chinese Sovereignty* (co-editor, 1996). He is general editor of the *Hong Kong Becoming China: The Transition to 1997* multi-volume series.

Alison W. CONNER teaches at the University of Hawaii School of Law. She was formerly a member of the Faculty of Law, the University of Hong Kong from 1986 through 1994. She has written extensively on Chinese legal history and modern Chinese law.

Mei-ling FUNG is an M. Phil student in the Department of Sociology, the University of Hong Kong whose field of study is immigrant Chinese in contemporary Canada.

Chin-Chuan LEE is Professor of Journalism and Communication at the Chinese University of Hong Kong and the University of Minnesota. Among his English publications are *Mass Media and Political Transition: The Hong Kong Press in China's Orbit* (co-author, 1991), *Sparking a Fire: The Press and the Ferment of Democratic Change in Taiwan* (1993), and *China's Media, Media's China* (editor, 1994).

Janet SALAFF is Professor of Sociology, University of Toronto, Canada. Her publications include *Working Daughters of Hong Kong: Filial Piety or Power in the Family?* (1981 & 1995), *State and Family in Singapore: Structuring an Industrial Society* (1988), and *Cowboys and Cultivators: the Chinese of Inner Mongolia* (1993).

Alvin Y. SO is Professor of Sociology, University of Hawaii. His recent publications include *Hong Kong-Guangdong Link: Partnership in Flux* (co-editor, 1995).

James T.H. TANG is a member of the Department of Politics and Public Administration, the University of Hong Kong. His books include *Britain's Encounter with Revolutionary China, 1949–1954* (1992), and *Human Rights and International Relations in the Asian Pacific Region* (editor, 1995).

Siu-lun WONG is Professor of Sociology and Director of the Centre of Asian Studies at the University of Hong Kong. He is a Hong Kong Affairs Adviser, and a member of the Selection Committee of the First SAR Government of Hong Kong. He is the author of *Emigrant Entrepreneurs: Shanghai Industrialists in Hong Kong* (1988), and co-editor of *Hong Kong's Transition: A Decade After The Deal* (1995).

Foreword

One Country as a Changed System

Hong Kong's integration with China is also China's with Hong Kong. The centralist revolution of the People's Republic is slowly ending because of trends on the mainland that officials there did not fully intend. As Communist Party conservatives fear, the "Hong Kong breeze" (*Gang feng*) contributes mightily to this current. The Beijing government's policies in Hong Kong, alternating between modern reformism and patronizing traditionalism, reflect a much wider politics pervading the whole country.

At the time of the 1997 handover, there was a sharp division of views about Hong Kong. Optimists predicted minimum change in the city's lifestyle and prosperity. Pessimists foresaw a quasi-feudal, clientelist style of politics and a loss of Hong Kong's economic vitality (especially to Shanghai). Yet a medial view is probably a more accurate prediction than either the optimists or the pessimists suggest — because China haltingly changes, too.

Hong Kong already became more effectively Chinese in 1989. The territory's politics were more "nationalized" then, not because most of its citizens chose this transformation, but because Tiananmen reminded them that they deeply care how the Chinese government rules. No country's public life is either wholly economic or wholly political, despite the different emphases on these points by optimists and pessimists respectively. Oversight of the economy, for Hong Kong people as for citizens in any other modern place, is a crucial aspect of government. So is responsible freedom.

Liberal pessimists in Hong Kong emphasize political values; economistic optimists stress material needs. But why should people in this city want to choose between rights and well-being? They will opt for both. In China too, the reform boom has diversified people's occupations and created higher per-capita incomes in large parts of the country. Occupational diversity in the PRC has greatly expanded. Although Hong Kong is economically the richest and politically the liveliest city in China, many other coastal places and a few inland ones are catching up quickly. Hong Kong is not alone, as a modern Chinese center of both politics and growth.

The China that Hong Kong joins is post-revolutionary. It may in the future become post-Leninist or more admittedly corporatist. The People's Republic will not become a procedural democracy overnight (if only because no country is wholly democratic). But on occasion, its leaders have suggested that national elections might be advisable — for some later generation. The "Basic Law" specifies 2007 as a year by which the methods of selecting Hong Kong's Legislative Council and Chief Executive might be amended. A democratic ideal has infected China, as well as Hong Kong. As the editor of this volume has written elsewhere, "Increasingly, Party leaders in southern provinces do not fear democratic elections. This process of liberalization may also be facilitated by deepening Cantonese and southern regional solidarity vis-à-vis Beijing rulers."[1]

There is much reason for pessimism, or for dissident demonstrations, in the short term after the mid-1997 transition. But in the medium term, a spate of reform leadership is overdue in Beijing. Hu Yaobang may have died and Zhao Ziyang may have retired, but their constituencies within the Chinese Communist Party and the broader mainland polity, including local power networks, have not disappeared. Over the long term, as the aftermaths of Cromwell or Napoleon or Stalin showed, revolutions do end. It should be no surprise that central leaders espouse centralism. They do not, however, always get results that they like.

Hong Kong has not been separate from China or its revolution. Poor immigrants have joined wealthy Chinese who have sought refuge in Hong Kong from inland rebellions at various times after the 1840s to the 1950s at least.[2] Flight from rebels or revolutionaries has made many Hong Kong Chinese family heads anti-political — not just apolitical. Window bars still grace the tops of rather safe residential high-rises in Hong Kong, perhaps in part because of their symbolic value: they keep neo-rebels out of family space. For fifteen decades, many in Hong Kong have seen politics as more violent than public.

This attitude, coming out of China, was nonetheless welcome to British colonial police, who wanted docile citizens — and to Chinese entrepreneurs, who wanted non-unionized workers. Privatism became the code of the business elites (both Chinese and foreign). Governors such as Pope-Hennessey or Patten have been roundly damned by tycoons for "political" efforts to extend participation in government — and thus perhaps pave the road to higher taxes. It will be surprising if future Chief Executives of the Special Administrative Region do not also speak about public needs far more than the city's plutocrats wish to hear.[3] These new governors, especially after the initial term, will be tied to the Beijing government not just to other Hong Kong business people. It would be amazing if China's central leaders do not seek future opportunities to expand their own political bases within Hong Kong, which are currently rather narrow and perhaps unreliable.

Government spending in Hong Kong has traditionally been minimal — or else devoted to subsidizing wages, lowering the general price of labor. Official money has gone to cheap housing since the mid-1950s, reservoirs since the early 1960s, transport loans in later decades, and universities by the 1990s when Hong Kong companies needed white-collar workers to help manage industries that had moved to Guangdong. Yet the state in Hong Kong, except through its effects on the price of labor, has directly instigated economic development far less than in Japan, South Korea, Singapore, Taiwan, or mainland China. This pattern may not change soon. Many semi-state PRC agencies are making money from their investments in Hong Kong businesses and land. These forces within China are likely to moderate Beijing conservatives' impulses to extract resources from the city.

Beijing conservatives are mainly concerned to preserve their established budgets and constituencies, much closer to China's capital, from erosion by reforms. Hong Kong liberals will surely give hard-liners occasions to hope against hope they might recreate the national discipline they nostalgically imagine from the PRC's first decades. So Hong Kong's democracy is "contested."[4] It may eventually prevail in some form, though; and specific battles over the local structure, aided but not determined by long-term trends, will shape the city's political system. Some of the factors in this process will come from Hong Kong. Many will come from other parts of China.

Without 1989, which was such a contest affecting Hong Kong, tycoons might have run the 1997 transition far more comfortably. Events are the sparks that call in the political participation of new groups. Patriotism, especially as regard the Taiwan issue, may generate such events. A Hong Kong superpatriot has already died in a symbolic non-state war against Japan over the small Diaoyu islands. Taiwan is not the same as Hong Kong, however, because the large island may be defended by the people who live there. Lu Ping, the PRC's commissar for Hong Kong who is better known for his expertise in politics than in epistemology, distinguishes information from advocacy — and he signals that Taiwan autonomy is a litmus case against free speech. Not just in Hong Kong, but also in other PRC cities, the question will nonetheless arise: If good Chinese on Taiwan can have high-level competitive elections, then why can we not? The Beijing elite's claim to the island, one of its most popular positions within China, partly conflicts with its case against political freedoms in China including Hong Kong.

Wealth is as great an attraction as freedom to mainland Chinese, and many notice that prosperity is found alongside rights, in both Taiwan and Hong Kong. Escapist "infotainment" prospers even in places where more truly informative media also exist.[5] But media do not communicate well if they are preachy, predictable, dull, or irrelevant to people's lives. Mainland Chinese reporters long ago discovered that "transparency" (*touming*, as it is called there) is crucial to effectiveness in communication. Evening papers in China are more often bought by readers than official morning papers for this reason — especially in large, socially diverse PRC cities, where the situation is rather like Hong Kong's.

Freedoms are tested in courts. Tycoons and democrats alike will need a stable rule of law in Hong Kong's future.[6] They may hope that Hong Kong's judicial system will not become merely a part of the executive, as is still the national norm. Reformers in Beijing may nonetheless raise confidence that laws can become more impartial, both in Hong Kong and in China. If they fail to do so, the habit of trying to substitute personal relationships for reliable laws may reach its limits. Both are needed, as the linked economies of the PRC and Hong Kong expand further.

Will Hong Kong remain very international? The answer is yes and no.[7] Chinese patriotism in Hong Kong became more active, rather than remaining latent, largely because of specific tensions at specific times with various governments, including China's. This process is sometimes ironic, but is was obvious in 1989. It may become so again after mid-1997. Sometimes repression, or fear of it, oddly nationalizes Hong Kong — when the repression is national as surely as when it has been foreign. The rate of continued Sinification may depend on future events whose emergence is hard to predict. At the same time, overseas forces are strongly affecting China. Specific historical occasions are again crucial: trade pacts and large foreign or Taiwan investments, the advent to China of Hong Kong and Overseas Chinese pop music, the birth of proto-democratic procedures in some ex-Communist countries, the assertion of authoritarianism as an ideal in other Asian countries, and other specifiable events such as China's negotiations with members of the World Trade Organization. Historical sequences and contexts, not just ethnicities, create political identification anywhere.

Hong Kong's influence on China is great, just as China's on Hong Kong has always been. The change of 1997 will certainly affect some aspects of life in China's most wonderful city. But the "Crown Colony" has long been replaced by a more vibrant "Territory" in any case. Hong Kong's example induces changes in China, some of which are political and will redound to the advantage of this city.

Lynn T. White III
Princeton University
May 1997

Note

[1]   Ming K. Chan, "Decolonization Without Democracy: Pluralist Politics," in Edward Friedman, ed., *The Politics of Democratization: Generating East Asian Experiences* (Boulder: Westview, 1994), p.177.

[2]   Janet W. Salaff, Siu-lun Wong, and Mei-ling Fung in their methodologically sophisticated chapter for this book show what most readers do not already know: that poor people *can* migrate. They intend to use kinship networks to find jobs, while rich emigrants use largely non-kin networks to make better lives. This may prove as true for mainland migrants to Hong Kong, as it has been for Hong Kong migrants abroad.

[3]   John P. Burns, in his chapter about the civil service for this book, also shows in different ways that there may be more continuity in Government and its personnel than other reports often suggest.

[4]   For much more, see Alvin Y. So's chapter in this book.

[5]   Chin-Chuan Lee, in his contribution to this book, provides a careful view of the media.

[6]   A comprehensive treatment of Hong Kong's legal transition is in Alison W. Conner's chapter below.

[7]   See the chapter in this book by James T.H. Tang.

Preface

As the historical moment of July 1, 1997 fast approaches, it is timely and necessary to look beyond the celebrations and festivities to reflect upon the unprecedented transformation of Hong Kong in the past decade and a half of transition towards Chinese sovereignty. It is of even greater significance to appreciate how the various transformative processes ushered in by the 1997 China factor have reshaped Hong Kong since the early 1980s to the extent that they formed a new baseline for the People's Republic of China's (PRC) Hong Kong Special Administrative Region (SAR). Indeed, China's handling of the 1982–1997 transition has revealed the policy bottomline on the Hong Kong issue as an integral part of Beijing's two major concerns — economic reform and modernization as well as national reunification with Taiwan.

Controlling the transition from British colonial rule to SAR status under Chinese sovereignty has been a crucial task for the PRC government; but Hong Kong's post-1997 development may pose an even greater challenge to Beijing. While Hong Kong under Chinese rule may bring countless benefits, it may also have unpredictable and serious domestic and external ramifications. There are many problematic areas in the relations between the central government and the SAR, and in the SAR's internal functioning and global linkages within the framework of the Basic Law. As exemplified by various landmark cases during the transition era, the clash of political cultures, conflicting interpretations of the Sino-British Joint Declaration and the Basic Law, divergent motives and hidden agendas have underlined, and more often, undermined Sino-British-Hong Kong negotiations and co-management of transition issues.

Even after the colonial veneer is removed, the differences in mentalities, institutions, procedures, assumptions, objectives and values between the people of Hong Kong and their mainland compatriots are so significant that the much heralded "one country, two systems" formula devised by Beijing will be put to serious test. If the countdown to 1997 has been an uneasy passage to Chinese sovereignty, with considerable ironies and turbulence, then developments in the SAR could well unfold along a hazardous course. In this sense, the demise of British colonialism in Hong Kong would not necessarily guarantee a smoother mainland-Hong Kong interface. Rather, the liquidation of colonialism-imperialism will force Beijing to deal with Hong Kong as a challenge of full-scale domestic integration. How Beijing deals with the opportunities afforded by Hong Kong's retrocession will signal to the world Beijing's ability to articulate an expanded Greater China. The ability to maintain harmonious co-existence and even genuine collaboration between the socialist mainland and capitalist Hong Kong will be a powerful testimonial to the longer term prospects of China's economic reform and international openness. These are some of the issues on the minds of observers of the fast paced Hong Kong story, which will soon become a new chapter in China's own book on state-building and national development.

The seven essays in this volume address some of the critical issues underlining the transition-transformation-integration process of Hong Kong becoming China. Starting in the mid 1980s, the authors review the past decade and a half of drastic changes in Hong Kong under the impact of the China factor with the aim of providing a more informed appreciation of the forces and dynamics that will continue to shape Hong Kong-Beijing interaction for some time to come. July 1, 1997 may turn a new page in Hong Kong's constitutional status and national identity, but it will not change overnight many of the built-in concerns and aspirations of the populace — free, creative and productive people which are Hong Kong's most valuable assets. Their hopes and fears, lives and work, collective demands and communal undertakings, have been shaped in a most profound and far-reaching manner by the China factor; yet their varied responses to the reintegration process have shaped the conduct of Beijing and the local authorities, and their voices could not be totally ignored by the elites of the new order.

These seven essays provide multi-disciplinary perspectives to articulate the major institutions and issues that shape the ongoing transformative processes, and help to define the challenges ahead. Ming Chan delineates the key dimensions of the China factor which dominates and manipulates the political arena of Hong Kong's transition. John Burn offers a comparative analysis of mainland China's and Hong Kong's civil service systems which are undergoing substantial changes now and beyond 1997. Alvin So suggests the root causes of Hong

Kong's recent political crisis as a case of "contested democracy" which might not end with the sovereignty transfer. Alison Conner brings into focus the still unsettled controversies in the legal system and the rule of law in this critical juncture of transition. Chin-Chuan Lee assesses the impact of regime change on the local media and the question of press freedom under communist Chinese sovereignty. Janet Salaff, Siu-lun Wong, and Mei-ling Fung use interview surveys to construct contrasting profiles of the family decision toward overseas migration as an important manifestation of "confidence crisis" toward 1997. Finally, James Tang observes the China-Hong Kong integration in a globalization and nationalization context.

Taken together, this volume of scholarly essays offers penetrating, in-depth analysis of the key dimensions in the first phase of the China-Hong Kong integrative and transformative process. As the China factor will carry increasing weight in Hong Kong's future development, the authors aim to provide an informed baseline to articulate the prospects of mainland-Hong Kong relations, the faithful implementation of the "one country, two systems" formula, Beijing's agenda of national reunification, and communism in China. Hopefully, an understanding of how socialist China and colonial-capitalist Hong Kong interacted before 1997 will shed light on how events will unfold after Hong Kong's full integration with the mainland. As the world watches the Hong Kong SAR on its new journey from July 1, 1997, this volume should serve as a useful guide.

Ming K. Chan
May 1997

Acknowledgments

Early drafts of six of the chapters in this volume were first presented in the double-panel "Hong Kong's Imperfect Transition to 1997: Part I, The Political Transformation, & Part II, The Social and Institutional Transformation" at the 48th Annual Meeting of the Association for Asian Studies, Honolulu, April 12, 1996. They have been revised and updated for inclusion here. The efforts of Gerard A. Postiglione, the organizer of the Part II panel, are deeply appreciated. His own paper on Hong Kong higher education is not included in this volume simply because it is committed for publication elsewhere. Likewise, the paper on party politics and elections in transitional Hong Kong by Ian Scott is not included for the same reason. Alvin So, who served as a discussant to the Part II panel, contributes a new essay for this volume.

On behalf of the contributors/panelists, I wish to thank Roger T. Ames, University of Hawaii, for chairing the Part I panel, James Watson, Harvard University, for chairing the Part II panel, and Diana Lary, University of British Columbia, for serving as discussant to the Part I panel. A particular intellectual debt is owed to Lynn T. White III of Princeton University whose very insightful comments have aided the revision of the papers into book chapters. We are indeed deeply honored by his illuminating Foreword to this volume. The helpful comments by Sonny Shiu-hing Lo, the University of Hong Kong, on Alvin So's chapter is also gratefully appreciated.

The service rendered by my research assistant, Roy Chi-Kwong Man at the University of Hong Kong in the preparation of this volume is acknowledged with thanks. Last but definitely not least, the friendly cooperation of the staff of Hong Kong University Press enabled the publication of this volume in a timely manner and this should be recorded here with profound appreciation.

Ming K. Chan
May 1997

1

The Politics of Hong Kong's Imperfect Transition: Dimensions of the China Factor

Ming K. Chan

After one-and-a-half century of British colonial rule, Hong Kong was mandated by the 1984 Sino-British Joint Declaration to become a Special Administrative Region (SAR) of the People's Republic of China (PRC) from July 1, 1997. China's policy toward Hong Kong is based on the concept of "one country, two systems" which supposedly allows the existing legal, economic and social systems to be preserved for fifty years until 2047. The political system, however, had to undergo fundamental and drastic changes in the transition to 1997. The processes of decolonization, localization, internationalization, democratization and politicization characterize the era of transition since the early 1980s, which also witnessed dramatic deterioration in Sino-British relations, especially following the 1989 Tiananmen Incident.

Despite the PRC's much-heralded "one country, two systems" formula for the future SAR, the China factor looms increasingly larger and closer to constituting direct interference with and serious obfuscation to British-sponsored reforms and infrastructural developments. Indeed, China has often tried to undermine the British-sponsored constitutional and administrative reforms, and to impede the introduction of direct elections and fuller scale representative government before 1997. The drafting of the Hong Kong Basic Law by Beijing, a process intended as a United Front exercise to win support for the power transfer, became a highly divisive and delegitimating experience, and exposed the illiberal, anti-democratic impulse of the PRC-local leftists-tycoons axis.

Sino-British discord, which first emerged in the aftermath of Tiananmen, deteriorated into open hostility when Governor Patten reversed the former British policy of appeasing Beijing with his 1992 electoral proposals. The bilateral non-cooperation led to the PRC's obstruction of the new airport and container terminal projects as well as the setting up of "a second stove" — the SAR Preliminary Working Committee (PWC) in 1993 as a preemptive shadow power organ. Since then, Hong Kong's transition to 1997 has become a tug of war for power and control of Hong Kong between London, Beijing and the local populace. Specifically, the PRC officialdom was determined to embark on its own "China-centered" approach to Hong Kong issues with the deliberate exclusion of British cooperation in the final years of transition. With this approach, Beijing has tried to bypass the British colonial authorities and deal directly with the people of Hong Kong — to galvanize their popular support for, and to absorb elite elements among them into, the PRC's preemptive power organs to manage Hong Kong affairs even ahead of the actual power transfer on July 1, 1997

In January 1996, the SAR Preparatory Committee (PC) was established by the PRC with 150 members (96 Hong Kong members and 64 mainland members). In the fall of 1996, the Preparatory Committee in turn created the 400-member SAR Selection Committee (all Hong Kong members). The two functions of the Selection Committee were to choose the first Chief Executive of the SAR government and to produce a "provisional legislature"; the latter would replace the fully elected Legislative Council formed in 1995 under British auspices. On December 5, 1996, shipping tycoon Tung Chee-hwa was chosen by the Selection Committee as the first SAR Chief Executive, and on December 21, 60 members of the SAR provisional legislature were also selected. Thus, by implementing the "China-centered" approach, Beijing already had its SAR key personnel and control mechanism firmly in place six months before the actual sovereignty retrocession, leaving very little room for the British colonialists or the local Hong Kong populace to conduct any last minute maneuvers against the PRC's dictate.

This essay adopts a bi-focal approach to highlight the key dimensions of the China factor in underlining Hong Kong's transition to 1997. It will first look at the PRC's own political requirements, especially in relation to national reunification. Then it will delineate the inter-related transformative processes in Hong Kong as unleashed or facilitated by the China factor since the early 1980s. The disequilibrium between the constraining pressures stemming from the PRC's "sovereignty obsession" toward Hong Kong and the liberalizing forces generated by the transformative processes in Hong Kong as impacted by the China factor has been responsible for many of the difficulties in Hong Kong's transition. These difficulties will continue to shape the early days of the new SAR, especially in state-society interactions and the relationship between the SAR and the central authorities in China.

Hong Kong's Retrocession and the PRC's Politics of Reunification

To appreciate Hong Kong's problematic transition to Chinese sovereignty, it is necessary to consider the impact of the China factor on Hong Kong's transformative processes. At the same time, it is equally important to understand the symbol and meaning on the other side of the coin, that is, the implications of Hong Kong's retrocession for the PRC's domestic agenda and policy objectives.

In a nutshell, Hong Kong's sovereignty is a critical issue in the PRC's politics of national reunification. In its continuous drive for reunification, China places particular emphasis on the resumption and actualization of sovereignty, as well as the maintenance of territorial integrity. During the past one-and-a-half decade of Hong Kong's uneasy transition, several major dimensions of the PRC's politics of reunification have been noteworthy because of their profound significance to the PRC's Hong Kong policy and other related aspects of Beijing's external reach. The following four dimensions will be discussed:

1. Hong Kong and the PRC-Taiwan/Macau links
2. China's "sovereignty obsession"
3. preemptive sovereignty assertion
4. military power as sovereignty actualization

Hong Kong and the PRC-Taiwan/Macau Links

Hong Kong's retrocession has been a key component in the Chinese politics of reunification. Hong Kong's absorption into and reintegration with the PRC is based on the "one country, two systems" formula. This formula is crucial for Hong Kong, as well as the other targets of Beijing's reunification efforts — Taiwan and Macau. It will serve as the basis of the post-1999 Macau SAR and is intended to be applied to post-unification Taiwan.

As a matter of fact, the earliest official PRC pronouncement on this "one country, two systems" concept was aimed at Taiwan. It first appeared as the fourth item in Marshal Ye Jianying's July 1981 "Nine Points" policy for Taiwan's peaceful reunification with the mainland.[1] Since 1984, the PRC officialdom has repeated time and again that the smooth and successful transition of Hong Kong to Chinese sovereignty will set an excellent example and provide ample positive proof for Taiwan's reunification under the same "one country, two systems" formula. Beijing further emphasized that Taiwan would be treated more generously than Hong Kong as Taiwan would be able to retain its own military forces. Despite the PRC's military threat — in the form of missile tests and live ammunition maneuvers in the Taiwan Strait — to coincide with Taiwan's first direct presidential election in March 1996, Beijing still insists on the positive showcase effects of Hong Kong's retrocession according to this formula.[2]

In a broader context of modern Chinese history, the resumption of sovereignty over Hong Kong in 1997 actually constituted a modification, if not quite an interruption, of the PRC's original design and schedule for national reunification. Until the late 1970s, the official PRC approach to national reunification was anchored in the late Premier Zhou Enlai's "Three Stages Strategy" which called for: first the resolution of the Taiwan problem, then the retrocession of Hong Kong from British colonial rule, and finally the recovery of Macau under Portuguese administration. In terms of geopolitical and strategic significance, territorial domain and population size, Taiwan is of much greater importance to the mainland's reunification agenda than Hong Kong and Macau. Unlike Hong Kong and Macau, which are still under foreign colonial rule, Taiwan as an island state claims to represent "China"; under the Nationalist regime Taiwan's ideological, political and economic system is different from the PRC's and it has considerable global ties. This poses a continued and serious challenge to the PRC's own legitimacy and full international status as well as strategic interests.[3]

A well-known case of Beijing's adherence to the "Three Stages Strategy" was the Chinese rejection of the Portuguese offer to return Macau in 1974. Soon after the 1974 Portuguese revolution, the center-left leadership in Lisbon wished to liquidate Portuguese overseas colonial vestiges and took the initiative to offer Macau back to the PRC. However, Beijing declined; it re-affirmed Chinese sovereignty over Macau but decided to leave unchanged for the time being the continuation of Portuguese administration of the territory.[4] The logic behind Beijing's tolerance of Portuguese rule in Macau was to avoid any premature change in Macau's status which might undermine the stability of Hong Kong — which Beijing was in no hurry to alter, pending a settlement of the Taiwan question.

It was the British that initiated the Hong Kong retrocession process. Governor Murray MacLehose visited Deng Xiaoping in 1979 and asked him about China's bottom-line on Hong Kong's future status. The need to secure some sort of bilateral agreement at least a decade ahead of the June 30, 1997 expiration of the New Territories' lease (which covers some 93% of Hong Kong's land domain), prompted the British to enter into negotiations with the PRC to resolve Hong Kong's future in September 1982. The resultant 1984 Sino-British Joint Declaration stipulated the end of British rule and the resumption of PRC sovereignty in Hong Kong from July 1, 1997. This covers not just the New Territories but the entire Hong Kong region including Hong Kong Island and the Kowloon Peninsula which were supposedly ceded to the British in perpetuity.[5]

Following the pattern of the Sino-British accord on Hong Kong, Beijing and Lisbon started negotiations on Macau's status in June 1986 and the Sino-Portuguese Joint Declaration on Macau was signed in April 1987, which stipulated the end of Portuguese rule on December 20, 1999.[6] These two agreements signaled a fundamental change in the basic Chinese strategy for national reunification, which became Hong Kong first, then Macau, and finally Taiwan. The rearranged priorities in Beijing's reunification agenda have much to do with the objective time constraints. In the case of Hong Kong, it is the 1997 expiration of the New Territories lease; in the case of Macau, it was Hong Kong's retrocession which prompted Beijing to terminate all vestiges of foreign imperialism and colonial rule on Chinese soil before the end of the twentieth century. While the PRC has yet to specify any time limit on recovering Taiwan, it is only natural that with the imminent return of Hong Kong, there would be greater pressure and a new sense of urgency to settle the Taiwan problem in order to fulfill the high-priority policy of national reunification.

From the PRC perspective, the "one country, two systems" formula as devised by Deng Xiaoping had been an effective and by-and-large successful framework to regain sovereignty and jurisdiction over Hong Kong from the British, and by extension, Macau from the Portuguese. Beijing also envisages that under this formula Hong Kong will maintain stability and prosperity, and continue its economic success and functional vitality to contribute to the mainland's reform and modernization. A flourishing HKSAR would also be a priceless asset in the PRC's global relations, especially with the Western industrial democracies. Hopefully, the continued success of Hong Kong under PRC rule will fully vindicate the "one country, two systems" formula as Beijing's grand design for national reunification in an era of domestic economic development and post-Cold War international rapprochement, thus facilitating a peaceful settlement of the Taiwan issue on Beijing's terms.

In reality, this ideal scenario of the Hong Kong SAR as a showcase and real-life laboratory for the positive effects of the "one country, two systems" formula for reunification under PRC sovereignty has so far failed to promote the desired effects on Taiwan. The authorities and populace in Taiwan do not find the Hong Kong model an attractive one for peaceful reunification with the mainland. On the other hand, interactions between Beijing and Taipei have definitely impacted on transitional Hong Kong, in some sense even turning Hong Kong into a frontline of political crossfires. Since Taipei lifted the ban on its residents' visit to the mainland in 1987, there has been significant increase in contact across the Taiwan Strait. Many Taiwan individuals have visited the mainland for family reunion, business purposes as well as cultural, academic and professional exchanges; similarly more mainland individuals have visited the island. Due to the lack of direct across-the-strait links in shipping, air traffic, trading and financial services, Hong Kong has played a very substantial, almost indispensable, role as the intermediary in these functional exchanges. In this respect, Hong Kong has contributed much to the intensification and proliferation of cross-the-strait interfaces, a crucial dimension of the Chinese politics of reunification. However, with its own impending change of status in 1997, Hong Kong's intermediary status and functional utility in the social and economic exchanges between the mainland and Taiwan will be altered.[7] In this context, the three pronouncements below — made during the first half of 1995 — deserve special attention.

First, in January 1995, Jiang Zemin, President of the PRC and General Secretary of the Chinese Communist Party, announced an "Eight Points" policy on the peaceful reunification between the mainland and Taiwan.[8] Second, in response to these eight points from the PRC, Taiwan's top leader Lee Teng-hui issued a generally positive "Six Points" reply in April 1995 which emphasized the peaceful exchanges while acknowledging the de facto separated and distinct jurisdictions of the two Chinese domains across the Taiwan Strait. Of interest to this essay is the last point in Lee's "Six Points" — "Both the mainland and Taiwan should jointly preserve and maintain the stability and prosperity of Hong Kong and Macau, and also to promote democracy in Hong Kong and Macau."[9]

From these two set of documents, relations across the Taiwan Strait seemed to be developing under a more harmonious and cooperative atmosphere with social and economic exchanges on the rise from the late 1980s to the mid-1990s. However, following Lee's June 1995 "private" visit to his alma mater Cornell University in the US, there has been a sharp and drastic deterioration in Beijing-Taipei relations. The PRC severely condemned Lee's American visit as an important proof that his "flexible diplomacy" was intended to create "two Chinas," "one China, one Taiwan," or even an "independent Taiwan." All of these were beyond the PRC's limits of tolerance in its politics of reunification. Soon after Lee's visit, Beijing staged two rounds of missile tests in the Taiwan Strait as part of its propaganda onslaught and psychological warfare against Lee's pro-Taiwan independence orientation. It was at this critical juncture that the PRC issued the official dictum on post-1997 HKSAR-Taiwan relations which constitutes the third pronouncement.

On June 23, 1995, PRC Vice-Premier and Foreign Minister Qian Qichen in his capacity as the Chairman of the HKSAR Preliminary Working Committee (PWC) announced the "Seven Points" of basic principles and policy guidelines on HKSAR-Taiwan links. While allowing for the continuation of all present private, unofficial exchanges, including economic and cultural ones, the future Hong Kong-Taiwan shipping and air links would operate according to a special inter-region traffic scheme as part of the "one China's domestic traffic arrangement." The entry and exit documents for Taiwan residents visiting the HKSAR would be arranged by the PRC central government. The central government also would regulate or authorize the SAR government to regulate any official contact between the governmental bodies of the SAR and the Taiwan region.[10] These "Seven Points" could be viewed as PRC's response to the last item in the Lee Teng-hui's "Six Points."

Beijing is obviously concerned with sovereignty and reunification implications if the HKSAR, as a part of China, is allowed to deal with Taiwan directly; hence the tight control over official contacts between Hong Kong and Taiwan. The direct involvement of the central government in regulating and approving official contacts is based on Beijing's insistence on the "one China" approach and its strong opposition to any resemblance to a "one China, one Taiwan" mode. Even under the "one country, two systems" formula the HKSAR government will have no right to form special ties with Taiwan. The across-strait tension following Lee's US visit definitely stemmed from Beijing's decision to tighten the screw. Qian's "Seven Points" also served as Beijing's rebuttal to the doubts often expressed by Taipei on Hong Kong's change of status in 1997 and its successful implementation of the "one country, two systems" formula. The restrictions outlined in the "Seven Points" could also preempt Taipei's proposed "Hong Kong-Macau Relations Regulations" which were supposedly to be enacted by Taiwan's legislative body before July 1, 1997. Despite the growing influence of the opposition party (the pro-independence Democratic Progress Party) in the legislative body, the passage of this set of regulations as law in Taiwan finally took place on March 18, 1997.[11]

Taiwan has not shown great urgency in fashioning a new official approach to Hong Kong's new status as a part of China. This is partly due to the different political circumstances of Taiwan and Hong Kong. Taiwan enjoys genuine home rule autonomy with an entrenched and increasingly liberal democratic government; Hong Kong is a colony ruled by foreign imperialists. Taiwan is strategically defensible while Hong Kong is not. The ability of staging a military defense against the mainland is a crucial and fundamental distinction between Taiwan and Hong Kong. The military stand-off between the mainland and Taiwan in the spring of 1996 — which necessitated US naval involvement in the Taiwan Strait — clearly illustrates this point. As Taiwan continues to strengthen its armed forces, with new aircraft, warships, and tanks due for deployment in the next few years, the strategic equilibrium across the Taiwan Strait should not be easily disturbed in the foreseeable future.[12] Finally, it is important to note that Taiwan is much less dependent on the mainland economy as has been the case of Hong Kong, both historically and especially since the 1970s. Thus, the lack of positive echoes from Taiwan's government and populace to Hong Kong's retrocession as a model for reunification is no surprise to informed observers.

The PRC's "Sovereignty Obsession"

To the PRC leadership, from the start of the Sino-British negotiations in September 1982, through the decade and a half of transition, to the establishment of the SAR polity in 1997 and beyond, the crux of the Hong Kong issue has always been the recovery and full-fledged actualization of China's sovereignty. The primacy as well as supremacy of genuine and complete sovereignty is the core of Beijing's politics of reunification and also a major guiding light in its external orientation. Specifically, the re-integration of Hong Kong with the motherland has been regarded as a matter of patriotic pride and national honor. Hong Kong was a concrete reminder of China's century-long humiliation by foreign imperialists, and the "unequal treaties" under which China had to accept "impaired sovereignty" on its own soil. Qing Dynasty China ceded Hong Kong to the British under the first of the unequal treaties, the 1842 Treaty of Nanking which settled the First Opium War (1989–42). The cessation of Kowloon came under the second unequal treaty, the 1860 Treaty of Peking which concluded the Second Opium War (1856–60). The 99-year lease of the New Territories, starting in 1898, stemmed from the foreign powers' "scramble for concessions" in the aftermath of the Sino-Japanese War (1894–95). (The Sino-Japanese War resulted in the cessation of Taiwan to Japan; hence the historical roots of separatism among some Taiwan natives.)[13] Thus, the retrocession of Hong Kong in its entirety (including the New Territories) means to the PRC a profound, long-delayed redemption of national humiliation and full sovereignty reassertion with clear implications for Taiwan's reunification. As such, Beijing could neither allow any compromise nor afford too much concession to foreign imperialism. Sovereignty means more than nominal status transfer with a change of flag; it requires the genuine and highly visible actualization of control and full jurisdiction.

It was against these historical burdens and realpolitik requirements that Deng Xiaoping flatly obliterated Margaret Thatcher's claim of validity for the three unequal treaties and also rejected the British offer to restore Chinese sovereignty over the entire Hong Kong region in exchange for a 50-year extension of continued British administration. This dispute over sovereignty (nominal versus actual) stalemated the Sino-British negotiations for a year. Only when the British (in late 1983) capitulated to China's demands for full sovereignty over the entire Hong Kong region could the negotiations proceed on the practical arrangements for the transition to 1997 and on post-1997 guarantees to preserve Hong Kong's freedom, stability and prosperity.[14] In contrast, the Sino-Portuguese negotiations over Macau took only ten months to reach an agreement because there was no dispute of Chinese sovereignty, Lisbon having acknowledged much earlier that it was only an administering but definitely not sovereign power over Macau.

Furthermore, not only were the 1982–84 Sino-British negotiations a highly secretive exercise in bilateral diplomacy, but the Hong Kong people were totally excluded from the process. Beijing insisted that the future of Hong Kong was a matter to be determined exclusively by the governments of the two sovereign powers with no room for Hong Kong's participation in whatever form or shape. Any attempt to include Hong Kong representation in the negotiations would constitute in Beijing's eyes a dangerous imbalance resembling a "three-legged stool" — although in real life, a stool with two legs is far less stable than one with three. The London-appointed Hong Kong Governor Edward Youde did take part in the negotiations, but he did so only as a member of the British government delegation. Beijing also denied a visa to the director of the Hong Kong Government Information Services Peter Tsao who originally planned to accompany Youde to Beijing as his personal press spokesman during the negotiations.[15]

The PRC's insistence on national sovereignty has been much more than just a matter of basic principle, abstract concept, or policy guidelines; its emphasis on sovereignty actualization demands concrete expression in all areas of policy implementation and practical arrangements, even down to the smallest details, leaving little room for compromise. In realpolitik terms, Beijing's exclusion of Hong Kong participation from the negotiations affecting its own future served several purposes. First, it prevented the British from using "Hong Kong public opinion" as an additional bargaining chip — if Hong Kong had been included, then London plus Hong Kong had two voices, and Beijing would be disadvantaged in having only one voice. Second, the exclusion of Hong Kong from the negotiations would reduce the complexity of the issues, especially transitional era matters and also post-1997 rights, entitlements, and obligations for which the two sovereign powers must bear responsibility toward the interests and demands of the Hong Kong people. Third, the PRC regarded Hong Kong as a municipal-level entity, a British administered colonial domain before 1997 and a SAR under the central government after 1997. Hence, Hong Kong must not be allowed to enjoy the status as a national-level entity in these state-to-state negotiations. Otherwise, it would send the wrong signal to Taiwan which is merely a provincial-level entity inside China in Beijing's eyes.

Of course, the British being an alien, expatriate regime, unelected and unaccountable to the Hong Kong people and suffering from an acute and incurable crisis of legitimacy and lack of popular mandate, could hardly counterbalance the PRC's nationalistic assaults. Moreover, given the time constraint of the expiration of the 1997 leasehold, and Hong Kong's economic and functional integration with the mainland (including the supply of water, food and raw materials), the British had very little bargaining power, especially as they could not play the "Hong Kong public opinion" card effectively.[16]

In fact, other than the few colonial diehards and anti-communist ultra-conservatives, the majority of the Hong Kong populace, who are of Chinese descent, could put up little resistance to the mainland's appeal to patriotism and nationalistic unity during the Sino-British negotiations. The best they could hope for was that the retrocession to China would also bring forth local democracy to replace British colonial rule. Unfortunately, the nationalistic fever also propelled the PRC officialdom into a militant, aggressive mode of decision making and policy implementation on almost all Hong Kong issues in the name of full sovereignty recovery and genuine sovereignty actualization. While supposedly this "sovereignty obsession" only aimed at the British colonial establishment and British influence, it would soon find concrete expression in the preemptive assertion of Chinese sovereign rights in the transitional period to 1997. Thus, a very important feature of the politics of transition was the PRC's attempt to gain control of Hong Kong even in the pre-SAR era of transition so as to lay a firm foundation for Bejing's undisputed sovereignty position after 1997.

Preemptive Sovereignty Assertion

In the 1984 Sino-British Joint Declaration, Annex III "Land Leases" stipulated that premium income from land transactions must be shared equally between the current British Hong Kong regime and the future SAR government, that a land commission should be set up with equal representation from the PRC and the British governments, and that the amount of the new land to be granted in the transitional period is limited to 50 hectares annually. From the above provisions it is clear that even before 1997 the Hong Kong government could only exercise limited jurisdiction on land matters while the PRC government, on behalf of the future SAR government, has already enjoyed some shared rights.[18]

Since the 1989 Tiananmen crisis, notwithstanding the PRC's repeated assurance of "high degree of local autonomy" and "Hong Kong people ruling Hong Kong", Beijing has adopted an increasingly militant preemptive posture to intervene in pre-1997 Hong Kong affairs. Its justification is that the current Hong Kong colonial regime derived its power from London and as such it could not claim to reflect or represent the genuine interests of Hong Kong. Thus it is absolutely necessary for the PRC government, as "the self-appointed" representative and guardian of the Hong Kong people and their future SAR government, to take practical measures to safeguard Hong Kong's long-term interest vis-a-vis British colonial conspiracy. In Beijing's view, after the resumption of sovereignty all HKSAR residents of Chinese descent shall naturally become PRC citizens. Since the central people's government is the defender and the promoter of Chinese national sovereignty, therefore, naturally and necessarily it should represent the PRC citizens in Hong Kong before and after 1997.

A major flaw in this line of reasoning is its disregard of the emerging democratic movement in Hong Kong. It is ironic that the PRC resorted to preemptive assertion of sovereignty on the ground that the colonial Hong Kong regime did not and could not speak for the Hong Kong people. Yet, at the same time, Hong Kong's domestic efforts in advancing democratic representation were frustrated and obstructed by the PRC and its Hong Kong supporters; the intention was to fulfill Beijing's dictum on Hong Kong's lack of a legitimate body to represent genuine local interest, thus the necessity for Beijing to fill this vacuum and appoint itself to speak and act for Hong Kong even before 1997. This approach was clearly manifested in the 1987–88 controversy regarding the introduction of direct elections to the Hong Kong legislature in 1988.[19]

Beijing and its Hong Kong supporters strongly objected to the introduction of direct elections in 1988 as this might preempt the yet-to-be-drafted HKSAR Basic Law. Part of the Beijing argument rested on the dubious point that drafting the Basic Law was a serious matter concerning national sovereignty and prerogatives that should be handled by the central government at the state level. Therefore, local political structure and electoral system should not be allowed to violate or contravene central government prerogatives in the exercise of national sovereignty.

However, at that time (1987–88) the drafting of the Basic Law was at a preliminary stage only — it was to be officially promulgated by the PRC National People's Congress two years later on April 4, 1990. Furthermore, the

Basic Law would come into force only from July 1, 1997; it has no validity before that date. To argue that the 1988 elections to the Hong Kong legislature (which would include some directly elected seats from geographical constituencies) would violate or damage the yet-to-be-created Basic Law (which was not be finalized until spring 1990 and then must wait until July 1, 1997 to take effect) was a blatant attempt at preemptive jurisdiction. Unfortunately, the British colonial regime under Governor David Wilson succumbed to China's pressure and backed down from its proposed electoral reform. Under the pretext of ensuring a "convergence" between Hong Kong's internal developments and the future Basic Law, the introduction of direct election (of only 30%, i.e. 18 out of 60 seats) of the legislature had to be deferred until 1991.[20]

In Beijing's view, local democratization could undermine the actualization of full sovereignty which means effective control of the HKSAR polity after 1997. Pre-1997 democratization will create an elected representative legislature enjoying legitimacy and popular support, thus checking the authority and reducing the effectiveness of the colony's authoritarian "executive-led" government. Furthermore, genuine local autonomy based on full-scale democratic participation and accountability may promote and reinforce localism, which carries the risk of encouraging separatism, thus undermining national unity and sovereignty. It is therefore ironic and self-defeating for Beijing to expect Hong Kong's "one country, two systems" model to be attractive to Taiwan and to lure it toward peaceful reunification. The people in Taiwan have already enjoyed a high degree of democratic autonomy and can freely exercise their rights to directly elect their local, provincial and central level legislators and chief executives. The derailment of Hong Kong's limited democratization illustrates the PRC's opposition to democracy and local autonomy, and is counterproductive to solving the Taiwan problem.[21] In the control of developmental projects and resources allocation, the PRC's record on Hong Kong offers another alarming example of preemptive sovereignty obsession.

In the aftermath of the 1989 Tiananmen Incident, mistrust between China and Britain deepened. Beijing has extended its official claim of the right to "co-management" of major infrastructural development projects and even a vetoing "consultation" role in other matters which straddle the 1997 transition date. An example of such PRC insistence on preemptive jurisdiction in transitional Hong Kong is the new airport project at Chek Lap Kok, which was first announced by the colonial regime in October 1989. Little progress could be made without Beijing's endorsement of this very expensive (more than HK$160 billion) project; approval in principle was obtained after a year and a half of negotiations which produced the 1991 Sino-British Memorandum of Understanding. In September 1991, British Prime Minister John Major had to travel to Beijing to sign this Memorandum (thus becoming the first major Western leader to visit the PRC after June 4, 1989). This Memorandum not only specified the financial responsibilities of the Hong Kong government for the new airport (including a huge reserve fund of at least HK$25 billion, and limiting debts to HK$5 billion unless with the prior approval of China), it also required the British regime to "consult" Beijing on all key decisions that transcend the retrocession date or affecting the transition, thus yielding to the PRC the power to "veto" any major Hong Kong matters ahead of actual power transfer.[22]

The more recent moves and gestures by PRC-appointed future SAR office holders and power organs seem to reconfirm their deliberate attempts to exercise control and exert influence ahead of July 1, 1997. For instance, the PRC originally demanded that it should have a say in drawing up the 1996–97 Hong Kong government budget (of revenues and expenditures), but at the end had to settle for being informed of the budget making process for 1996–97. Beijing was able to play a role in making the 1997–98 budget which covers the April 1997–March 1998 period, thus transcending the date of retrocession.[23] After his appointment in early December 1996, Tung Chee-hwa repeatedly insisted that he should be addressed as the "Hong Kong SAR Chief Executive", not as the "Chief Executive-designate". While it may seem to be only a minor matter of wording, the fact remains that Tung has yet to be officially sworn into office, and the SAR will only come into existence on July 1, 1997.[24] Furthermore, the SAR provisional legislature, despite the PRC foreign minister's reassurance to the contrary, has started to hold formal meetings to conduct legislative work in Shenzhen across the border from Hong Kong (where it might be subject to legal challenge as an "unlawful body" as it lacks legal/constitutional basis in the Sino-British Joint Declaration and the Basic Law).[25] All these cases are indicators of how the mentality of preemptive actualization of Chinese sovereignty has been translated into actual operational mode in the final stage of Hong Kong's transition.

Military Power as Sovereignty Actualization

The 1984 Sino-British Joint Declaration stipulates that the PRC can station troops in the HKSAR after 1997 for national defense. Even before the bilateral agreement was reached, PRC paramount leader Deng Xiaoping publicly condemned in May 1984 as "nonsense and false utterances" the statement by senior diplomat Huang Hua that China would not deploy the People's Liberation Army (PLA) in Hong Kong after 1997. Deng stressed that the presence of the PLA was necessary to demonstrate the recovery of sovereignty from Britain and China's sovereign rights in Hong Kong.[26] (Deng was then Chairman of the Central Military Affairs Commission.) This becomes the dictum that presence of military force means the actualization of national sovereignty.

Both the Joint Declaration and the Basic Law state very clearly that the central government will have direct jurisdiction in matters of national defense and international relations involving the HKSAR. Therefore, Chinese military presence in the form of stationing PLA troops should be considered a normal, natural and even necessary act of state in exercising sovereign prerogatives.

Deng's high-profiled, public pronouncement reflected Beijing's concept of national sovereignty and its insistence on the full actualization of such sovereignty. It could also mean that the PRC military establishment takes great pride in its up-front role in the defense of territorial integrity, the pursuit of national unity, and upholding national sovereignty.

An interesting case of the military's direct role in Hong Kong's transitional arrangements is the exceptional breakthrough in the June 1994 Sino-British agreement on the transfer of British military sites and facilities to the PLA in 1997.[27] This agreement on military facilities is the only significant item of Sino-British cooperation since October 1992 when Governor Chris Patten's electoral reform proposal angered Beijing and triggered a three-year long Sino-British confrontation until summer 1995. At the peak of the hostility, Governor Patten was denounced by the PRC officialdom as the "sinner of a millennium." The PRC held major infrastructure projects (such as the new airport at Chek Lap Kok and the container terminal No. 9) hostage while the Sino-British Joint Liaison Group made little progress on many substantive issues straddling 1997. Thus, the accord on military facilities reflected the powerful influence and even direct involvement of the PRC military in the politics of sovereignty retrocession and reunification management. At this juncture in the mid-1990s, there seems to be also a clear preference for aggressive action through military pressure in the PRC approach to Taiwan, which is the only remaining and the most significant target of Beijing's national reunification drive.

Such a "military presence as sovereignty actualization" mentality toward both Hong Kong and Taiwan also reflected the PRC's domestic crisis of ideological faith, legitimate authority and power succession. With the demise of the Communism-Maoism orthodoxy, and the questionable appeal of "economism" (i.e. economic reform and development, but also uneven growth and distribution of gains, official corruption and economic crimes), Chinese nationalism is the only major focus to galvanize mass support and to buttress the government's legitimacy, authoritativeness, and popular appeal; in short, the survival of the Beijing leadership depends on evoking strong feelings of nationalism.[28] Hence, dramatic and militant manifestations of nationalism directed toward Hong Kong (with its explicit anti-British and anti-imperialism/colonialism overtone) and Taiwan (with its overt anti-separatism and anti-American interference message) are necessary measures — and Hong Kong's British heritage and colonial institutions are such delightful ready-made targets for the PRC's ultra-nationalistic sovereignty assertion. Beijing will not and cannot afford to yield any room in the actualization of sovereignty over Hong Kong's pre-1997 transition and post-1997 control; it will be a prime showcase of nationalistic fulfillment under the Chinese Communist Party leadership.

In this same context, as the PLA is of the same bureaucratic rank as the State Council (the organ of civilian administration) in the PRC's political hierarchy, the active and high-profiled Chinese military presence in the HKSAR can be a matter of great domestic realpolitik importance. When the PRC resumes full sovereignty over Hong Kong, both the government and the military ought to be equally, fully represented and be seen to play an up-front, more than symbolic, role.[29] Of course, the future SAR Chief Executive, unlike the British Governor in the colonial era (who is the commander-in-chief of all the British forces in Hong Kong), will have no authority over the PLA forces stationed in the SAR. The Chinese troops in the SAR will have a separate chain of command directly accountable to the central military authorities in Beijing.

The China Factor and Hong Kong's Transformative Processes

In each and every aspect of life in Hong Kong, the China factor has been of increasing importance since the early 1980s. By 1997 it has become the single most dominant factor shaping Hong Kong public affairs, government decision making and policy implementation, as well as Hong Kong's various external links and extensive global interactions. This political tornado has engulfed Hong Kong to such an extent that it has virtually created a new political culture — including the rising tide of politicization, national identity awareness, political value orientation, and future prospect articulation — among the Hong Kong people. The increasingly close relationship between Hong Kong and the Chinese mainland in trade, manufacturing, investment, transportation, finance, skills and technology transfer has created an intimate economic interdependence, even functional integration between the two with the China factor as the principal force underlining and underwriting Hong Kong's economic growth and tertiarization since the late 1970s.[30]

As such, changes in the PRC polity and economy will have decisive effects on Hong Kong's stability and prosperity in the transition to 1997 and beyond. Although Hong Kong is still under British administration until June 30, 1997, and the Basic Law guarantees that the HKSAR will enjoy a high degree of autonomy after that date, in actual conduct as well as policy pronouncements and commentaries on Hong Kong affairs, the PRC officialdom has repeatedly interfered with and at times even directly encroached on Hong Kong's internal affairs. The PRC's preemptive strikes into local affairs, especially since the fall of 1992 when Sino-British discord escalated into a war of words and functional non-cooperation because of Beijing's opposition to Governor Patten's proposed electoral reform, have turned the China factor into a rather destabilizing force with negative effects on public confidence in Hong Kong's future.[31]

Nonetheless, since the early 1980s, the China factor has been the accelerator, stimulant and even mid-wife to potentially constructive processes which are transforming Hong Kong into a post-colonial, cosmopolitan, more self-conscious and truly modern Chinese community. In a sense, the China factor necessitates fundamental change in the Hong Kong polity and socio-cultural mentality that could yield great opportunities and new dynamics to meet challenges in Hong Kong and China in the next century.

Decolonization

The decolonization process, gradual and snail-paced at first, has shifted to a rather rapid and fuller-scale effort during the last decade. There are the basic constitutional reforms and institutional adaptations to prepare for the 1997 power transfer which means the end to British colonial rule, the PRC's resumption of sovereignty, and the establishment of an autonomous SAR polity. Not only must the personnel and management culture of the government undergo drastic change, in other areas and institutions of public life, community affairs, professional and academic qualifications, education system and curriculum, the once omnipotent British style or London-derived nomenklatura, designs, norms and practices can no longer maintain their officially sanctioned monopolistic status as the approved or "superior" standards.

Public policy decisions and functional requirements can no longer blindly follow British examples, subscribe to British policy or rely on British input and output. It becomes unacceptable to confuse UK interest with genuine Hong Kong interest. However, the inevitable decline of the British will not lead to the usual end result of the classic Western decolonization process — independence for the local domain and its people. The PRC will replace the UK as the new sovereign master; Hong Kong will enjoy a carefully prescribed system of autonomy as a Special Administrative Region with another kind of dependency on the central authorities in Beijing. Judging from the rather high-handed interference, intimidating threats and preemptive assaults from the PRC officialdom in recent years, the suspicion that Hong Kong is in fact becoming the target of Beijing's "re-colonization" attempt is not entirely unjustified.[32] The latest examples of this "colonial resurrection" under Beijing's wing are the PRC's patronage and high-profiled appointments of ex-colonial elites (mostly conservative, pro-big business, and illiberal, even anti-democratic, former British-appointed but non-elected, colonial legislative/executive councillors) to such SAR organs as the PWC, PC, Selection Committee, the SAR provisional legislature and the SAR executive council.[33] For instance, former colonial Executive Council Senior Member Sir S.Y. Chung has been appointed as the "convenor" of the SAR executive council by Tung Chee-hwa while Rita Fan, another ex-colonial appointed Legislative Council and Executive Council member, was installed as president of the SAR provisional legislature in January 1997.[34] This "elite transfer" from the colonial regime to the SAR polity is definitely not the ideal manner for full actualization of genuine Chinese sovereignty or for building local autonomy based on democratic principles. Political expedience and the need to preserve "continuity and stability" seem to be Beijing's main excuses to enlist and reactivate the service of these ex-colonial appointees to buttress its SAR oligarchy and plutocracy regime.

Localization

This is a parallel development to decolonization with direct impact on the civil service personnel policy as the Basic Law requires the holders of top government positions to be Hong Kong Chinese without foreign right of abode.[35] The localization of leadership and senior management personnel also extends to public bodies and other social organizations; it is not simply a byproduct of decolonization but a natural and healthy development. Until recently leadership positions in Hong Kong have been the preserve of expatriate personnel, but given the increasingly strong local identity, popularization of education, significant increase in the technological skills, academic qualifications and professional experience of the Hong Kong populace, they should be capable of and responsible for managing their own affairs.[36] In fact the localization of government and public sector personnel is in full compliance with the global trends in human rights. There is much merit in offering equal opportunity to qualified Hong Kong residents, and it also meets the requirements for rational human resources deployment and fair and non-discriminatory employment practices. The use of Chinese as an official and legal language and the change in school curriculum and textbook contents are crucial elements in localization and the training of local talents.

The continued employment of non-local Chinese in the civil service, public organizations, academic institutions, and private concerns are guaranteed by the Basic Law, which only requires the SAR Chief Executive, senior officials (about two dozen), and the chief justice of the Court of Final Appeal to be local Chinese, and which also limits non-Chinese SAR citizens to 20% of the membership of the legislature.[37] While boasting the populace's self-esteem in decision making and leadership, the current drive toward localization — with its clear anti-colonial and non-British overtone — might, after 1997, become a parochial and even xenophobic tendency under the spell of ultra-nationalistic sentiments, . This would depend very much on the PRC's ideo-cultural lines and its relations with the outside world. Furthermore, localization will logically serve as a solid foundation for the "high degree of autonomy" on which the PRC has been placing strong restrictions recently.

Internationalization

As a parallel development to decolonization, but on the other side of the coin of localization, is the expanding range and complexity of Hong Kong's global linkages. With the tremendous growth, outreach and diversification of its economy, Hong Kong has assumed an increasingly significant functional role and strategic vitality as a world-class commercial, transportation, financial and communication hub on the Pacific Rim. Hong Kong is presently the eighth largest world trade entity, the busiest container port, the fourth ranking financial center in the world as well as the gateway to and the largest external investor in the fast-growing PRC economy.

In its multifold functional capabilities, economic power projection, and intermediary role for the Chinese mainland, Hong Kong has been highly internationalized. The gradual fading out of the British colonial raj with its London-centered orientation, and the absolute decline of British economic hegemony and monopolies, yielded room for Hong Kong to expand its external ties. The resulting pluralistic international influences have already substantially enriched the economic and cultural lives of Hong Kong people and enlarged their political horizon, especially with the worldwide promotion of democratic values and human rights. Furthermore, the massive overseas exodus of Hong Kong people for education, business as well as migration and settlement have enlarged and deepened Hong Kong's very impressive international networks in human terms. The attention and concern for Hong Kong in the international media, academia, and political circles, especially on the issue of its reintegration with China, also help to strengthen Hong Kong's global linkages and presence on the world stage.

However, in the world trend toward democratization and human rights awareness, the future SAR's global connections would be of the utmost concern to China. The PRC has often looked with suspicion at Hong Kong's relationship with the outside world as potentially dangerous and capable of undermining Beijing's sovereign prerogatives in security, defense, and foreign policy. In fact, the PRC was displeased with the 1992 US-Hong Kong Policy Act which was interpreted as American interference in Chinese domestic affairs and an attempt to drive a wedge in Beijing-SAR relations.[38] More recently, with about a hundred days left before the power transfer, both the PRC foreign minister and SAR Chief Executive-designate Tung Chee-hwa have tried to counter the generally negative images of Hong Kong under Communist Chinese rule as projected in the world press. They even condemned some local political leaders (such as Democratic Party Chairman Martin Lee) for "bad mouthing" the SAR in front of international audience on this score.[39] The very strong international linkages enjoyed by Hong Kong in this sense can be both an asset and a liability in future SAR-PRC central government relations.

Democratization

This is the most problematic transformative process underlining the whole transitional era. The PRC's "one country, two systems" formula contains the pledge for a high degree of autonomy, and both the Joint Declaration and the Basic Law call for a fully elected legislature and an elected Chief Executive as the foundation of the SAR polity. Thus, it seems that the 1997 sovereignty retrocession could have paved the way for Hong Kong's decolonization with elected/ representative democracy.

Unfortunately, there has been a big gap between rhetoric and reality. On the one hand, the scope and pace of British democratization efforts differed substantially from the demands and the expectations of the majority of the Hong Kong people. A gradualist and small steps approach was adopted by the colonialists with support from the conservative elites and big business interests. They were afraid that the rapid emergence of a fully and directly elected legislature would undermine administrative efficiency and executive authority, and give rise to grassroots interest at the expense of big business privileges under colonial patronage. On the other hand, the PRC officialdom has sharply different understanding and appreciation of democracy, especially the electoral process, public accountability, and constitutional limits to executive power, which are contrary to its tradition of absolute control and rule by man.

Chinese party/state cadres, with their ideological preconceptions, harbor deep fear and blatant mistrust of the Western-style democratic system; to them, a directly elected legislature and Chief Executive based on one-person-one vote and universal franchise would lead to a truly autonomous Hong Kong that is not easily susceptible to Beijing's control or manipulation. Thus, Chinese cadres, local conservative elites, and traditional pro-Beijing leftist elements consider that the "elections" stipulated in the Joint Declaration mean other type of electoral arrangements different from the direct election by universal franchise as practiced in many industrial democracies. This crucial difference between the two schools of democratization has divided the local political scene, limited the scope and pace of democratic reforms, and contributed much to the deterioration of Beijing-Hong Kong-London relations.[40]

Of course, the impact of the 1989 Tiananmen Incident further added to the strain and stress in Hong Kong-Beijing tensions over democratization. In the immediate aftermath of the incident, there was an urgent sense of crisis in Hong Kong that galvanized strong popular support, forcing the diehard opponents of democratization such as pro-Beijing unionists and conservative tycoons to lie low or even accept limited electoral reform. (However, their change of heart was short-lived and superficial, as by late 1989 they had mostly retuned to Beijing's fold.) The PRC leadership, suffering from the post-crisis sense of insecurity, paranoia, and international condemnation, decided to tighten its control on Hong Kong. While Beijing had to allow a slightly larger number of directly elected elements in the pre- and post-1997 Hong Kong legislature, it added a new provision on "subversion" in the Basic Law's final draft, so as to curb the democratic politicians who were regarded as "subversives".

The twisting course to pre-1997 partial democracy has been characterized by heated partisan debates, polarization of political allegiance, sectorial conflicts, colonial betrayal and even government falsification of public opinion in Hong Kong.[42] Externally, tension and stress were raised by Beijing's condemnations, threats, and preemptive maneuvers including the creation of extra-constitutional, non-legitimate power organs not stipulated by the Basic Law. The bottomline of the Sino-British discord, which manifested itself in the non-cooperation in political and legal matters, is Beijing's desire for maximum preemptive control over Hong Kong affairs even before 1997 in opposition to both the sunset colonial regime and the awakened Hong Kong Chinese.

Politicization, Identity Consciousness and the Double Crisis of Confidence

The China factor and the processes of decolonalization, localization, internationalization, and democratization combined to raise the level of political awareness and also sharpen an identity consciousness among the Hong Kong populace. The traditional image of political apathy of the Hong Kong Chinese, who were only interested in economic well-being, is no longer valid. There has been a rising tide of heated debates, active participation, and widespread collective action regarding public affairs, community issues, and of course, the transition to 1997 and the prospects of the future SAR.[43] The people of Hong Kong have received valuable lessons in civic education and gained first-hand experience in citizenship during the past 15 years as provided by the 1982–84 Sino-British negotiations, the 1985–90 Basic Law drafting process, the 1987–88 and 1992–94 electoral reform controversies, as well as the 1985, 1988, 1991, and 1995 Legislative Council elections. Even the selection of the first SAR Chief Executive in late 1996 — by the China-appointed Selection Committee — entailed pseudo-campaigns by the three candidates; they worked hard to court the support of the public which did not have a single vote. The very fact that such "campaigning" had to take place (even through this only generated more publicity and widespread interest instead of genuine public participation) shows how the political culture has changed in the transition era.

The decolonization/localization/democratization processes leading supposedly to a high degree of autonomy in the future SAR have given birth to a new political culture and civic mentality. This has encouraged and empowered popular participation in and societal mobilization for both electoral campaigns and pressure groups/sectorial politics. There are concerns for the inevitable political change, and a new assertiveness to fill in the space created by the colonial regime's fadeout and as yet unoccupied by the SAR power structure. These feelings have energized an unprecedented wave of public affairs activism and promoted popular discourse on political rights, citizenship, and national identity. The improvements in education, level of affluence, skills, and civic sophistication have yielded a population, most of whom are native-born Hong Kong belongers, more ready and prepared to have a voice and even a hand in matters affecting their life and work as well as their future prospect under a different sovereign.

Indeed, the Hong Kong people have been transformed from colonial subjects into citizens of a distinct Chinese community, and this is an unmistakable result of the rapid and intensive popular politicization of the transition era. Yet their newly gained sense of "Chineseness" has compelled them to be more attentive and mindful of developments in the PRC.[44] Paradoxically, this heightened China-awareness has often led to greater tension and even deepened the mistrust between the Hong Kong Chinese and the mainland communist regime.

No longer could the Hong Kong Chinese take comfort under the British colonial regime, which until the 1980s had deliberately discouraged political activism, national consciousness, and the emergence of a political culture of participation, representation and accountability. The 1997 sovereignty retrocession has forced many local residents to wake up and face reality outside the colonial cocoon. Unless they secure other alternative arrangements, they will soon become, in legal and administrative terms, citizens of a special administrative region of the PRC. The majority have little option to alter their status. Besides being Hong Kong residents, they also share distinctively Chinese attributes culturally, socially, biologically, and often economically. Thus the political and constitutional construct of a self-embraced or externally imposed identity of being or soon becoming a Chinese national, a permanent resident of the Hong Kong SAR and also a citizen of the PRC is an accepted fact of life to many.[45] This heightened sense of political consciousness and increasingly clear notion of status, identity, and citizenship also underline several related phenomena that galvanized into a crisis mentality under the 1997 syndrome — the "double crisis of confidence."

First, political awareness promotes a widespread realization that the people of Hong Kong were not, are not, and cannot be the master of their own fate. Not only were they excluded from the secretive 1982–84 Sino-British Joint Declaration negotiations and the 1993–94 Sino-British talks on the Patten electoral reforms, they are still the prawns and victims in the ongoing discord and struggle for control between the two sovereign powers. Because of their inability to alter the decisions made by Beijing and London, the local community feels helpless and pessimistic about the promised autonomy that would preserve their existing rights and freedom.

Second, as a direct response to the increasingly powerful China factor, there is a natural echoing effect of Chinese nationalistic allegiance among many Hong Kong Chinese, especially the younger generation, that goes beyond socio-cultural identity but transcends into political reorientation. The resultant patriotic impulses, combined with the belief in the inseparable bond binding the fate of Hong Kong with the mainland, have propelled many Hong Kong Chinese to engage actively in PRC political events as Chinese nationals' natural contribution to their motherland.

A well-known example is the outpouring of sympathy and overwhelming support in Hong Kong for the spring 1989 Tiananmen democratic movement. More than a million people in Hong Kong took to the streets in massive demonstrations, funds and supplies were dispatched to the Beijing student activists, and later assistance provided for the escape and exile overseas of mainland dissidents. While these activities stemmed from genuine patriotic concern for motherland China, they provoked Beijing's wrath. The PRC leadership condemned such conduct as Hong Kong people's interference in China's internal affairs and "subversive behavior against the central state".[46] This is a tragic "conflict of patriotism" because the newly acquired identity of the Hong Kong people — as Chinese nationals and soon-to-be PRC citizens — endowed them with a powerful commitment to China. Unfortunately their moral allegiance and political sympathy with the democratic cause (for both Hong Kong and the mainland) rendered them unacceptable to the anti-democratic authorities in Beijing. The crux of the problem is a "dilemma of loyalty" — with their newly discovered nationalism, patriotic sentiment, and sense of belonging, most Hong Kong Chinese identify with China the nation-state, its people, territory, history and culture; but they have no allegiance to the PRC regime, its communist party leadership or official policies.

Third, the feeling of helplessness and pessimism reinforced a pervasive sentiment of bitterness and serious mistrust toward the officialdom in both London and Beijing.[47] This has induced a significant portion of Hong Kong people to seek security and an alternative future prospect by writing off Hong Kong and reducing their own stake in the territory. A clear manifestation of this lack of confidence has been the high rate of emigration.

Since the 1980s, Hong Kong has witnessed massive emigration waves, with an annual average of over 1% of its total population "relocating" to Canada, the United States, Australia, New Zealand, Singapore, the United Kingdom, and other destinations aboard. This outward-bound human traffic has created new "Hong Kong towns" overseas. Domestically it has resulted in a "brain drain" of professional and managerial personnel, thus affecting the availability of human resources for the local economy and public sector. Such a pattern of "voting with your feet" as a self-preservation measure by Hong Kong people with valuable skills and economic assets became particularly obvious after the June 1989 events and has yet to show any sign of serious decline.[48]

The "double crisis of confidence" is derived from frustration toward the current and the incoming sovereigns. On the one hand, many Hong Kong people harbor serious doubts about the post-1997 prospects of the Hong Kong SAR as a free, democratic society enjoying prosperity and stability under Chinese communist dictatorship. On the other hand, they also doubt the ability and will of the colonial regime in maintaining a fair, clean, effective, and responsive administration and also in standing up firmly to PRC pressure and interference in the sunset years of British rule. Furthermore, there is the feeling that the British colonial connections have been a liability which added to the current difficulty in the much strained China-Hong Kong relationship. London's assumption of all responsibilities for Sino-British negotiations without direct input from the Hong Kong people has created a perception of British betrayal or sellout of genuine Hong Kong interests in exchange for British advantage in China. Also, the

PRC's attacks on the British colonial establishment under Governor Patten have inevitably impacted on the local populace's attitude toward both the Beijing and London regimes.

Indeed, since the 1980s, Hong Kong people have found themselves in a precarious balance between the UK and the PRC, and they could not remain innocent or ignorant bystanders to the unfolding dramas of an imperfect transition. They are being victimized by the crossfires of Sino-British hostilities which escalated into crisis proportions in the aftermath of the Tiananmen Incident. The international condemnation of the PRC's brutality reflected a new mistrust of Beijing's true intentions and unchanged nature as a Communist dictatorship with little regard for human rights and civil liberties despite a decade of "reform and opening."

The British government was forced to acknowledge Hong Kong's "crisis of confidence" and adopted the following measures to rebuild local confidence toward 1997:
1. the granting of the right of abode in the UK to some 50,000 qualified Hong Kong families,
2. the enactment of a Bill of Rights,
3. the building of a new airport as a sign of "prosperity", and
4. the improvement in the scope and pace of pre-1997 democratization, especially the number of directly elected legislators.[49]

The PRC leadership, disgraced and shocked by the severe and negative global response to the Tiananmen crackdown, felt more insecure and even paranoid. They became less tolerant to the democratic aspirations of the Hong Kong populace and suspected an anti-China, anti-communist conspiracy behind the British measures to restore confidence after Tiananmen.[50]

The results of the first-ever direct elections to the Legislative Council in September 1991 seemed to confirm Beijing's suspicions. With a voter turnout rate of nearly 40%, the pro-democratic lobby captured two-thirds of the votes and 17 of the 18 directly elected seats (in the 60-member legislature), and all the pro-PRC candidates were defeated. This amounted to a Hong Kong referendum on the June Fourth events with a total repudiation of the PRC's policy.[51] Beijing then stepped up its opposition to the democratic movement in Hong Kong lest the example of "prosperity and stability with democracy" in the SAR should threaten the Communist Party's control on the mainland.

The controversies over the 1992–94 electoral reforms deepened the Sino-British confrontation and led to Beijing's preemptive assaults against the colonial regime and non-cooperation over almost all transitional issues. In mid-1993 Beijing set up, without any legal or constitutional basis as specified by the Joint Declaration or Basic Law, the SAR Preliminary Working Committee (PWC) as a "second stove" or "shadow government think tank." The following year, after the Hong Kong legislature had passed Governor Patten's electoral reforms, Beijing decided to abolish the earlier agreed upon "through train" formula under which the last colonial legislature, elected in 1995, would serve beyond 1997 till 1999, two years into the SAR. Instead, the PRC will install an "SAR provisional legislature" to replace the 1995 elected legislature which will be disbanded on July 1, 1997.[52] Furthermore, despite the Sino-British Memorandum of Understanding signed in September 1991, Beijing withheld its endorsement of the new airport project (which straddles 1997) until the summer of 1995.

The Legislative Council elections held in September 1995, the last under British auspices, seem to be another setback to the PRC's attempt to restrict Hong Kong's democratic development. Although the voter turnout rate (36%) was lower than that in 1991, nearly a million voters took part to choose 20 directly elected legislators and 30 indirectly elected "functional" seats (plus 10 electoral college selected seats). The pro-democracy camp again captured the lion's share of the seats: the Democratic Party 19, the Association For Democracy and People's Livelihood 4, and other pro-democracy independents 6. The pro-Beijing Democratic Alliance for Betterment of Hong Kong won only 6 seats, but its top three leaders were all defeated in direct election contests. All together, the democratic camp captured nearly 64% of the popular vote. Beijing refused to accept the election results and questioned the fairness of the electoral system as a British conspiracy to perpetuate pro-British, anti-China influence.

To counter the colonial government's measures to restore local confidence, the PRC contemplated — via the PWC and PC — tight controls over SAR permanent residency requirements (targeting those Hong Kong people with foreign passports/rights of abode). The PWC and PC also proposed to "resurrect" or "reinstall" six "original" Hong Kong laws which were extensively amended in the early 1990s to avoid contravening the 1991 Bill of Rights.[54] In late 1995, the PRC officialdom attacked the Hong Kong government's increased spending on welfare as dangerous "welfarism" — despite the high surplus in the budget. This constituted a blatant interference in local policy making and resources allocation which is fully in the purview of Hong Kong's autonomy.[55]

Thus it seems that the PRC, in the final transition era, has emphasized its assertion of "sovereignty" at the expense of the earlier promised "high degree of autonomy" so cherished by the Hong Kong people. Perhaps unintentionally, Beijing's recent behavior gave substance to the "crisis of confidence" scenario. With only a hundred days left before the transfer of sovereignty, it has unmasked its perception of how the SAR should be governed — to maintain firm control, Beijing will "preserve" Hong Kong as an outdated, unjust, uncaring and undemocratic colonial polity with many of the British-groomed ex-colonial elites installed in the new SAR power organs. This is indeed an ironic twist of fate that few could have anticipated at the start of the Hong Kong reintegration process one and a half decade ago.

The Challenge Ahead

Ironically, Hong Kong democratic activists were among the first in the local community to embrace Chinese sovereignty retrocession in the early 1980s. However, in the aftermath of the June Fourth events, their dedication to the democratic cause has made them "subversives" in the eyes of the Beijing officialdom. While deliberately excluding these activists from the transition era power structure — such as the PWC, PC, and Selection Committee — the PRC government has systematically recruited retired officials, former British proteges and "colonial defectors" who opposed the sovereignty retrocession in the early 1980s. Such "united front" tactics provoked the anger and criticism of leading long-time PRC supporters and pro-Beijing grassroots circles as a most dubious kind of allegiance building and loyalty transfer. To many Hong Kong people, these "old batteries" from the British colonial dust bin hardly seem to be the right pillars to support the future, post-colonial SAR under Chinese sovereignty.[56]

While history does not necessarily repeat itself, it is worthwhile to note the tragic experience following mainland China's recovery of a former colonial island domain 50 years ago. This refers to the February 28, 1947 incident in Taiwan when the Nationalist government under the Guomindang brutally suppressed the local protests stemming from widespread and legitimate grievances and serious gaps between the rulers and the ruled.[57] The bitter memories of the thousands who perished in the massacre have poisoned relations between the Nationalist regime and provincial natives with lingering negative effects on the prospect for mainland-Taiwan reunification.

The real success of the China-Hong Kong reintegration does not merely rely on the faithful actualization of the Basic Law provisions or the proper functioning of the SAR institutions. Rather, it is in the winning of the hearts and minds of the six million plus Hong Kong Chinese who will shed their colonial past and become Chinese nationals. To achieve this is the greatest challenge ahead for Hong Kong's future sovereign.

Even if one discounts the basic issue of communism versus capitalism, there are sharp discrepancies between the Chinese mainland and Hong Kong in terms of:

1. size, scale, and magnitude;
2. level of socio-economic development, income, and lifestyle;
3. popular mentality, ideo-cultural orientation, and world view; and
4. legal, political, economic systems, and administrative practices.

It would therefore require considerable self-restraint, tolerance, patience, goodwill, and trust on the part of the PRC leadership in its approach to the Hong Kong SAR and its citizens.

If the record of the past decade and a half of imperfect transition is any indication, this will be an extremely demanding task for the PRC. How it copes with this Hong Kong challenge will affect both its cherished reunification with Taiwan and its relations with Hong Kong's many global partners, including the US and other industrial democracies, which are of importance to Beijing's strategic and economic concerns.[58]

Looking ahead, the success or failure of the SAR under Chinese sovereignty — in preserving the best of Hong Kong for the benefit of its people and its new mainland masters — will be the greatest challenge for the PRC leadership. For instance, if the Hong Kong SAR continues to function as an economically prosperous, socially free and politically democratic Chinese community of pluralist and cosmopolitan flavor, much credit will be given to the late-Deng Xiaoping's "one country, two systems" formula. But if by then, a prosperous economy, a free society and a democratic polity were still elusive to the people in major Chinese cities like Shanghai, Tianjin, Wuhan and Guangzhou, the standard "one country, two systems" explanation would not be an adequate or satisfactory rationalization for the sharp contrast between them and their Hong Kong brothers and sisters. It would not require too much cynicism to suggest that the Hong Kong SAR's success could no longer be attributed to British management or colonial legacy, but to the fact that it does not practice communism. Thus the relative underdevelopment in terms of economic prosperity, social freedom, and political democracy for mainland China would have to be attributed, fairly and squarely, to communism. On the other hand, if the Hong Kong SAR can no longer enjoy economic prosperity, social freedom, and political democracy, the people of Hong Kong and their global social-economic partners would naturally place the blame on the suffocating interference by Hong Kong's communist masters. Again, the failure of the Hong Kong SAR would be no credit to communism in China.

Therefore, in either the bloom or doom scenario for the SAR's future prospect, Chinese communism cannot be the winner. Hong Kong as part of China will set in motion a very crucial and fundamental challenge to the communist polity and ideology on the mainland. Of the three benchmarks of success (i.e. economic, social, and political performance), it is relatively easy for the Beijing leadership to deliver improvement on the economic front with tangible material gains, as has been the case since the 1980s. However, if Beijing continues to promote economic modernization, the subsequent material improvement and popular affluence will inevitably create the conditions and expectations for social liberalization, which in turn will generate demands for political democratization. Unfortunately, social liberalization and political democratization still have no place on the agenda of the Chinese communist regime today. With economic and social transformation, greater momentum toward liberty and democracy would be generated and the foundation of communist rule would be undermined ultimately; the Communist Party's claim to power would only be the coercive capacity of the gun.

To bridge the gulf between the SAR and the mainland, Beijing will not only have to strengthen the institutional linkages between the two, but also must consider social, economic and other issues. One option to reduce the great disparity in living standards, lifestyles, liberty and rights of the people in the two Chinese communities would be to bring down the high level of prosperity, freedom, and democracy enjoyed by the SAR.[59] But this will carry an extremely high economic and political cost, for both Beijing's cherished reintegration with Taiwan and for its international relations, especially with the Western industrial democracies. The other option, more genuinely beneficial in the long-term interest of the Chinese nation, would be to devote all resources and efforts to accelerate the economic reform and modernization of the mainland. But then Beijing also must be prepared to accept the natural and inevitable by-products (social freedom and political democracy) of economic well-being and popular affluence in order to reduce the disparities between the SAR and the mainland (and by extension, between the two Chinese communities across the Taiwan Strait). By taking this latter approach, the economic modernization as unleashed by Deng in the late 1970s and Hong Kong's retrocession in 1997 will be intertwined to create the overwhelming stimulants and imperatives to proceed with reform beyond the economic sector. Of course, one may argue, this would sow the seeds for the fundamental transformation, if not the ultimate demise, of communist rule in mainland China.

In this sense, Hong Kong's integration with the mainland, under the "one country, two systems" formula with a 50-year schedule for post-retrocession adjustment and transformation, may well be the more challenging phase for Hong Kong. As such, how the Chinese communist leadership manages the Hong Kong SAR will shape its agenda for domestic modernization and reform, its patriotic drive for national reunification, and its functional-strategic relationship with the global community in the twenty-first century. If the tiny Hong Kong SAR, with 6.3 million people in 400 square miles, is not exactly a young David in the world of economic success and global significance, then would mainland China, as the home to 1.2 billion Chinese in 3.7 million square miles, turn out to be the Goliath in this challenge of full integration after 1997?

While there is no simple or easy answer to the above question, the past 15 years of Hong Kong's transformation have yielded concrete examples of the PRC's policies and measures on the Hong Kong issue which have already laid a platform for the SAR's political and institutional functioning in the immediate post-transfer era. Even as the colonial era is approaching its final sunset in Hong Kong, thereby removing the British factor from the Sino-British discord over transition matters, the British departure does not mask the many still unresolved problems in Hong Kong as it is about to embark on its SAR phase of development.[60] How these problems are resolved by the new SAR regime and between the SAR and the PRC central authorities will be crucial to the process of further transformation leading to Hong Kong's full integration with China by 2047.

Hopefully, by then Hong Kong would have made its greatest contribution to China by promoting balanced and enlightened economic, social, and political developments on the mainland. It will be under such auspicious conditions that the end of Hong Kong's SAR status shall signal a full-scale reintegration of the two prosperous, free, and democratic communities within one China.

Notes

1. On Ye's "Nine Points" and the PRC's "peaceful offensive" toward Taiwan in the 1980s, see Lai To Lee, *The Reunification of China: PRC-Taiwan Relations in Flux* (New York: Praeger, 1991), pp. 8–11.

2. *South China Morning Post*, March 23, 1996 and *Ta Kung Pao*, same date.

3. For a balanced overall view of this issue up to the early 1990s, see Lai To Lee, *The Reunification of China*.

4. Camoes C.K. Tam, *Disputes Concerning Macau's Sovereignty Between China and Portugal* (1553–1993) (Taipei: Yung-yeh Publishers, 1994), pp. 255–262.

5. On the 1982–84 negotiations, see Robert Cottrell, *The End of Hong Kong: The Secret Diplomacy of Imperial Retreat* (London: John Murray, 1993) and Mark Roberti, *The Fall of Hong Kong: China's Triumph & Britain's Betrayal* (New York: John Wiley & Sons, revised edition, 1996), part I. Also see *Sing Tao Daily* May 20, 1997, p. A-14.

6. Camoes Tam, pp. 273–318; also see Shiu Hing Lo, *Political Development in Macau* (Hong Kong: Chinese University Press, 1995), pp. 21–31.

7. See Byron S.J. Weng "Mainland China, Taiwan and Hong Kong as International Actors" in James Tang and Gerry Postiglione, eds., *Hong Kong's Reunion with China: Global Dimensions* (Armonk, N.Y.: M.E. Sharpe, 1997). Also see the recent volumes published by Taipei's Institute for National Policy Research on Taiwan-Hong Kong links in the 1997 context, Wei Min, ed., *Taigang guanxi: jizhi ji fazhan* (Taiwan-Hong Kong Relations: Mechanism and Development) (Taipei: Yeqiang chubanshe, 1996) & Hung-mao Tien & Yun-han Chu, eds., *Yi jiu jiu qi quodu yu Taigang quanxi* (The 1997 Transition and Taiwan-Hong Kong Relations) (Taipei: Yeqiang chubanshe, 1996).

8. *Ta Kung Pao*, January 31, 1995.

9. *Hong Kong United Daily*, April 9, 1995.

10. *Sing Tao Daily*, June 23, 1995.

11. For the passage of "Hong Kong Macau-Relations Act" by Taipei's Legislative Yuan, see *Ming Pao* (Hong Kong), March 19, 1997, and *Central Daily* (Taipei), March 19, 1997.

12. The author is most grateful to Professor Lynn T. White III of Princeton University for his insightful suggestions on this key point.

13. Hu Sheng, Imperialism and Chinese Politics (Beijing: Foreign Language Press, 1953) remains the PRC's authoritative academic study on the issue from a historical perspective. Hu, currently president of the Chinese Academy of Social Science, was a member of the PRC's Hong Kong Basic Law Drafting Committee, 1985–1990.

14. Robert Cottrell, *The End of Hong Kong*.

15. James T.H. Tang & Frank Ching "The MacLehose-Youde Years: Balancing The 'Three Legged Stool', 1971–86," in Ming K. Chan, ed., *Precarious Balance: Hong Kong Between China and Britain,* 1842–1992, (Armonk, N.Y.: ME Sharpe, 1994), pp. 149–172.

16. James Tang & Frank Ching , "The MacLehose-Youde Years," in *Precarious Balance*, p. 159.

17. A recent study of the PRC's sovereignty concern over Hong Kong issues from the angle of the Basic Law is Enbao Wang, *Hong Kong, 1997: The Politics of Transition* (Boulder: Lynne Rienner, 1995), chapter 5.

18. See Sino-British Joint Declaration, Annex III. At the end of March 1996, the total assets of the Land Fund Trust was valued at over HK$110 billion. How should the SAR government manage this sum after July 1, 1997 has recently sparked some debates, *Ta Kung Po,* March 4, 1997, and *Hong Kong Economic Journal,* same date.

19. See Ming K. Chan, "Democracy Derailed: Realpolitik in the Making at the Hong Kong Basic Law, 1985–90," in Ming K. Chan & David Clark, eds., *The Hong Kong Basic Law: Blueprint For "Stability and Prosperity" Under Chinese Sovereignty?* (Armonk, N.Y.: M.E. Sharpe, 1991), pp. 8–17.

20. Frank Ching, "Toward Colonial Sunset: The Wilson Regime, 1987–92" in *Precarious Balance,* pp. 189–191.

21. *Wen Wei Po,* July 21, 1993.

22. On the airport project see, Government Information Services' *Hong Kong 1996* (Hong Kong: Government Information Services, 1996), chapter 16. Despite this 1991 memorandum, due to Sino-British political discord over Governor Patten's October 1992 electoral reforms, no breakthrough was achieved until June 1995 when detailed arrangements to fund and manage the airport project were agreed upon by the two sides.

23. *Ta Kung Po,* March 5–7, 1997 on the Sino-British budget agreement. Also *Hong Kong Economic Journal,* March 7, 1997 "Editorial" on the PRC's input into the 1997–98 budget.

24. *Sing Tao Daily,* January 10, 1997 (see p. 13, also p. 16 for Governor Patten's response and p. 10 for the political cartoon).

25. Local democratic activists formally lodged a complaint with the Hong Kong police on March 7, 1997 against an individual member of the SAR provisional legislature who formally set up an office in Hong Kong, see *Sing Tao Daily,* March 8 and 10, 1997. Also *South China Morning Post,* March 10, 1997.

26. *Wen Wei Po,* July 21, 1993.

27. Hong Kong Government Information Services, ed., *Hong Kong 1995,* (Hong Kong: Government Information Service, 1995), p. 60.

28. The rising tide of nationalism as the channel to enhance political legitimacy and popular support in the PRC is delineated in *Far Eastern Economic Review,* November 9, 1995, pp. 20–28.

29. The author is deeply indebted to Professor Lynn White of Princeton University for his insightful suggestions on this important point.

30. The functional and economic integration between the PRC and Hong Kong has been particularly intimate and productive in the regional context of Hong Kong's link with the neighboring Guangdong province, see, Ming K. Chan, "All in the Family: The Hong Kong-Guangdang Link in Historical Perspective," in Reginald Y. Kwok and Alvin Y. So, eds., *The Hong Kong-Guangdong Link: Partnership in Flux* (Armonk, New York: M.E. Sharpe, 1995), pp. 31–63; also see other essays in that volume.

31. On the 1992–94 Sino-British discord over the Patten reform, see John Burns "Hong Kong in 1992: The Struggle for Authority," *Asian Survey,* V. 33, no. 1, (January 1993), pp. 22–31, and "Hong Kong in 1993: The Struggle Intensifies," *Asian Survey,* V. 34, no. 1, (January 1994), pp. 55–63; and Suzanne Pepper, "Hong Kong in 1994: Democracy, Human Rights, and the Post-Colonial Political Order," *Asian Survey,* V. 35, no. 1, (January 1995), pp. 48–60.

32. Ian Scott, "Political Transformation in Hong Kong: From Colony to Colony," in *The Hong Kong-Guangdong Link,* pp. 189–223.

33. All these PRC organs share, to an alarmingly high degree, interlocking and

overlapping personnel whose composition by appointment from Beijing magnified the very acute lack of genuine legitimacy and popular mandate.

34. In *South China Morning Post,* March 9, 1997, p. 9 the "Focus" section carries a special feature interview with Rita Fan by Jonathan Brande. Also see, S.Y. Chung's interview in Sally Blyth and Ian Wotherspoon, *Hong Kong Remembers* (Hong Kong Oxford University Press, 1996) pp. 47–54.

35. See Basic Law article 101.

36. On the pre-1997 public sector reform, see, Jane Y.C. Lee and Anthony B.L. Cheung, eds., *Public Sector Reform in Hong Kong: Key Concepts, Program-to-Date and Future Directions* (Hong Kong: Chinese University Press, 1995).

37. See Basic Law articles 67, 90, and 101.

38. Ming K. Chan, *Global Dimensions of Hong Kong's Transition Toward 1997* (Milwaukee: University of Wisconsin-Marquetee University Center for International Studies Occasional Paper #95–03, June 1995), pp. 12–18. This 1992 US-Hong Kong Policy Act is also a cousin to the 1979 US-Taiwan Relations Act but minus the provisions on defense, arm sales, etc.

39. *Ta Kung Po,* March 5, 1997; *South China Morning Post,* February 14, 1997. Martin Lee's offending piece, "A Message from Hong Kong to Davos," appeared in *Asia Wall Street Journal,* February 5, 1997, p. 8. Also see *Sing Tao Daily,* March 7, 1997.

40. Ming K. Chan, "Democracy Derailed: Realpolitik in the Making of the Hong Kong Basic Law, 1985–90," in Ming K. Chan and David Clark, eds., *The Hong Kong Basic Law: Blueprint for "Stability and Prosperity" under Chinese Sovereignty?* (Armonk, New York: M.E. Sharpe, 1991), pp. 3–35.

41. This is article 23 in the Basic Law.

42. A detailed study of this subject is Ming Sing, "The Democracy Movement in Hong Kong, 1986–1990," (D.Phil. thesis, University of Oxford, 1993)

43. See Michael DeGolyer and Janet Lee Scott, "The Myth of Political Apathy in Hong Kong," *The Annuals of the American Academy of Political Science,* V. 547. *The Future of Hong Kong* (September 1996), pp. 68–78.

44. Ming-kwan Lee, "Community and Identity in Transition in Hong Kong," in *The Hong Kong-Guangdong Link,* Table 5.6 points out that according to a 1990 survey of 1957 respondents, 56.6% regarded themselves as HongKongese; 25.4% as Chinese, 13.8% as both, 1.2% as either; 3% don't know/no opinion/no answer in their claimed identity. In a 1995 survey conducted by Asia-Pacific Research Institute, Chinese University of Hong Kong, among the 408 respondents, 50.2% claim to be HongKongese, 30.9% as Chinese, 15.4% as both, 1.2% either, 2.2% don't know/no opinion, see Lau Siu-kai, "HongKongese or Chinese: The Problem of Identity on the Eve of Resumption of Chinese Sovereignty over Hong Kong," (Unpublished paper, 1996).

45. On the transition era identity change, see Ming-kwan Lee, "Community and Identity in Transition in Hong Kong," in *The Hong Kong-Guangdong Link,* pp. 119–132.

46. For the June Fourth events' impact on Hong Kong democratization, see Ming K. Chan, "Democracy Derailed," pp. 17–25.

47. According to a survey conducted by the Social Science Research Center, University of Hong Kong, in October 1996, the over 200 respondents expressed greater trust in Hong Kong government: 60%, than in British government in London: 27%, with only 23% expressing trust in the PRC government. Such results are reported in Robert Chung Ting-yiu, ed., *Pop Press* (Hong Kong: Social Science Research Centre, The University of Hong Kong), Vol. 3, No. 3, November 1996.

48. On the migration waves and overseas Hong Kong settlements, see, Ronald Skeldon, ed., *Reluctant Exiles? Migration from Hong Kong and the New Overseas China* (Armonk, New York: M.E. Sharpe, 1994).

49. On the British post-June Fourth confidence-building measures, see Frank Ching, "Toward Colonial Sunset: The Wilson Regime, 1987–92," in *Precarious Balance,* pp. 173–197, and also Ming K. Chan, *Global Dimensions,* pp. 8–10.

50. Ming K. Chan, *Global Dimensions,* pp. 16–18.

51. On the 1991 election results and implications for party politics, see Ming K. Chan, "The 1991 Elections in Hong Kong: Democratization in the Shadow of Tiananmen," in George T. Yu, ed., *China in Transition: Economic Political and Social Developments* (Lanham: University Press of America, 1993), pp. 229–250, and Ming K. Chan, "Decolonization without Democracy: The Birth of Pluralistic Politics in Hong Kong," in Edward Friedman, ed., *The Politics of Democratization: Generalizing East Asian Experiences* (Boulder: Westview Press, 1994), pp. 161–181.

52. John Burns, "Hong Kong in 1993," and Suzanne Pepper, "Hong Kong in 1994."

53. The 1995 election results are based on the reports in *South China Morning Post* and *Sing Tao Daily,* September 19 and 20, 1995. Also see Ian Scott "Party Politics and Elections in Transitional Hong Kong", *Asian Journal of Political Science,* V. 4, No. 1 (June 1966).

54. For reports and comments on the PRC's proposal to trim the Bill of Rights and the "restoration" of old colonial laws, see *Far Eastern Economic Review,* November 16, 1995, "Editorial," p. 7, and "Hold Your Ground: Colony protests at China's efforts to trim Bill of Rights," p. 36.

55. For the official PRC attack on Hong Kong government's "welfarism" and also the name-calling of Governor Patten as a "dictator," see *South China Morning Post* and *Sing Tao Daily,* November 29 and 30, 1995. Also see *Far Eastern Economic Review,* November 9, 1995, p. 36 on Hong Kong's inadequate welfare provisions. In the 1997–98 budget, welfare spending was increased by a mere 9.4%, perhaps due to PRC pressure; see *South China Morning Post,* March 7–8 1997, and *Sing Tao Daily,* same dates.

56. The late Dorothy Y.C. Liu, a Hong Kong member of the PRC's National People's Congress, coined the term "old batteries" to describe these "colonial turncoats" that staffed the PWC and PC. Her sentiment is well received among the local populace.

57. Tse-han Lai, Ramon Myers and Wou Wei, *A Tragic Beginning: The Taiwan Uprising of February 28, 1947* (Stanford: Stanford University Press, 1991).

58. For recent examples of international concern for Hong Kong's future, see then US Consul-General in Hong Kong, Richards W. Mueller "America's Long-term Interest in Hong Kong," *The Annals of the American Academy of Political and Social Science,* V. 547 (September 1996), pp. 144–152.

59. Bruce Buneo de Mesquita, David Newman, Alvin Rabushka, *Red Flag Over Hong Kong* (Chatham, New Jersey: Chatham House Publishers, 1996), which presents a bleak picture for the SAR's future, is a recent example of international pessimism.

60. Michael Yahuda, *Hong Kong: China's Challenge* (London: Routledge, 1996) offers a long-term articulation of Hong Kong's return to China as a unique turning point for China's own future development from a British perspective.

2

Civil Service Systems in Transition: Hong Kong, China, and 1997

*John P. Burns**

The most important content of China's Hong Kong policy is to acquire sovereignty and effective control over the territory in 1997. A core target of control is the Hong Kong government, especially the civil service. Implementation of the policy and other policies related to Hong Kong is conditioned in part by the experience of China's leaders with its own civil service.

During the last stage of the transition to Chinese rule, the British and Chinese governments have clashed on several issues relating to the management of the Hong Kong civil service. These have included: the extent to which the civil service should be accountable to the legislature; the nature of civil service neutrality; and the criteria for selecting the Hong Kong Special Administrative Region's (SAR) principal officials.

China's own experience of managing its civil service is changing in each of these areas. First, the people's congress system in China is becoming less of a "rubber stamp" as delegates represent the interests of their functional and sectional constituency, and begin more actively to scrutinize the work of the government. This bodes well for a more activist Legislative Council (Legco) in Hong Kong after 1997 than many may have realized. Still, the latitude permitted to the Legco may not be enough to satisfy public opinion.

---

* The author gratefully acknowledges the support of the Hong Kong Research Grants Council which provided funding for the research needed to write the essay.

Second, China's civil service is developing a norm of neutrality vis-a-vis society and groups in the economy as the state takes on a new regulatory role. This may reinforce Beijing's view that the Hong Kong civil service should remain neutral. Third, selection criteria for promotion in the civil service have in practice undergone considerable change since the 1970s when personal relations or *guanxi* played less of a role, to the 1980s and 1990s when arguably personal relations became more important for personnel decision making in the absence of institutionalized regulations. Chinese authorities expect to make promotions based in part on *guanxi*. Appointments to senior positions in the Hong Kong civil service may be no exception.

Background

As Hong Kong approaches its 1997 political integration with China, the legitimacy of its colonial institutions has declined. Efforts by the government to improve administrative efficiency through performance pledges and public sector reform[1] have probably slowed the decline, but it is real enough.

No where is it more evident than in the recent re-emergence of corruption in Hong Kong. Substantial increases in both private sector and civil service corruption[2] in Hong Kong are symptomatic of malaise in the territory. From 1992 to 1993, reports of corruption brought to the Independent Commission Against Corruption (ICAC) jumped by an alarming 44%. They continued to increase in 1994, but fell by modest amounts in 1995 and 1996 (see Table 2.1). Complaints against the police have largely followed these trends, although from 1995 to 1996 they increased again, as did complaints against other government departments.

Table 2.1

Corruption Reports in Hong Kong, 1992–96

Subject	1992	1993	1994	1995	1996
Police	454	614 (+35.2)	667 (+8.6)	561 (−18.9)	576 (+2.6)
Other Goverment Departments	578	751 (+29.9)	714 (−5.0)	687 (−3.8)	728 (+5.9)
Private Sector	1166	1798 (+54.2)	1830 (+1.7)	1630 (−10.9)	1651 (+1.3)
Public Bodies	59	113 (+91.5)	101 (−10.6)	109 (+7.9)	131 (+20.2)
Elections	19	8 (−57.9)	289 (+3512)	247 (−14.5)	22 (−91.1)
Total Reports	2276	3284 (+44.3)	3601 (+9.6)	3234 (−10.1)	3108 (−3.9)

Note: Percentage change over previous year in brackets.
Source: Independent Commission Against Corruption, March 4, 1997.

From 1994 to 1995, ICAC prosecutions of police officers increased from to 443.[3] In 80% of these cases, police officers were involved with other offic in corruption that, according to an ICAC official "showed chilling similarities the syndicates which ran amok in Hong Kong in the 1960s and 1970s."[4] From 1991 to 1995, corruption complaints against some other civil servants, such as hygiene inspectors, hawker control officers, and licensing staff also increased dramatically (by 42%).[5] Surveys of youth opinion reveal that corruption was more acceptable as a business practice to young people in Hong Kong than it was a decade ago. According to the ICAC, the sharp rise in corruption is related to 1997 ("the so-called 'fast buck' syndrome and people's fear of Chinese rule").[6] If this is true, then corruption should begin to decline during the latter half of 1997. But the current trend is indicative of the declining legitimacy of colonial Hong Kong's political institutions.

During the 1980s and 1990s, corruption in China also increased dramatically. From 1988 to mid-1993, for example, the Supreme People's Procuratorate accepted more than 430,000 cases of corruption, of which it investigated more than 220,000 cases,[7] averaging about 44,000 cases per year. By 1995 the same body investigated more than 63,000 cases of corruption,[8] an increase of more than 30%. In 1994, authorities estimated that in poor Anhui province, for example, one in five cadres was "on the take."[9] A year later authorities exposed the worst case of corruption since 1949, which reportedly implicated a Chinese Communist Party (CCP) Politburo member, Chen Xitong, the first party secretary of the Beijing Municipal Committee and former Mayor of Beijing. In 1996, 18 people were charged in the case with collectively embezzling RMB 18 3 billion yuan from the public purse.[10]

Increasing corruption in China may have contributed to increasing corruption in Hong Kong. Legal immigrants from China to Hong Kong, who have been arriving at the rate of 38,000 per year in the 1990s,[11] may have brought more tolerant attitudes about corruption with them. The experiences of Hong Kong's business community in China, where a significant amount of the territory's manufacturing has been re-located, (that bribery is necessary and effective) may have encouraged them to bring these habits back to Hong Kong. Cross border opportunities for corruption thrown up by the heavy volume of traffic at the border in recent years (more than 22,000 vehicles per day, mostly goods vehicles, pass through three checkpoints),[12] understaffing of border check points and inadequate regulation have attracted customs officers in the Hong Kong Customs and Excise Department to accept bribes as well.[13]

When China announced in 1994 the collapse of the pre- and post-1997 legislative "through train" arrangements that had been implied by documents attached to the Basic Law,[14] a powerful symbol of continuity and stability in the transition was lost. To be sure, even these arrangements permitted the Chinese government to vet each legislator and to remove any legislator Beijing authorities wished from the "through train". The Basic Law laid down no "through train" arrange-

t for other institutions, such as the Judiciary, apart from the provision that
he judicial system previously practised in Hong Kong shall be maintained . . ."
article 81). The delay in establishing the Court of Final Appeal (it will now be
set up from July 1, 1997) further robbed the Judiciary of such a role. Although
the Basic Law provided that civil servants serving the Hong Kong government
prior to 1997 could all continue in some capacity (article 100), by giving the
central government in Beijing the authority to appoint the future Chief Executive and the 27 principal officials (article 48(5)), no "through train" was
contemplated for top civil servants either. Maintaining the continuity and stability of the civil service and its management systems became an important part of
China's policy for gaining effective control of Hong Kong.

Hong Kong's civil service, numbering 182,675 people or about 3% of the
population in 1996,[15] is distributed among more than 40 different departments
and agencies. At the apex sit 1,052 directorate officers, who make up less than
1% of the total civil service (about 17% of the directorate are Administrative
Officers). Another 2,800 officers make up the senior manager or professional
group, who supervise about 34,000 junior and middle managers or professionals.[16]

Although the wastage rate among civil servants has remained a steady 5% or
so in recent years,[17] and has recently declined to about 4%, reflecting the worsening employment situation in Hong Kong, the intention of many senior and
experienced officers to take early retirement has worried succession planners.
According to information tabled in Legco by the Hong Kong government, by
1997, 30% of the civil service will be eligible for early retirement.[18] Official
Chinese government concern about a possible exodus of senior civil servants
was reflected in a document, "Several Opinions," issued in December 1995 by
Beijing's transition organ, the Hong Kong SAR Preparatory Committee's Preliminary Working Committee (PWC).[19] The document stated:

> . . . the British government should make regular reports to the Chinese government
> on the latest position relating to the resignation, early retirement and normal retire-
> ment of civil servants. The Chinese government should be notified as soon as
> possible on any case of resignation, early retirement or normal retirement of direc-
> torate officers.[20]

According to a survey carried out in late 1993, 34.7% of directorate officers
indicated that they intend to leave government before 1997.[21] Nearly 37% of the
respondents indicated that they were worried about their career in the civil
service after 1997, and more than half were concerned that the Beijing authorities would become involved in Hong Kong's major policy decisions before
1997.[22] With the colonial political system in decline, measures to stabilize the
civil service have taken on special significance.

Government Policies

Both the Chinese and Hong Kong governments have taken steps to maintain the stability of the civil service. First, the Chinese government's policy on the hand over provides for continuity — "all those employed by the government before 1997 may continue to work for the SAR government on terms of service no less favourable than before."[23] Second, the Chinese government has reassured civil servants that the current methods for calculating their compensation, the institutions used, and the levels of compensation will be maintained after 1997. The Basic Law, for example, lays down that civil servants may all "retain their seniority with pay, allowances, benefits and conditions of service no less favourable than before" (article 100). It goes on to make assurances that pensions will be paid as before (article 102), and that those bodies, such as the Standing Commission on Civil Service Salaries and Conditions of Service that have advised government on pay matter shall continue to perform the same functions (article 103). In December 1995, the Preliminary Working Committee re-iterated this position, specifically identifying the Standing Commissions and the Public Service Commission as bodies that will continue to perform their functions for the SAR government.[24] The PWC also called for the creation of a pension reserve fund to help to ensure that civil service pensions are paid by the SAR government.[25]

To quiet civil service fears about pensions, the Hong Kong government has set up a special reserve fund to help defray the costs of pensions, which previously had come wholly from recurrent expenditure. In spite of these reassurances, Hong Kong civil servants especially in the middle and upper ranks, cannot but help notice that their salaries are hundreds of times higher than the salaries paid to their counterparts on the mainland.[26] Ministry of Finance officials in Beijing have privately described Hong Kong's civil service compensation system as a "high salary system."[27]

Third, the Chinese government has reiterated that the existing Civil Service Regulations will continue in force after the handover, except for any revision to delete matters that have "a colonial connotation."[28] The Basic Law (article 103) makes the same pledge. The Colonial Regulations and Letters Patent, however, will no longer be in force after July 1, 1997, their position having been taken by the Basic Law.

To preserve the executive-led nature of the future SAR polity, the Chinese government has also decided that the Civil Service Regulations should not be codified into law.[29] The regulations can be more easily amended if they are internal — free from the debate and scrutiny of the legislature. Apparently authorities in Beijing anticipate that the future Hong Kong Legco will be more troublesome to manage than the current National People's Congress in China, where plans are well advanced to pass a "Civil Service Law."

Since 1984, the Hong Kong government has also taken steps to stabilize the civil service. The authorities have, for example, set up additional consultative mechanisms within the service at central level to facilitate increased representation on terms of service matters especially from among blue collar workers, the disciplined services, and the police.[30] Better monitoring of succession planning has been introduced by decentralizing the production of the plans to policy branches and the departments concerned.[31]

The Hong Kong government has stepped up the pace of localization to meet the Basic Law's requirement that top officials of the SAR not hold foreign passports or have the right of abode overseas. In 1983, for example, 51.4% of the directorate was staffed by expatriates. Nearly 33% of the senior manager and professional grades were in the hands of expatriates, as well.[32] By 1996, although expatriates or those appointed on overseas terms of service made up less than 1% of the civil service, they held 25.5% of directorate positions and nearly 19% of senior manager/professional positions.[33] That is, their numbers were still substantial. In 1996 there were still significant numbers of expatriate Administrative Officers (see Table 2.2).

Large numbers of expatriates could be found in the police (683, down from 1103 in 1983), the Judiciary/Legal group (184, down from 233), and in some technical departments, such as architectural services (58), and housing (43, down from 110).[34] Localization of the Legal Department (which employed 92 expatriates in 1995), and in 1996 was still presided over by an expatriate Attorney General, has been agonizingly slow and tension ridden.[35] Only recently has government taken steps to bring in from outside local lawyers, such as D.R. Fung, the Solicitor General and P.V.T. Nguyen, the Crown Prosecutor, to staff senior positions in the department.

Other steps taken by the government have included: pushing the use of written Chinese in internal government communication, and between the government and the public (to this end an Official Languages Agency was recently estab-

Table 2.2

Administrative Officer Grade, by terms of service, 1996

	Local	Overseas
Secretary	5	2
AO Staff Grade A	18	4
AO Staff Grade B1	13	4
AO Staff Grade B	40	13
AO Staff Grade C	85	39
Senior AO	76	16
AO	156	0
TOTAL	393	78

Source: Civil Service Branch, March 22, 1996.

lished within government[36]); stepping up the provision of training in Putonghua for civil servants[37]; organizing China studies programs at the territory's tertiary institutions for large numbers of senior and middle-level civil servants; organizing familiarization trips for civil servants to visit counterpart agencies in various parts of China, especially in Guangdong, Shenzhen, and Fujian provinces; and sending groups of civil servants, especially Administrative Officers, to Qinghua University in Beijing for five-week intensive language training and lectures on the politics and administration of China. The practice of sending Administrative Officers to Oxford for training has been replaced by plans to send them to Beijing and the USA (to the University of Michigan). Interviews with civil servants reveal that competence in written Chinese has now become a selection criteria for senior civil servants. In spite of the fact that scores of delegations of Chinese and Hong Kong civil servants visit each other each year, the shock of becoming a civil servant of the SAR of the People's Republic of China in July 1997 is likely to be profound.

Issues in the Transition

A number of critical issues have emerged in the course of the transition. They include: the extent to which the civil service should be accountable to the legislature; the nature of civil service neutrality; and the criteria for selecting the principal officials of the future SAR government. These issues have presented dilemmas for both governments. The British government is pledged to intensify cooperation with China to achieve a smooth transition, on the one hand, but is unwilling to undermine the authority of the Hong Kong government, on the other. The Chinese government also wants to inherit a strong, executive-led Hong Kong government, but wants the government to take direction from its appointed SAR "provisional legislature."

Civil Service Accountability

According to the Sino-British Joint Declaration, the British government has responsibility for the governance of Hong Kong until June 30, 1997.[38] In 1991, however, both countries agreed that during the last stages of the transition they would intensify closer cooperation to achieve a smooth transition. The agreement appeared to give the Chinese government authority to veto major policies, the implementation of which would straddle the handover date, including the formation of the 1997–98 budget. Subsequently such rights were conceded to the Chinese government. According to official agreements, only if consensus is achieved by the British and Chinese sides on these issues can policy be implemented.[39] It could be argued, therefore, that the civil service in practice has been accountable to both sovereigns during the last years of the transition.

The Chinese government has stressed its policy that the future SAR government will be accountable through the Chief Executive to the central government in Beijing.[40] Its statement on the civil service, issued by the Preliminary Working Committee in December 1995, did not mention the need for civil servants to be accountable to the legislature. Undoubtedly the Chinese government sought to stress the executive-led nature of the SAR government in this statement. Still, the Basic Law requires the government of the SAR "to be accountable to the Legislative Assembly."[41]

The constitutional powers of the colonial Legislative Council make it an advisory body. According to the Letters Patent, the Governor may 'disallow' any law made by Legco (Letters Patent, VIII). In practice, however, the government has granted the legislature considerable authority to influence policy. No where is this clearer than in the Legislative Council's Standing Orders, which give the Council's Finance Committee the power to veto all items of government expenditure.[42] Since the 1985 enactment of the Powers and Privileges Ordinance, Legco has also had the power to order civil servants to appear before it and answer questions.

According to the 1993 survey of directorate officers, mentioned above, nearly 60% believed that they should be accountable to the legislature,[43] a remarkable development for a body whose constitutional position is so weak. The same respondents overwhelmingly (71.8%) believed that they should not be accountable to the Chinese government before 1997. Virtually the same number believed that they should be accountable to the central government after 1997, and that this should take the form of "regularly reporting and explaining policies" to the Beijing government.[44] Still, intriguingly half of the respondents believed that, after 1997, decisions of the Chinese government "could not override" decisions of the Hong Kong government.[45] The same survey revealed that substantial numbers of these senior civil servants were "worried about Beijing governing Hong Kong people" after 1997. In spite of the findings, which seem to support the current practice of being accountable to Legco, and see future accountability to the central government in relatively weak terms, vertical accountability is well established in Hong Kong.[46]

In 1996, the Preparatory Committee for the SAR, established by the National People's Congress under the Basic Law, formally voted to set up a provisional legislature to replace the legislative "through train."[47] Almost immediately the civil service became embroiled in controversy about this decision. The Governor of Hong Kong, reiterating a position he had taken months earlier when the possibility of a provisional legislature was first mooted, denounced the decision as a violation of the Basic Law and "a black day for democracy."[48] The Basic Law says nothing about a provisional legislature.

Next, the Chinese government's spokesman on Hong Kong matters, Lu Ping, head of the Hong Kong and Macau Affairs Office (HKMAO), observed that "it goes without saying that senior officials who wish to join the SAR government must recognize the provisional legislature and at the same time cooperate with it."[49] These views were interpreted by some in Hong Kong as requiring a declaration of support for the provisional legislature from candidates for top civil service positions in the post 1997 government. This would have forced them to directly contradict the policy of the current head of the Hong Kong government. Subsequently, New China News Agency (NCNA) in Hong Kong issued a clarification. Civil servants were not required to declare their position on the provisional legislature, the NCNA spokesman said. Rather they should keep silent on the issue. "Those officials who have already expressed their opposition [such as Chief Secretary Anson Chan Fang On-sang and Secretary for Constitutional Affairs Nicholas Ng Wing-fui] but want to remain in the SAR government will face a question of how to justify that to the public," the NCNA spokesman said.[50]

The incident exposed a dilemma for China's policy on accountability to the legislature. On the one hand, authorities prefer a strong, executive-led government that is not closely supervised by a legislature. On the other, they prefer the provisional legislature, whose members will all be selected by the Preparatory Committee, to be recognized as a strong, legitimate authority.

Civil service accountability in China is also in transition, which may explain some of the confusion. Long regarded both inside China and abroad as a "rubber stamp,"[51] the people's congress system has in the 1980s and 1990s begun to establish an identity of its own. Not only do delegates act as agents of the party, but they also articulate the interests of their functional or geographic constituency.[52] In recent times, delegates have voted in substantial numbers against the nominees of the party for senior state posts in a handful of cases, and have opposed draft laws on such issues as state-owned enterprise bankruptcies and government restructuring.[53] China's Hong Kong policy makers are making policy for Hong Kong based on these trends in the mainland. Other things being equal, they may be more willing than is sometimes realized for the legislature in Hong Kong to play an activist role. However, the central government will brook no opposition, including opposition from the legislature of Hong Kong, in its drive to assert sovereignty and effective control over the territory.

Neutrality

According to their official policies, both the British and Chinese authorities highly value a neutral civil service for Hong Kong. Although the Hong Kong government has sometimes been accused of favouring big business,[54] in more recent times the government has appeared to be more even handed, balancing the needs and interests of various sectors of the community. In the face of criticism from the business community, the government has increased welfare spending for the communities' poorest people; imposed regulation on the financial, securities, and banking sectors; and, in the face of rising unemployment, limited the number of laborers that may be imported into Hong Kong.

A central plank of the Chinese government's transition strategy has been to court big business in Hong Kong.[55] Ironically, this has led the Chinese government, for example, to repeatedly denounce the Hong Kong government's budget for social welfare as 'too high' and likely to lead to budget deficits.[56] The Chinese government has also supported the efforts of big business to import more and more manual laborers, especially from the mainland. The Chinese government's position on this issue is complicated, however, by its close ties to the 'pro-Beijing' Hong Kong Federation of Trade Unions, which has opposed the imported labor scheme because it tends to drive down wages in the territory. The appointment of business tycoon, Tung Chee-hwa, Chairman of Oriental Overseas Container Line, as the Hong Kong's SAR's Chief Executive-designate in December 1996, clearly demonstrated the big business orientation of China's Hong Kong policy.

Because of economic reform in China, mainland society is becoming more pluralistic. New groups and classes are emerging, especially in China's cities. China's market-oriented reforms call for a more regulatory state that acts as a monitor or referee for the market.[57] That is, the state in China must now begin to adopt a neutral role vis-a-vis society, a position that is increasingly recognized by officials. Thus, the authorities publicly rebuked civil servants in Sichuan and Jiangsu provinces who had developed relationships that were considered to be too close to local "business tycoons" because the businessmen could then expect favoured treatment.[58] These actions indicate a growing awareness among officials in China that neutrality vis-a-vis the market is essential for efficiency.

The Hong Kong government has also valued political neutrality for the civil service, and its regulations place restrictions on the rights of civil servants to freedom of speech and political participation enjoyed by other citizens. For example, according to Civil Service Regulation No. 520, public servants in Hong Kong may not publish anything of a "political or administrative nature" without the prior approval of their head of department, a restriction which would appear to prevent them from speaking out on any public issue. Although civil servants may vote in elections, they may not stand for office without first resigning from the civil service.[59] In 1991, however, as more seats in Legco were open to direct election, the government relaxed its prohibition on civil servants participating in political activities. According to guidelines issued in October 1990, in anticipation of the elections, all civil servants except the police, directorate officers, administrative officers, and information officers, may join political parties and engage in political activities so long as they do not conflict with their official duties.[60] In 1995, civil servants voted in a newly created functional constituency, representing the "community, personal, and social services sector," and helped to elect a retired senior civil servant (the former Secretary for Health and Welfare) as their representative to Legco.[61]

The Chinese government's position on these matters appears to be more restrictive. According to the PWC's Several Opinions:

> The principle of civil servants remaining politically neutral should be maintained after 1997. Therefore, there should be restriction on civil servants' participating in politics. Provisions concerning participation in politics by civil servants embodied in the existing Civil Service Regulations should be maintained.

Then follows a list of the provisions contained in the Hong Kong Civil Service Regulations that prohibit civil servants from uttering anything of a "political or administrative nature," taking up outside work without permission, "convening or participating in a public assembly to discuss any government measures, distributing any political publications, or signing or inviting others to sign any public petition relating to government measures or plans." The documents also points out, "civil servants are not allowed to participate in any other activities which are inconsistent with the principle of their remaining politically neutral."

The Preliminary Working Committee did not go on to reaffirm the guidelines issued by the Hong Kong government in October 1990 that considerably relaxed restrictions on political participation for most civil servants. Still, in 1996 the Preparatory Committee criticized the Hong Kong government's refusal to allow civil servants to join the PC's Selection Committee, which chose the Chief Executive-designate and the provisional legislature. The Hong Kong government maintained that the provisional legislature had no basis in law and was contrary to the Sino-British Joint Declaration and the Basic Law.

In the view of the Chinese government, the neutrality of some senior members of the Hong Kong government has been called into question because of their support for Governor Chris Patten's 1992 political reforms and his criticisms of China's decision to set up the provisional legislature.[62] Yet, as we have seen, at one stage the Chinese government demanded that these same civil servants publicly support its proposal for the provisional legislature as a condition for their future employment by the SAR government. That the Chinese government backed off from this position is a recognition that civil service neutrality requires civil servants to vigorously support the duly constituted political authority of the day. There may be lingering suspicions in Beijing, however, that the Hong Kong civil servants actually believe what they say.

The experience of political neutrality in Hong Kong could not be further removed from the policy and practice on the mainland. Civil servants in China, like other citizens, are encouraged to participate actively in mobilized activities to support Chinese Communist Party policy. No prohibitions exist on civil servants (many of them CCP members) voting, participating in political activities, or running for office, nor apparently are such prohibitions thought to be necessary. "Civil service neutrality" is only appropriate, mainland officials argue, for bourgeois states with two-party systems, and even then it is mostly a sham.[63]

The policy of the Chinese government on political neutrality is also based on practice. In May-June, 1989, hundreds of civil servants joined student demonstrators in Tiananmen Square and marched behind banners in support of student calls for more democracy.[64] As a result of this experience, when the "Provisional Regulations on Civil Servants" was published in 1993, authorities added a paragraph, not found in earlier drafts, that prohibited civil servants from:

> spreading views which are harmful to the government's reputation, organizing or joining an illegal organization, organizing or joining an anti-government activity such as a meeting, demonstration or show of strength, or organizing or participating in a strike.[65]

In China, these restrictions apply to civil servants and non-civil servants alike. No government can permit its employees to join illegal or anti-government organizations or activities. In China, however, questionable methods are used to determine the legality of organizations and official tolerance for unorthodox views is very narrow. "Civil service neutrality" that permits government officials to participate in anything other than officially approved activities in China is strictly prohibited. These views may find there way into new restrictions on the political activities of Hong Kong civil servants after 1997.

In practice, the neutrality of the civil service in Hong Kong has been undermined by corruption, just as corruption has impeded China's push to establish a neutral regulatory state. In so far as corruption has become a serious problem in the two places, it permits individuals to redirect public resources for private benefit. Neutrality, however, requires a level playing field. Questions about the extent to which well-connected Chinese state-owned enterprises operating in Hong Kong will be treated the same by the SAR as other economic entities continue to be raised. Indeed, the immediate dismissal of former Immigration Department head, Lawrence Leung Ming-yin, in July 1996 resulted in part due to questions about his unreported business dealings with businessmen in Hong Kong and China which could have compromised his position.[66]

Selecting the SAR's Principal Officials

A third area of controversy has surrounded the selection of principal civil servants for the SAR government. According to the Basic Law the appointment and promotion of civil servants shall be on the basis of their "qualifications, experience, and ability" (article 103), language lifted from the Hong Kong official Civil Service Regulations (Regulation No. 109). The Basic Law requires, in addition, that principal officials of the SAR government come only from among "Chinese citizens who are permanent residents of the SAR with no right of abode in any foreign country" (article 101). In practical terms, these policies require the localization of all senior positions in the civil service, a process that was speeded up since 1984 and that has had its own internal dynamics.[67]

To help it identify the principal officials in the months before the SAR government was set up, and as a matter of principal, the Chinese government demanded that the Hong Kong government turn over to the central government all archives, including all civil service personnel files.[68] According to Chinese government policy, the files will remain in Hong Kong,[69] but authority over them should be transferred by Britain to the central government in Beijing and not directly to the future Chief Executive of the SAR.

Since late 1994, the Chinese government has asked to see the files so that it could determine among other things which civil servants have the right of abode in a foreign country. The Hong Kong government has replied that this sort of information is not contained in the files.[70] Indeed, their position is that no information on the foreign passports of civil servants is kept by the government.

The Hong Kong government has refused to hand over the personnel files of candidates for principal positions in the SAR government.[71] Instead the Civil Service Branch of the Government Secretariat prepared summaries of what it considered to be relevant career information (most of which was probably available to the public in the Staff Biographies serial, compiled by the Civil Service Branch). The summaries also included confidential evaluations contained on personnel appraisal forms, which, with the consent of the civil servants involved, were handed to officials of the NCNA in Hong Kong. In addition, throughout 1996 a series of informal gatherings was held between senior Hong Kong government officials and officials of the NCNA and the HKMAO.[72] The meetings were held at the Jockey Club in Happy Valley, and reports of these meetings, including color photographs with detailed seating charts, were published in the local press. These reports only served to underline the gap in understanding and communication between officials of both sides.

China's formal civil service selection criteria stress both political integrity ("redness") and ability ("expertise").[73] Based on the political needs of the leadership, authorities have sometimes emphasized one criteria at the expense of the other. Still, China's emphasis on political integrity (which often becomes corrupted into personal loyalty to the leader, a criteria that probably features to some extent in all civil service systems in practice), stands in strong contrast to the system currently practiced in Hong Kong. Encouraged by the practice on the mainland, the post-1997 government may begin to consider this criteria, however.

Central leaders in Beijing make appointments/promotions to leadership positions in provincial governments based in part on personal knowledge of the candidates involved. According to official regulations in China, they are required to do so. Surveys reveal that in practice in China the most important criteria for promotion in the civil service are seniority, performance (measured by one's superior), and whether one had obtained more education during employment. Access to the latter, in turn, depends to a great extent on personal relations or *guanxi*. According to Bian, personal relations was also critical for changes in occupation or job transfers.[74] The Hong Kong government's attempt to limit the contact between its senior civil servants and authorities in Beijing undoubtedly frustrated attempts to build personal ties between them. It has probably undermined the confidence of authorities in Beijing that they will be able to identify the appropriate people (loyal but capable) to run Hong Kong.

Reflecting this situation and China's desire to stabilize the civil service, it came as no surprise that China approved virtually all serving principal officials to retain their current posts after July.[75] Among the 27 appointments announced on February 20, 1997 for the SAR government, replacements were found for only two posts. The incumbent Attorney General, a British expatriate, will be replaced by a new Secretary for Justice, who is a local solicitor and founding member of the Democratic Alliance for Betterment of Hong Kong, a pro-China political party funded through the NCNA. The current Director of Transport will replace the Commissioner of the ICAC, who had announced months earlier that he would retire from the the the post. Continuity and stability of the civil service, a cornerstone of the policies of both China and Hong Kong, has been preserved in these appointments.

Conclusion

Economic reform in China has put strains on the mainland's Leninist political institutions. New groups and classes are emerging, especially in China's cities. To meet any potential challenge from these groups, the authorities have reacted with a mixture of co-optation, exhortation, and repression. During the recent past the party has encouraged, for example, private entrepeneurs to apply for party membership. Subtle changes in the people's congress system have provided more room for voice. Through the media and propaganda system the party continues to urge Chinese citizens to be patriotic and to consider the interests of the nation as a whole. When people take to the streets, as they did in May-June 1989, however, they are met with repression.

China's policy on Hong Kong has been formulated in the context of this experience. Recovering sovereignty and exercising real control over Hong Kong is, of course, Beijing's top priority. How the policy will be implemented, however, depends on the China's experience of managing issues such as accountability, neutrality, and selection in its own civil service.

Notes

1. See John P. Burns, "Administrative Reform in a Changing Political Environment: The Case of Hong Kong," *Public Administration and Development,* Vol. 14 (1994), pp. 241–252.

2. The Prevention of Bribery Ordinance outlaws unauthorized kickbacks and bribery in both the public and private sectors.

3. *South China Morning Post,* January 1, 1996.

4. *South China Morning Post,* January 7 and February 4, 1996.

5. *South China Morning Post,* February 5, 1996.

6. *South China Morning Post ,* January 7, 1996.

7. *Xingzheng renshi yu guanli* [Administrative personnel and management] January 1994, p. 22.

8. *Wen Wei Po* [Wenhui bao] (Hong Kong) March 13, 1996.

9. *South China Morning Post ,* January 5, 1994.

10. *South China Morning Post,* April 5, 1996.

11. *Hong Kong 1995: Review of 1994* (Hong Kong: Government Printer, 1995), p. 445.

12. *Hong Kong 1995: Review of 1994,* p. 264.

13. *South China Morning Post,* March 19, 1994. A senior customs officer and nine others in the customs service were convicted of accepting bribes to permit stolen cars to be smuggled into China.

14. The "Decision of the National People's Congress on the Method for the Formation of the First Government and the First Legislative Council of the Hong Kong Special Administrative Region" (adopted on April 4, 1990) [Abbrev. Method] states: "If the composition of the last Hong Kong Legislative Council before the establishment of the Hong Kong SAR is in conformity with the relevant provisions of this Decision and the Basic Law of the HKSAR, those of its members who uphold the Basic Law of the HKSAR of the PRC and pledge allegiance to the HKSAR of the PRC, and who meet the requirements set forth in the Basic Law of the Region may, upon confirmation by the Preparatory Committee, become members of the first Legislative Council of the Region" (section 6). The relevant provision appears to be that the last Legco be composed of 60 members, 20 of whom are returned by direct elections in geographical constituencies, 10 returned by an election committee, and 30 returned by functional constituencies (Method, section 6). The requirements set forth in the Basic Law state that members should be Chinese citizens who are permanent residents of Hong Kong with no right of abode in any foreign country. However, up to 20% of Legco members may come from among permanent residents who are not Chinese citizens (article 67).

15. Civil Service Branch statistics on the World Wide Web [http://www.hku.hk/csb], as of April 1, 1996.

16. Civil Service Branch, *Civil Service Personnel Statistics, 1995* (Hong Kong: Government Printer), p. 5.

17. Civil Service Branch Statistics on the World Wide Web [http://www.hku.hk/csb], as of April 1, 1995.

18. *South China Morning Post,* June 7, 1995.

19. In the wake of their dispute with Governor Chris Patten over his plans for political reform in Hong Kong, in July 1993, Chinese authorities set up the Preliminary Working Committee, composed of both mainland and Hong Kong members. The PWC was tasked with studying transition issues and making recommendations on how they should be handled. Before it was disbanded in December 1995, it issued several policy statements.

20. See "Yuweihui guanyu baochi xianggang gongwuyuan duiwu he zhidu wending de ruogan yijian" [Preliminary Working Committee, "Several opinions on maintaining the stability of the Hong Kong civil service corps and system"] December 8, 1995 in *Wen Wei Po,* December 9, 1995. [Abbrev. Several Opinions]

21. Jane C.Y. Lee, "Political Accountability of Senior Civil Servants in Hong Kong: A Study of the Bureaucrat-Politician Relationship," paper prepared for the International Conference on the Quest for Excellence: Public Administration in the Nineties, City Polytechnic of Hong Kong (February 26, 1994). Questionnaires were sent to all members of the directorate. There were 606 satisfactory responses, for a response rate of 56%.

Almost half of the those saying that they would go belonged to the age group 51–55. Substantial numbers of younger directorate officers also indicated their intention to leave.

22. Lee, p. 16.

23. Basic Law, article 100. This article makes special mention of the police, which played a critical role defending the government during the 1966 and 1967 riots. All police officers may continue in the service. According to official policy there will be no revenge taking or "settling of old scores" after 1997 (See Several Opinions, section 5). The Basic Law also lays down that special treatment of foreigners (such as those on overseas or expatriate terms of service) may not continue after 1997 (article 103).

24. See Several Opinions, section 13.

25. See Several Opinions, section 14.

26. According to 1993 data, the Chinese Premier's salary was about RMB 1,200 yuan per month, while the Chief Secretary of the Hong Kong government was being paid HK$180,000 per month. A provincial bureau chief, who lived in subsidized housing, may have earned RMB 800 yuan per month, while a department head (D7) in Hong Kong, who also lived in subsidized housing, may have earned HK$115,000 per month.

27. Interviews, Beijing, October 1994.

28. See Several Opinions, section 15.

29. See Special Opinions, section 15.

30. *Hong Kong, 1995: Review of 1994,* p. 44.

31. Civil Service Branch, Human Resource Management (Hong Kong: Government Printer, 1995).

32. Ian Scott and John P. Burns, eds., *The Hong Kong Civil Service: Personnel Policies and Practices* (Hong Kong: Oxford University Press, 1984), p. 30.

33. Civil Service Branch statistics on the World Wide Web [http://www.hku.hk/csb] and *Civil Service Personnel Statistics, 1995,* p. 5.

34. *Civil Service Personnel Statistics, 1995,* pp. 14–18.

35. See Ian Scott and John P. Burns, eds., *The Hong Kong Civil Service and Its Future* (Hong Kong: Oxford University Press, 1988), pp. 102–104.

36. *South China Morning Post,* March 18, 1996.

37. See *South China Morning Post,* February 1, 1996, concerning the provision of putonghua training for ICAC investigators. See also the *Report of the Working Group on the Use of Chinese in the Civil Service* in *South China Morning Post,* September 18, 1995.

38. Sino-British Joint Declaration on the Future of Hong Kong (September 26, 1984), Annex II, section 5.

39. "Memorandum of Understanding," July 4, 1991 in *South China Morning Post,* July 5, 1991 and "Beijing Can Veto Major Proposals in next budget", *South China Morning Post,* March 15, 1992.

40. See Several Opinions, section 19.

41. Basic Law, article 64.

42. Norman Miners, *The Government and Politics of Hong Kong* 5th ed. (Hong Kong: Oxford University Press, 1991), p. 134.

43. Lee, p. 8.

44. Lee, p. 18.

45. Lee, p. 18. 50.9% disagreed or strongly disagreed with the statement: "Decisions of Chinese government leaders could override that of the Hong Kong government."

46. Terry Lui, "Changing Civil Servants' Values," in Ian Scott and John P. Burns, eds., *The Hong Kong Civil Service: Personnel Policies and Practices* (Hong Kong: Oxford University Press, 1988), pp. 139–140.

47. *Wen Wei Po,* March 25, 1996. According to the recommendation of the Prelimi-

nary Working Committee, the provisional legislature will be composed of 60 people, all from Hong Kong. It will be "elected through consultation" by the 400 member Selection Committee that is to choose the future SAR Chief Executive. The members of the provisional legislature will be identified in 1996. See *South China Morning Post,* October 8, 1994.

48. *South China Morning Post,* March 25, 1996.

49. *South China Morning Post,* March 30 and April 3, 1996. Lu Ping also reportedly said that the majority of senior civil servants would want to serve the SAR government. "If I invited you, would you come forward?" he asked reporters. "For any principal official, if I wanted to appoint him, would he come forward? For us, it's simple. If he's earning $10,000, even if we were to offer him $9,000, he's got to come. But certainly, we won't do it, we won't give him a penny less." This was widely reported as showing contempt for local civil servants. See Fanny Wong, "So unfair to our civil servants' *South China Morning Post,* April 3, 1996.

50. *South China Morning Post,* March 30, 1996.

51. Liao Gailong, "The '1980 Reform' Program in China, Part IV," in John P. Burns and Stanley Rosen, eds., *Policy Conflicts in Post-Mao China: A Documentary Survey with Analysis* (Armonk, NY: M.E. Sharpe, 1986), pp. 87–102.

52. Kevin O'Brien, "Agents and Remonstrators: Role Accumulation by Chinese People's Congress Deputies," *The China Quarterly* No. 138 (June 1995), pp. 359–380.

53. See *Wen Wei Po,* February 7, 1993; Lincoln Kaye, "Bureaucrats beware," *Far Eastern Economic Review* (1993), p. 13; and Josephine Ma, "Bankruptcy law in doubt," *South China Morning Post,* February 12, 1996.

54. Lau Siu-kai, *Society and Politics in Hong Kong* (Hong Kong: Chinese University Press, 1982), p. 28.

55. See, David Wallen and Gren Manuel, "Patten Attacks Handover Tycoons," *South China Morning Post,* February 9, 1996.

56. See, for example, *South China Morning Post,* November 29, 1995.

57. Victor Nee, "Peasant Entrepreneurship and the Politics of Regulation in China," in Victor Nee and David Stark, eds., *Remaking the Economic Institutions of Socialism: China and Eastern Europe* (Stanford: Stanford University Press, 1989), pp. 169–207.

58. *Zhongguo qingnian bao* [China Youth News] March 30, 1996, quoted in *South China Morning Post,* March 31, 1996.

59. A.B.L. Cheung, "The Civil Service," in Sung Yun-wing and Lee Ming-kwan, eds., *The Other Hong Kong Report 1991* (Hong Kong: Chinese University Press, 1991), p. 51.

60. Cheung, p. 51.

61. *South China Morning Post,* September 19, 1995.

62. See the commentary in *Wen Wei Po,* March 31, 1996 and Catherine Ng, "Plea for neutral civil service" *South China Morning Post,* April 1, 1996.

63. Li Ruhai and Zhu Qingfang, *Zhongguo gongwuyuan guanlixue* [Chinese civil servant management] (Beijing: Falu chubanshe, 1993), p. 19.

64. See the evidence of their participation in Michel Oksenberg, Lawrence Sullivan, and Marc Lambert, eds., *Beijing Spring, 1989, Confrontation and Conflict: The Basic Documents* (Armonk, NY: M.E. Sharpe, 1990), pp. 283–284.

65. Ministry of Personnel, *Provisional Regulations on Civil Servants* (Beijing: Ministry of Personnel, 1993) article No. 31. This prohibition had not appeared in earlier drafts of the regulations.

66. *South China Morning Post,* January 23, 1997.

67. In 1994, in the face of a law suit from expatriate civil servants faced with termination of their contracts to localize the civil service, the Hong Kong government

announced that was prepared to allow expatriate civil servants to transfer to local terms of service. The proposal provoked outrage from unions representing local civil servants, who successfully lobbied Legco to freeze the policy. A year later, a modified policy that permitted expatriate civil servants to transfer to local terms if they agreed to be demoted by one grade was approved by Legco. Expatriate civil servants sued the government, but lost. Some expatriate civil servants have successfully applied to be re-employed on local terms of service.

68. See Several Opinions, sections 23 and 24.

69. See Several Opinions, section 24.

70. *South China Morning Post,* January 18, 1995. "China's top official in charge of Hong Kong affairs, Lu Ping, yesterday issued a blistering warning to the Government about its refusal to hand over information on civil servants to Beijing."

71. No Kwai-yan, "Britain warned it must give archives to China," *South China Morning Post* , December 9, 1995. See also Connie Law, "Beijing asks for information on who is staying after '97," *South China Morning Post,* December 10, 1995.

72. These gatherings followed many months of acrimony over the Hong Kong government's ban on civil servants meeting with members of the Preliminary Working Committee, which China had set up soon after the Governor's October 1992 announcement of political reforms in Hong Kong. See "Pressure mounting to lift ban on contacts" *South China Morning Post,* October 21, 1994 and "Detailed rules issued for [civil service]-PWC links" *South China Morning Post,* October 7, 1994.

73. *Provisional Regulations on Civil Servants,* article 38.

74. Yanjie Bian, "*Guanxi* and the Allocation of Urban Jobs in China," *The China Quarterly* 140 (December 1994), pp. 991–998.

75. *South China Morning Post,* February 21, 1997.

3

The Tiananmen Incident, Patten's Electoral Reforms, and the Roots of Contested Democracy in Hong Kong

Alvin Y. So

On December 11, 1996, pro-democracy activists scuffled with riot police outside the Hong Kong Convention Centre, where the 400 member Hong Kong Special Administrative Region (SAR) Selection Committee was voting for a Chief Executive to rule Hong Kong after 1997. The pro-democracy activists — including Legislative Council (Legco) members Emily Lau, Andrew Cheng and Lee Cheuk-yan — erected a "a tomb of democracy" outside the building and shouted "oppose the phony election." Lying down on the road, the activists were dragged away and then detained by the police for over four hours.[1]

On December 16,1996, the Democratic Party said it would burn all 114,589 signatures it had gathered in support of its party whip Szeto Wah's campaign as the "unofficial" Chief Executive candidate. The Democratic Party boasted that while the Chief Executive of the first post-1997 government was selected by only 400 members of the Selection Committee appointed by Beijing, Szeto Wah was chosen by 114,589 people in Hong Kong. The signatures had to be burned to ease the public's fear of the possibilities of retaliation by Beijing after the handover.[2]

On December 20, 1996, the eve of electing candidates to the SAR provisional legislature — which would replace the current popularly elected Legco in mid 1997 — British Foreign Secretary Malcolm Rifkind challenged Beijing to defend the legality of the provisional legislature in the International Court of Justice. In addition, members of the Democratic Party chanted "oppose the provisional legislature, oppose the rubber stamp" outside the local branch of Xinhua News Agency, China's *de facto* consulate in Hong Kong. The pro-democracy activists condemned the provisional legislature as illegal and unconstitutional — it was not even mentioned in the Basic Law which was to serve as Hong Kong's mini-constitution after 1997.[3]

On January 20, 1997, a legal panel of the SAR Preparatory Committee decided to repeal or amend 25 laws protecting human rights and permitting peaceful demonstrations. Pro-democracy groups described the Preparatory Committee's move as a blow to democracy that would dent international confidence in post-1997 Hong Kong.[4]

The above news headlines show that Hong Kong's democratization has become more contested as the 1997 transition drew near. Thus, while Hong Kong's East Asian neighbors (Taiwan and South Korea) seem to enjoy democratic consolidation in the 1990s, Hong Kong's democratic transition is marred by narrow electoral competition, feuding over electoral rules, delegitimation of the future SAR legislature, and widespread concern with the worsening of civil liberties.

What then explains the emergence of a "contested democracy" in Hong Kong? The existing literature offers a prevailing power dependency explanation of Hong Kong's democracy.[5] In this perspective, the Hong Kong government is seen as a dependent polity controlled by London and Beijing, whereby the incumbent London government is responsible for Hong Kong's present, while the Beijing government controls its future. Both London and Beijing command overwhelming resources, especially the coercive ones. Hong Kong people have no credible bargaining strength with either power, except perhaps through an exodus of people. London and Beijing set the rules of democratization, while the Hong Kong people are denied the right to participate in the shaping of their own future. Following this argument, "contested democracy" is a product of the Beijing-London feud over which government will have more control over Hong Kong in the transition to 1997.

The power dependency perspective tends to paint a picture of powerless local elites and apathetic masses in Hong Kong. Both the local elites and the masses are seen as being manipulated by London and Beijing.[6] In this contrast, a "third wave democracy" study perceives elites as agents and political actors — elites can bargain, negotiate, compromise, and make strategic decisions on democratization.

Using a "third wave democracy" framework, it can be argued that there are, not two, but four different types of elites and masses influencing the path of Hong Kong's democratization:

1. **London** and the pro-British forces run the colonial government of Hong Kong and enlist international support.
2. **Beijing** and pro-mainland forces will be Hong Kong's rulers in 1997. **Big Business** controls the economic resources of Hong Kong and has served as the ruling class before the onset of democratization.[7]
3. **Service professionals** influence the mass media and enjoy a strong track record in past electoral victories.[8]
4. The **grassroots population**'s strength lies in their mere numbers at the ballot box.[9]

In addition, a "third wave democracy" study would highlight the construction of elite alliances. Anti-democracy alliances regularly decompose, realign, and reconstitute, as do the pro-democracy alliances. In this respect, the crucial research questions are: What explains the rise, transformation, and decomposition of elite alliances? How exactly have shifting elite alliances shaped the contour of democratization in Hong Kong?

This chapter argues that two new elite alliances had emerged in Hong Kong in the 1990s: an anti-democratic "unholy alliance" between communist Beijing and Hong Kong's Chinese businesspeople versus a pro-democratic "popular alliance" between service professionals and the grassroots population.[10] Although the unholy alliance was more powerful, the popular alliance was not without strength. The aim of this chapter is to show how the historical event of the Tiananmen Incident in 1989 and the decolonization politics of Governor Patten in the early 1990s led to the emergence and transformation of the unholy alliance and the popular alliance, leading to a contested democracy in the 1997 transition.

Impact of the Tiananmen Incident on Hong Kong

The late 1980s was a period of democratic frustration in Hong Kong. Growing power of pro-democracy forces from service professional backgrounds (like social workers, teachers and professors, lawyers, and journalists) triggered an "unholy alliance" between big businesspeople and Beijing. The Basic Law drafting process was then used by Beijing and big businesspeople to imprint a restricted democracy system into the mini-constitution of Hong Kong. The service professionals did put up a fight for a populist democracy system — they wanted the Hong Kong government to fulfill its promise to introduce direct directions to the Legco in 1988, and they protested against the business sector's restricted democracy model both in the Basic Law drafting process and in the streets. Nevertheless, overwhelmed by the conservative alliance of Beijing-big businesspeople-London, failing to mobilize the grassroots population on issues concerning the Basic Law, and lacking unity and strategic planning, the service professionals' populist democracy package was defeated. As the restricted democracy system was written into the draft Basic Law, many service professionals became disillusioned about their democracy project. Some even thought of emigration and setting up a democratic front overseas to oppose the conservative alliance.

However, the Tiananmen Incident in 1989 opened up a whole new era for the democratization of Hong Kong, enabling the service professionals to effectively contest the restricted democratic model in the Basic Law.

Democracy Protest

Thanks to the power of the mass media, the democracy movement in China became a principal obsession of the Hong Kong people between April and June of 1989. As Joseph Chan and Chin-Chuan Lee point out, "television instantaneously brought scenes of joyous marches, hunger strikes, and tanks into their living room, as a powerful reminder that whatever China did in Beijing was inescapably pertinent to Hong Kong's well-being."[11]

An estimated 1 million Hong Kong people (about one-sixth of the colony's population) showed up to protest against the Beijing government on May 21, and there were numerous large-scale rallies afterwards. Many protestors wore yellow headbands that said "Support the Beijing Students," or T-shirts scrawled with "Long Live the Democratic Movement." On May 27, over 150 entertainers, including most of the Hong Kong's biggest pop stars, held a twelve-hour concert to raise money for the students in Beijing. Over US$1.5 million was collected during the concert, bringing the total raise in Hong Kong to more than US$3 million.[12]

On June 4, when the news reached Hong Kong that Chinese troops had moved into Tiananmen Square to crush the student movement, an estimated crowd of over 200,000 Hong Kong people gathered at the Happy Valley Race Course to mourn the students. They sat for five hours and listened to emotional speeches from the activists in the democracy movement, community leaders, and movie stars.13

The Tiananmen Incident shook the political landscape of Hong Kong and nearly turned it upside down. As Sai-wing Leung explains, "it was so dramatic that it drew around the clock coverage by Hong Kong mass media, so emotional that it ignited the nationalist feeling of many Hong Kong Chinese, so appealing that it rekindled the democratic aspiration of the local populace, and so tragic that it made most of the Hong Kong people moan, weep, and thunder."[14]

The historical event of the Tiananmen Incident, then, profoundly impacted Hong Kong's democratization. First, it greatly empowered the service professionals; their democracy project was given a chance of rebirth after its near-fatal defeat in the Basic Law struggles. Since the service professionals took the lead in organizing mass protests, they emerged as the popular leaders against authoritarianism. They were no longer seen in the mass media as fame-hungry, status-seeking, and self-interested politicians. In fact, Martin Lee, Szeto Wah, Yeung Sum, and Lau Chin-shek emerged as "highly visible, widely accepted, charismatic" leaders promoting the cause of democratization in Hong Kong.[15] The service professionals, furthermore, were more united than before. A new organization called "Hong Kong Alliance in Support of the Patriotic Democratic Movement of China" was formed. Szeto Wah was the president and Martin Lee the vice-president of the Alliance, and most leaders of the Alliance became leaders of the Joint Committee for Democracy. After the Tiananmen Incident, this Alliance further gave birth to a political party named "United Democrats," whose members publicly declared that they were committed to promote democratization in Hong Kong because they did not trust the Beijing government to protect their freedom.

Second, anti-democracy forces decomposed during and in the aftermath of the Tiananmen Incident. Moved by the large-scale demonstrations in Hong Kong and worried about the prospect of Beijing's intrusion into Hong Kong's politics, many big businesspeople were prepared to accept a faster pace of democratization.

Third, at the height of the Tiananmen affair, Beijing lost its credibility with the Hong Kong public; mainland Basic Law drafters canceled a visit to Hong Kong; Louis Cha (who formulated the conservative mainstream model adopted in the draft Basic Law) resigned in protest against Beijing's suppression of the student demonstrators. The "leftist" presses, unions, and schools in Hong Kong were much divided and paralyzed; some even publicly pledged their support for the student protesters at Tiananmen Square.[16] For example, Hong Kong's communist press broke party ranks to endorse the student movement in China. *Wen Wei Po*, a pro-communist newspaper funded by Beijing, published a stark, four-character editorial "Deep grief, bitter hatred" on May 21, 1989, the day after martial law was declared in Beijing.

Fourth, the protest marches during the Tiananmen Incident expanded the support of the service professionals among the grassroots population. Whereas the service professionals' democracy project attracted an average turnout of about 500 in previous demonstrations in the late 1980s, the same project attracted tens of thousands and up to one-and-a-half million in mid-1989. Furthermore, threatened by rapid inflation, growing unemployment, the pending importation of laborers, and the escalation of real estate prices, the grassroots population was more receptive to the welfare program as advocated by the service professionals than before.

Finally, the Tiananmen Incident consolidated a new Hong Kong ethnic identity vis-a-vis a Chinese national identity. In Ming-Kwan Lee's survey in 1990, more than half (56.6%) of the respondents regarded themselves as "HongKongese," only 25% as "Chinese."[17] The "HongKongese" identity that emerged during the Tiananmen Incident possessed an anti-Beijing component, as it was invoked to assert against the taken-for-granted "Chinese" identity. Lee's survey shows that a tiny portion of the Hong Kong respondents (less than 10%) neither trusted the Beijing government nor were prepared to regard "political allegiance with the PRC" as a necessary criterion for defining "Chineseness." Maria Tam's survey in 1994 also reports that 90% of the interviewees felt negatively about the Beijing government, particularly on its supposed lack of rule of law and freedom.[18]

The Business Community's Reaction

At the height of the Chinese democracy movement in late May 1989, many businesspeople who were members of the Executive and Legislative Councils (Omelco), moved by the demonstrations in Hong Kong and Beijing, were prepared to accept a much faster pace of democratization than that proposed by the draft Basic Law. Although Martin Lee and Szeto Wah wanted at least half the legislature directly elected in 1991 and the entire body directly elected by 1997, they eventually came to a compromise with their business colleagues' proposal.

The so-called "Omelco Consenus" model proposed that one-third of the Legco be elected in 1991, then 50% be elected by 1995, and 100% by 2003. The Chief Executive of the Special Administrative Region would also be directly elected no later than 2003.[19]

The strategic alliance between service professionals and businesspeople over the issues on democratization, however, was a transient and fragile one. As the emotions of Tiananmen Incident subsided, businesspeople gradually withdrew their support of rapid democratization. Although they abstained from unnecessary confrontations with the democrats, they maintained low-key participation, if still participated at all, in ceremonies that commemorated the events of June Fourth.[20]

In the aftermath of the Tiananmen Incident, many businesspeople who developed connections with the Thatcher government initiated a drive towards emigration. Thus Hon-Kwan Cheng, a Legco member who represented the Engineer constituency, charged that "Britain has both a moral obligation and a constitutional responsibility to support its subjects in their hour of need. We believe that the British Government ought to provide all 3.25 million BDTC or BNO passport holders an assurance or insurance policy by granting to them the right of abode or the right of entry".[21]

London's Policy Toward Hong Kong

Since London could not possibly allow 3.25 million Hong Kong British subjects to come and live in the United Kingdom (this would double the size of the minority population in Britain!), it needed to formulate policies to restore confidence in Hong Kong so as not to be accused of washing its hands off Hong Kong after signing the Joint Declaration in 1984.

The Foreign Affairs Committee of the House of Commons immediately called for a faster pace of democratization to provide the best and surest base for the future of Hong Kong. On June 30, 1989, the FAC released its report recommending:

1. half of the 60-member Legco be directly elected in 1991 and the entire body by 1995.
2. the first Chief Executive of the Hong Kong Special Administration Region (SAR) be elected by a democratically constituted electoral college six months before the transfer of sovereignty on July 1, 1997; subsequent chief executives be elected by universal suffrage; and
3. a bill of rights be introduced in existing legislation to ensure they do not breach international human rights covenants.[22]

However, the committee's report was not binding on the London government.

Still, anti-British sentiment continue to rise in Hong Kong right after the Tiananmen Incident, as seen by the hostile reception for British Foreign Secretary Geoffrey Howe by the Hong Kong people in early July 1989. Howe's visit was apparently intended to show the people of Hong Kong that the British government did care about them. However, Howe was greeted by several thousand vocal protesters at the airport. When delivering a speech at a lunch hosted by the Governor, Howe was heckled by some elected District Board members. The elected members put up a banner condemning "Shame on the Thatcher government — Irresponsible and Hypocritical Government." Then they walked out yelling, "Shame! Shame!" to a round of applause.[23]

Due to the pressures from Hong Kong people and the British Parliament, the London government finally agreed to offer several packages to restore public confidence in Hong Kong; namely, the speeding up of democratization, the introduction of a human rights bill, the granting of UK citizenship to some selected Hong Kong people, the launching of massive infrastructure projects (such as building a new airport and container terminals) and the substantial expansion of tertiary education.

In sum, a strategic alliance was built during the Tiananmen Incident among service professionals, businesspeople, the London government, and even some "leftist" supporters for the promotion of democratization in Hong Kong in mid-1989.

Beijing's Reaction

This strategic alliance surely alarmed Beijing. Beijing not only worried about its inability to control the colony, it now also feared that Hong Kong's democracy had become so strong that it could spread across the border to revitalize the Chinese democracy movement on the mainland. Subsequently, Beijing adopted a much hardened policy toward Hong Kong's democratic movement than before the Tiananmen Incident.

Beijing tried to pressure the British to outlaw the use of Hong Kong as "a subversive base against China," while it also continued to coopt corporate leaders and fortified the control of "leftist" organizations. Beijing warned the Hong Kong public not to interfere in China's domestic affairs. Toward the pro-democracy forces, Beijing attempted intimidation by publicly attacking their leaders — Martin Lee and Szeto Wah — in its official newspaper *The People's Daily* on July 21, 1989. Lee and Szeto were accused of trying to subvert the Chinese government, and warned that they would be arrested and charged if they ever set foot on the mainland. Lee and Szeto were also expelled from participation in the Basic Law Drafting Committee.[24]

Toward the members of the Executive and Legislative Councils, Beijing dismissed their democratization and emigration proposals as part of a British conspiracy, which aimed to perpetuate British interests at the expense of Chinese sovereignty. Beijing insisted that the Basic Law Drafting Committee would not even consider "the Omelco Consensus." As Ming Chan further notes, *"The Comments on the Basic Law (Draft)* issued by Omelco in October 1989 had to be sent via British diplomatic channels to the Chinese authorities who regarded this a British-'tinted' reflection of local views."[25]

In response to the UK nationality package, Beijing labeled the package as another conspiracy to perpetuate British rule in Hong Kong beyond 1997. The package, Beijing insisted, would either drain the pool of talents required to keep Hong Kong prosperous or leave behind a group of people whose loyalty was to Britain rather than China.[26] Beijing was especially disturbed by the prospect that all senior officials of the Hong Kong government after 1997 would hold British passports. Beijing was worried that administration of the Hong Kong government could grind to a halt should these senior officials decide to leave en masse after 1997.

The Promulgation of the Basic Law and the 1991 Elections

The Changing Sino-British Relationship

The Sino-British relationship obviously worsened in the aftermath of the Tiananmen Incident. Beijing strongly condemned London for the speeding up of democratization in Hong Kong, the passing of the human rights bill, and the granting of UK passports to almost a quarter million Hong Kong residents. Not only had Beijing criticized London openly, it even threatened not to take back the illegal immigrants from the mainland that the Hong Kong government repatriate across the border in October 1989.[27] On the other hand, Beijing badly needed London's cooperation during the transition to 1997. Without the support of both the business community and its local "leftist" organizations, Beijing had little option but to form a tactical alliance with London at this critical historical conjuncture.

A tactical Beijing-London accommodation was initiated when London took special action to pacify Beijing in late 1989. William Ehrman, Political Advisor of the Hong Kong government, wrote a letter to Xinhua News Agency to explain that "The Hong Kong government has no intention of allowing Hong Kong to be used as a base for subversive activities against the People's Republic of China. Xinhua should have noticed the arrest of the April Fifth Action Group [an anti-Beijing radical organization-Trotskite] outside their National Day reception. . . . that the Hong Kong government has recently rejected a proposal for a permanent site for a replica statue of democracy."[28]

In addition, London arranged several visits to Beijing by sending Percy Cradock (former British ambassador to Beijing and personal advisor to Prime Minister Thatcher), Hong Kong Governor Wilson, and new British Foreign Secretary

Douglas Hurd to explain its policy to the Chinese officials between November 1989 and January 1990.[29] Finally, London and Beijing reached a last-minute compromise on the 1991 and 1995 elections, which was reflected into the Basic Law.

The Finalization of the Basic Law

On the one hand, the British government tolerated Beijing to insert into the Basic Law two controversial new clauses relating to subversion and internationalization. There was a new clause (article 23) requiring the Hong Kong SAR legislature to pass laws prohibiting acts of subversion against the central government. In addition, there was a clause prohibiting political activities of foreign/international political organizations and groups in Hong Kong, or local political groups from establishing international links with foreign political organizations or groups.[30] As Mark Roberti remarks, this clause could prevent Chinese dissidents from using Hong Kong as a base of subversion against the central government after the handover.[31]

On the other hand, with agreement on the 1997 "convergence" of election arrangements, the British government was able to increase the portion of directly elected seats in Legco to 18 in 1991, to reduce the senior civil servant official seats from 10 to 3 and appointed members from 20 to 17, and to increase functional constituency seats from 14 to 21 in 1991. In the last election in 1995 before the handover, there will be no more appointed members or official seats. The number of functional constituency seats will increase from 21 in 1991 to 30 in 1995; the number of directly elected seats from 18 in 1991 to 20 in 1995; and the ten remaining seats of the 60-member Legco will be selected by an election committee.[32] Thus the pre- and post-1997 "convergence" requirements did in fact restrict the pace and scope of democratization in the transition era under British rule. As Ian Scott remarks, "the Basic Law is a profoundly antidemocratic document."[33] Beijing favors a restricted democracy which enables it to rule Hong Kong through surrogates and collaborators from the big business; the functional constituencies, with their small electorates, allow for greater manipulation in the selection of business and pro-Beijing candidates than large electorates in the directly contested seats.[34]

Furthermore, Beijing and London reached an understanding that there would be a "through train," i.e., the legislature's members elected in 1995 would be allowed to serve as the first legislators of the HKSAR until 1999, if the 1995 legislature was constituted according to the Basic Law.[35]

It is interesting to note that the final efforts before the promulgation of the Basic Law in April 1990 bore the imprint of Beijing and London, with very little direct input from Hong Kong people. On the other hand, big businesspeople already imprinted their pro-business, anti-welfare policies into the draft Basic Law, although a few had rethought the pace of democratization during the

Tiananmen Incident. But as the emotion about the Tiananmen Incident died down and as Beijing affirmed its commitment to the business community, big businesspeople saw no particular need to ask for revision of the draft Basic Law. On the other hand, after the Tiananmen Incident, the service professionals lost faith in China's promise of a high degree of autonomy under the Basic Law. They perceived the whole Basic Law drafting exercise as merely a "political show" to deceive the Hong Kong public.[36] If Beijing could declare martial law and move tanks into the Tiananmen Square, what good was a piece of paper called the Basic Law to protect the rights and freedom of Hong Kong people?[37]

In fact, the final promulgation of the Basic Law on April 4, 1990 was an anticlimax. By then the mass media in Hong Kong already shifted their attention to the promulgation of the Nationality Package in the British Parliament on April 5, 1990.[38] In this respect, the Basic Law failed to acquire the "sacredness" that other constitutions attained. Promulgated in 1990, the Basic Law was "polluted" by Beijing's action at Tiananmen Square.

Still, the legal and constitutional framework for post-1997 Hong Kong was now in place. Within minutes of the announcement that Beijing officially passed the Basic Law, the Hong Kong government announced that 18 directly elected seats in the Legco would be introduced in the 1991 election, prompting the formation of political parties in Hong Kong.[39]

Party Formation and Political Labels

The first political party formed was the United Democrats of Hong Kong (UDHK), established on April 23, 1990. The United Democrats was headed by Martin Lee and Szeto Wah, who remained the leader of the Hong Kong Alliance in Support of the Patriotic Democratic Movement in China. As such, the United Democrats was labelled "anti-Beijing" because of the group's overlapping leadership role in the Hong Kong Alliance and the latter's support for the democratic movement in China. In 1990, the United Democrats included some 220 activists who were also members of Meeting Point (MP), the Hong Kong Affairs Society (HKAS), and Association for Democracy and People's Livelihood (ADPL). The United Democrats were mostly service professionals from the ranks of social workers, teachers, university professors, independent union activists, church leaders, and lawyers. The United Democrat's platform was to speak up for the interests of Hong Kong, safeguard Hong Kong rights against Beijing's interference, and maintain a high degree of autonomy for Hong Kong.[40]

Many businesspeople, however, still worried about welfare spending and adversarial politics in Hong Kong. Some of them formed the Liberal Democratic Federation (LDF) on November 6, 1990, with the objective of supporting candidates to run in the 1991 elections. Members of the LDF were mostly well-known businesspeople in the Basic Law committees and appointed members of the Legco, including Maria Tam, James Tien, and Hu Fa-kwong.[41]

Finally, a pro-Beijing group emerged. The Hong Kong Citizen's Forum (CF) was established by Cheng Kai-nam (a pro-Beijing "moderate" school teacher) and Tam Yiu-chung (a leader of the pro-Beijing Federation of Hong Kong Trade Union). The Citizen's Forum supported Chinese nationalism and aimed to prepare pro-Beijing people to contest the 1991 elections.[42]

The above discussion delineates the profound impact of the Tiananmen Incident on Hong Kong's democratization. Before 1989, the terms "democracy" and "the democrats" had yet to receive widespread acceptance in Hong Kong society. However, after the million-person marches to support the democracy movement in China in May 1989, the terms "democracy" and "the democrats" became hegemonic in Hong Kong's political discourse. Not only the service professionals were proud to declare themselves as democrats, but big business and pro-Beijing forces were also forced to adopt a democratic label, talk in the democratic discourse, and play the democratic games. Thus the conservative forces called themselves the Liberal Democratic Federation in order to appeal to the pro-democratic sentiments in Hong Kong society.

Mobilizing the Grassroots Population

Ming Chan observes that the United Democrats had a large organized labor component among its top leadership.[43] Six of its 30 Central Committee members, including Szeto Wah and Lau Chin-shek, were leaders of major independent unions and veterans of labor protests and community movements. In addition, many core members of the United Democrats were very experienced in collective mobilization and electoral campaigns. Tuen Mun's Ng Ming-yum, Shatin's Lau Kong-wah and Wong Hong-chung, and Eastern HK Island's Man Sai-cheong were typical examples. When these local activists joined the United Democrats, they brought with them their own local networks and power bases. Sai-Wing Leung also points out that the success of the United Democrat candidates was partly due to their long-term efforts in community construction, district betterment, and social movements.[44]

Interest in local community and grassroots affairs was revitalized with the coming of the direct elections in 1991. The securing of support and endorsements from resident organizations (livelihood concern groups or district groups), the setting up of local party chapters at the community level, and the use of protest action against government policies were the principal strategies used by the democratic candidates in their campaigns. Ta-lok Lui remarks that the political penetration and institutionalization of the United Democrats at the community level even replaced local-resident livelihood organizations by making their action redundant.[45]

During the electoral campaigns, the United Democrats articulated a set of pro-welfare and anti-Beijing issues to appeal to the grassroots. Analyzing campaign materials and platforms, Ming-kwan Lee reports that United Democrat candidates, apart from their anti-Beijing stand, scored very high on pro-welfare issues, such as endorsing a progressive income tax system, demanding a bigger welfare budget and the introduction of a central provident fund, opposing the importation of labor, and favoring the strengthening of labor rights through unionization and collective bargaining.[46] Based on indepth interviews with Legco candidates, Jane Lee reports that most candidates chose to focus on attacking government policies which directly affect everyday livelihood and welfare programs. By demonstrating their commitment to improve general welfare, these candidates used a set of common expressions, such as "to fight for," "to guarantee," "to protect," and "to take care of" the interests of the grassroots; or "to urge," "to monitor," "to supervise," or "to oppose" government on some specific social legislation and policies, such as the importation of labor and price increases.[47] Stephen Tang finds that supporters of the United Democrats came from grassroots populations living in public housing as well as service professionals who enjoyed a relatively higher occupational status and were relatively well-educated.[48] In this respect, the United Democrats were now able to forge a populist alliance with the grassroots through the institutionalization of Legco direct election in 1991.

Election Outcome

The democratic activists won a landslide victory, capturing two-thirds of the popular votes and 16 of the 18 directly elected seats. From the democratic camp, 12 of the 15 United Democrat candidates won, two of the three Meeting Point candidates won, the single candidate from the APDL won, and an independent candidate formerly the chair of the Journalists' Association and a strong democratic advocate also won. The remaining two directly elected seats were won by moderates.[49] Since the democrats won 16 directly elected seats and five of the 21 functional constituencies, they formed a fairly solid democratic camp in the Legco together with a few other liberal-minded independents.

On the other hand, the business and the pro-Beijing political groups were heavily defeated in the direct election contests. Business' Liberal Democratic Federation polled only 5.1% of the vote, while pro-Beijing organizations received only 7.9% of the vote. None of their candidates were elected.[50] As a result, their influence in the Legco was considerably weakened than before.

What explains the remarkable success of the democrats in the 1991 elections? Since both the United Democrats and many pro-Beijing candidates (such as Tam Yiu-chung) were pro-welfare, a pro-welfare stand by itself could not explain the electoral victory of the United Democrats and the defeat of the pro-Beijing candidates. As such, many analysts argue that the China factor was clearly on the agenda during the electoral campaigns, and it powerfully shaped electoral results. For instance, United Democrat's Lau Chin-shek challenged his "leftist" unionist opponent Chan Yuen-han by asking her opinion about helping participants in the 1989 democracy movement to flee China.[51] Various surveys indicated that voters acquired a "HongKongese" identity; they strongly distrusted the Beijing government after the Tiananmen Incident; they feared Beijing's intervention in Hong Kong affairs; and they preferred a more responsive and autonomous Hong Kong government. That was why they voted against the pro-Beijing candidates but supported the United Democrats for their outright criticisms of Beijing policies.[52]

What, then, explains the failure of businesspeople and corporate professionals in winning the direct election seats? Businesspeople had little experience in community organization and grassroots mobilization. They never claimed to seek a mass base and remained a collection of notables with ties to Beijing and the colonial government of Hong Kong.[53] In addition, Siu-lun Wong points to the undercurrent of distrust and ambivalence toward the business sector. Wong's survey shows that 45% of the respondents disagreed with the idea that the business leaders were honest and dependable.[54] Ming-kwan Lee also reports that the overwhelming majority (75%) of the respondents to his survey agreed with the view that "the wealthy people and the big bosses have already had their safety exits arranged; they are here only to make the last killing."[55]

Thus, since the early 1990s, the institutionalization of direct elections consolidated the popular alliance between the service professionals and the grassroots population. This popular alliance enabled the Democratic Party to become a formidable force in the legislature and in fact transformed the mode of operation in the Legco. There were new rules (allowing more debates on motions and adjournment), a new secretariat, new standing committees, and even a historical bill to reprove the Governor of Hong Kong.[56] The growing power of the pro-democracy forces probably influenced London's policy toward the last phase of decolonization as well.

Patten's Electoral Reforms

London Changed Its Position

It is interesting to note that the Sino-British relationship sharply deteriorated during this last phase of colonial rule. From 1984 to 1991, London generally adopted a cooperative policy toward Beijing over the political development of Hong Kong. London was willing to postpone the introduction of direct elections in Hong Kong until 1991 (the year after the promulgation of the Basic Law) as Beijing had demanded. Prime Minister John Major went to Beijing in September 1991 for the signing of the new airport memorandum. This marked the first significant break in the West's isolation of China following the 1989 Tiananmen Incident. Furthermore, London was willing to "consult" Beijing on all major matters straddling 1997 in order to get Beijing's approval for the new airport project. Nevertheless, after his Beijing visit, Major decided in December 1991 to remove David Wilson (an exponent of the cooperative policy), and in April 1992, after the Conservative victory in the British general election, appointed Chris Patten as the last Governor of Hong Kong.

It must be pointed out that London's new democratic package was introduced at a time when the political structure of Hong Kong had largely been settled by the terms of the Basic Law promulgated in 1990. The scope for constitutional reform in Hong Kong in the early 1990s, therefore, was seriously restricted and it was almost too late for London to make any significant change in Hong Kong's political structure.

As such, what explains the sudden shift in London's policy toward Beijing in 1992? First, London's new position may be a result of the diminishing influence of the "old China hands" in British Foreign Office (who always advocated a cooperative policy toward China) and a growing influence of politicians over British policy towards Hong Kong's future.[57] Second, Norman Miners suggests that Patten, as a politician rising from the electoral ranks, believes passionately in democracy and the maximum feasible participation of the people in the government.[58] Third, London's democratization policy could be seen as an effort to construct a more positive image of the Conservative Party. Patten's democratic project was publicized at the Conservative Party conference at Blackpool in 1993. At the time of Patten's appointment as Governor, London knew there would be no flood of Hong Kong Chinese into Britain after 1997 because of the passing of the Nationality Act several years ago. Thus, Patten's democratic project would pose no real threat to a xenophobic Conservative Party which was in turmoil over immigration to Britain.[59] Fourth, as the parliamentary report of the House of Commons Foreign Affairs Committee acknowledged, the balance of world power and public opinion had shifted massively against China since the Tiananmen Incident, so there was less concern with Beijing's opposition to democracy reforms in Hong Kong.[60] Fifth, Suzanne Pepper suggests that London may be concerned about how history might judge them if they did not make the extra efforts to prepare their last colony for self-rule, given the expectation that Chinese communism would soon be doomed and go the way of its European counterparts.[61] Finally, John Major's September 1991 visit to Beijing did not bring about the desired results (the airport project did not take off), so there was the need for a new course of action toward Beijing.

Crafting a New Alliance

In order to enhance its bargaining power with Beijing, Patten needed strong support from the Hong Kong public. Upon his arrival, Patten immediately set up a new Business Council. But since big business already developed strong ties with Beijing through mainland trade and investment, Patten had little success in securing their support. Many corporate chiefs, in fact, wrote the Business Council off in private as a "Patten publicity stunt."[62]

Subsequently, Patten tried to craft a new populist alliance with the service professionals who emerged as a significant political force in Hong Kong since the Tiananmen Incident. First, Patten announced ambitious programs for improving social welfare, social security, education, health, public housing, and environmental protection — programs which would greatly increase the demand for service professionals.

Second, when nine Unofficial Members of the Executive Council (Exco), all of whom had been appointed by Governor Wilson, offered their courtesy resignations when Patten took office, seven were surprised that their offers were accepted. The members dropped from the Exco included Allen Lee, Selina Chow, Edward Ho, and Rita Fan — the four founding members of the pro-business Cooperative Resources Center which was the prototype of the Liberal Party.[63] Then Patten appointed several service professionals who were more sympathetic to democratization into the Exco, but also several prominent business elites, one of whom — Tung Chee-hwa — was later appointed by Beijing to be the SAR's first Chief Executive.

Third, Patten adopted a more open style of leadership: he took to the streets, shake hands with local residents, gave interviews to journalists, and dispensed with some of the secrecy that had always surrounded the Hong Kong Governorship.[64]

Finally, Patten replaced Wilson's "convergence" discourse with a new "democratization" discourse to redefine state-society relations in Hong Kong. Ngai-ling Sum points out that Patten treated citizen participation as an essential precondition for securing Hong Kong's future prosperity.[65] In his maiden policy speech to the Legco in October 1992, Patten underscores that "the best guarantee of Hong Kong's prosperity for as far ahead as any of us can see or envisage is to protect our way of life. . . . An integral part of this way of life . . . is the participation of individual citizens in the conduct of Hong Kong's affairs."[66] For Patten, subsumed under citizen participation are concepts such as a lower voting age, the replacement of corporate voting by individual voting, wholly elected legislature, direct representation, accountability, and the rule of law.

Electoral Reforms

After his popularity rating in Hong Kong soared, Patten was ready to take on Beijing. Without consulting Beijing in advance, Governor Patten sparked the Sino-British conflict in October 1992 with his electoral proposals seeking to increase the pace of democratization for Hong Kong. Patten's strategy was to adhere to the wording of the Basic Law (which will allow only 20 legislative seats returned by popular direct elections, 30 seats elected by functional constituencies, and 10 seats elected by an electoral committee by 1997, thus setting the limits on the 1995 elections), but he exploited the various loop-holes and filled in the many grey areas not too clearly defined in the Basic Law document.

Patten's electoral proposals can be summarized as follows:[67]

- To lower the voting age from 21 to 18 so that more young people will be eligible to vote in the Legco elections.
- Single vote, single seat: Since the 1991 system of double-member constituencies was criticized by the democrats, Patten proposes to give each voter a single vote for a single directly elected representative in a single seat for each of the 20 direct election geographic constituency seats.
- Functional constituency revisions: Before 1992, the 21 existing functional constituencies in the Legislative Council were decided largely on a corporate/institutional basis, e.g., each bank has a vote for the financial constituency. Patten proposed to replace corporate voting by individual voting in the existing functional constituencies. In addition, Patten wanted to redefine the nine new functional constituencies so that each would include the entire working population working in that sector. This redefinition of the functional constituencies would broaden the voting franchise from a few thousand corporate bodies to around 2.7 million people by giving every employed person the opportunity to elect to the Legislative Council a member to represent him or her at the workplace.
- Stronger local administration: Patten suggested to abolish all appointments to the local District Boards and Municipal Councils, so their members would be all directly elected.
- The election committee: Those elected in local District Boards would then make up the Election Committee to elect the remaining 10 members of the Legislative Council. In the Basic Law, however, it was stated that the Election Committee should be elected indirectly by corporate bodies, members of the Legco, and representatives on the National People's Congress and the Political Consultative Conference.

In other words, under Patten's plan, all members of the Legislative Council would be directly or indirectly elected by the people of Hong Kong in 1995. Following the categories of the Basic Law, Patten could claim that his proposals for constitutional reforms were quite compatible with the provisions of the Basic Law.[68]

British Prime Minister John Major and Foreign Secretary Douglas Hurd expressed their full backing for Patten's reforms and reiterated that the reform package would not violate the Joint Declaration, the Basic Law, or the seven Sino-British diplomatic letters exchanged during 1990–91. By mid-November 1992, the Canadian, Australian, and US governments also publicly stated their support for greater democracy in Hong Kong.[69]

In Hong Kong, 40 human rights and service professional groups organized public support for Patten's proposals through political advertisements, press conferences, public meetings, and demonstrations outside the Xinhua News Agency Hong Kong Branch Headquarter. Subsequently, opinion polls conducted in Hong

Kong in late 1992 showed that a clear majority of those surveyed approved of Patten's proposals and his performance, although this was coupled with a strong popular wish that confrontation with China be avoided.[70]

Beijing's "Triple Violation" and Nationalism Discourse

As expected, Beijing's reaction to Patten's proposals was highly negative. Patten was given a cold reception when he visited Beijing in October 1992. Beijing demanded that Patten's proposals be withdrawn, or else Beijing would take unilateral drastic actions with regard to both the political system and the proposed new airport project. Beijing regarded Patten's proposal as a plot to prevent China from regaining full sovereignty of Hong Kong, to plant pro-British elements in the political establishment after 1997, and to spread the virus of democracy to the mainland.[71]

According to Ngai-ling Sum,[72] Beijing pursued a discourse that clustered around "violation," "nationalism," and "negative metaphors" to fight back against Patten's democratization discourse. First of all, Beijing accused Patten of the "Three Contraventions." The first contravention: without prior consultations with the Chinese side, the British side suddenly and unilaterally made public Patten's constitutional package. This violated clause 5 of the Joint Declaration. The second contravention: the proposed electoral arrangements (the 1995 election committee and the new functional constituencies) of the Legco were major changes to the existing structure. This violated clause 3 of the Joint Declaration which states that political development in Hong Kong should be incremental and gradual. The third contravention: the Basic Law stipulates that the District Board is not a political organization. Yet Patten proposed to enlarge the power of the District Board by allowing board members to become the election committee to elect 10 Legco councilors. Beijing further accused London of breaching the agreement and the understanding reached between the two foreign ministers as evident in their exchange of letters in early 1990.[73]

Apart from the violation discourse, Beijing also promoted a discourse of nationalism. *The Beijing Review*, for instance, invoked China's "historical shame" and charged that "Hong Kong was plundered by Britain during the Opium War which was launched to invade China during the last century; they will never forget the shame, and without wiping out this shame, the Sino-British relationship can never become harmonious."[74] This "historical shame," then, was invoked to condemn British colonialism, to justify Hong Kong's reunification with the Chinese motherland, and to the Hong Kong Chinese as an integral part of the Chinese people in China rather than as subjects of a foreign colonial power.

Third, negative metaphors were used to construct unfavorable political images of Patten and his reform package. *Wen Wei Po* drew on metaphors such as "serpent," "prostitute," "two-headed snake," and "sinner of the millennium" to castigate Patten in the following terms: The hypocrisy of London in starting to introduce democracy to Hong Kong after 150 years of colonial rule; the indecency of London in violating signed agreement and mutual understanding; and the criminality of London in creating obstacles to China's national reunification with Hong Kong.[75]

Besides using an anti-colonial, nationalistic, and negative metaphor, Beijing also cultivated its own political group — the Democratic Alliance for Betterment of Hong Kong (DAB) — in Hong Kong. The DAB, in fact, was inaugurated the day after Patten's arrival in Hong Kong in 1992. The chairperson of DAB is Tsang Yuk-sing, the principal of what used to be known as a "patriotic" (i.e., pro-Beijing) high school. Endorsing Beijing's view, Tsang criticized Patten for "inventing a new cunning devices in the constitutional package which will enable him to transcend the pace of political reform set by the Basic Law."[76] Since 1992 the DAB is composed mainly of pro-Beijing "service professionals" and acted as a pro-Beijing patriotic party in the Hong Kong political arena, recruiting members, offering seminars, holding press conferences, and contributing commentaries to the mass media so as to promote the national reunification of Hong Kong with the "motherland."

In addition, Beijing also fought back at an economic level. Beijing threatened that economic "contracts, leases, and agreements" signed by the Hong Kong government would not be honored after 1997 unless they had been approved in advance by China.[77] Thus the construction of the new airport and container terminal number 9 was also affected. Beijing's move was intended to force the business community to take a firm stand against Patten's electoral reforms.

In March 1993, the Sino-British conflict intensified as Patten published his proposals in the government gazette. However, just before the proposals were debated for enact into law by the Legislative Council, Beijing agreed in April 1993 to hold talks. This occurred after London agreed that the talks should be based not directly on Patten's 1992 proposals, but on the Sino-British Joint Declaration, the Basic Law, and "previous understandings" reached through diplomatic exchanges by the two sides.

The Talks

The 17 rounds of talks in Beijing from April to November of 1993, nevertheless, failed to produce concrete results because Beijing proved unyielding on all issues. John Burns points out that the two sides disagreed on the following three major issues:[78]

1. The "through train" — London pressed Beijing to establish objective criteria prior to the 1994–95 elections for determining who could "ride the through train" beyond 1997, but Beijing insisted that this was a matter for the Preparatory Committee to decide in 1996.

2. The functional constituencies — Although London compromised by narrowing the scope of functional constituencies to one million voters, Beijing still

insisted that these voters must be limited to clearly identifiable corporate bodies.
3. The election committee — London and Beijing disagreed on the composition of a committee to elect ten members to the legislature in 1995. London argued that the committee should be made up of locally elected members, while Beijing insisted that the committee should be constituted by functional constituencies and appointed members.

Beijing and London at first agreed on the principle of "starting from the easier part and then moving on to the more difficult part." The negotiations, however, broke off after the seventeenth round in November 1993, when the two sides could not agree upon either the above three "major issues" or three other "simple issues" — the lowering of the voting age, the "single-seat, single vote system" for the 20 direct election seats, and the abolition of appointed seats on the lower councils.[79]

What explains the breakdown of the talks? Percy Cradock suggests that Beijing's unyielding position possibly reflected uncertainty about the succession to Deng Xiaoping, as no Beijing official had enough confidence to be flexible.[80] In addition, for Patten, there were apparently technical constraints. Patten had long insisted that time was running out; if the talks led nowhere, he would have to present his proposals to the legislature as soon as possible in order to make preparations for the District Board elections in September 1994, Urban/Regional Council elections in March 1995, and the Legco elections in September 1995.

The Second Stove

In order to discredit Patten's reform package, Beijing repeated its threat to sack any legislative member elected under a system it did not approve when it would resume the exercise of sovereignty over Hong Kong on July 1, 1997, and it would even dismiss the other tiers of government (the District Boards and the Municipal Councils) as well. This signalled the end of the "through train" agreement spelled out in the Basic Law, by which legislators elected in 1995 could stay in office until 1999, thus invaliding the design for the pre- and post-1997 institutional and personnel "convergence."

In addition, Beijing accelerated preparations for a shadow government, called "the second stove," to be installed in Hong Kong when it reverts to Chinese sovereignty. In June 1993, Beijing appointed 57 members to the Preliminary Working Committee (PWC) for the Hong Kong Special Administrative Region Preparatory Committee. The PWC had five sub-groups covering political, economic, legal, cultural and education, and security issues. The political and legal sub-groups were instructed to have their members immediately embark on plans for an alternative body to the legislature elected in 1995 under the Patten proposals.[81]

Furthermore, Beijing tried to consolidate its "unholy alliance" with big business in Hong Kong. During March and May 1994, Beijing appointed the third batch of Hong Kong Affairs Advisors, the first batch of 274 District Board Advisors, and another 13 members into the PWC. These appointees included pro-China political figures, DAB members, District Board chairpersons, heads of the major universities, former Hong Kong civil service senior officials, and big businesspeople.[82] In order to isolate the pro-democracy forces, no member from the United Democrats was appointed as advisor or as PWC member.

The Enactment of Patten's Proposals

In the midst of Beijing's offensives, Patten held firm and decided to proceed with his reform proposals even without Beijing's blessing. Patten's new tactic was to split his election proposals in two. In December 1993, the Legislative Council was first to be asked to consider legislation for the three "simple issues." When they were easily passed in February 1994, Patten immediately presented the three "major issues" to the legislature for debate, and he declared July 1994 as the deadline for passing them.

At the Legco session in late June 1994, only 23 votes could be counted on as firmly in favor of Patten's "three major issues," while another 23 legislators would definitely vote against Patten's proposals.[83] After a record 17-hour marathon debate from June 29 to June 30, Patten's reform proposals were passed in the Legco by a narrow margin of a single vote.[84]

In August 1994, Beijing responded to Patten's reform victory by passing a resolution in the National People's Congress (NPC) to dissolve the last British colonial era Legco on July 1, 1997. In December 1994, the political subgroup of the Preliminary Working Committee proposed to set up a "provisional legislature" to avoid any legislative vacuum after the transfer of sovereignty in 1997.[85] For Beijing, a provisional legislature was necessary because London had been uncooperative and destroyed the basis and mechanism of the "through train" — the arrangement under which the members elected to office in the 1995 election could serve a full four-year term in the Legco until 1999.[86] In addition, the Preliminary Working Committee wanted to speed up the election of the Chief Executive for the SAR government. The early selection of the Chief Executive was aimed to undermine the authority of the British-Hong Kong administration, rendering it impotent to introduce major structural or policy changes in the last phase of transition.[87]

Societal Polarization and the 1995 Elections

Party Formation

Patten's democratic proposals prompted political party formation in Hong Kong.

In order to prepare for the coming District Board elections in September 1994, the Urban/Regional Council elections in March 1995, and the Legco elections in September 1995, the United Democrats merged with the Meeting Point to form the Democratic Party in April 1994. The manifesto of the Democratic Party said it would seek to further unite democratic forces, strive for a high degree of autonomy and an open, democratic government, and would promote welfare and equality in Hong Kong. In addition, the Democratic Party tried to appropriate the discourse on nationalism for its own political purposes. Thus its manifesto stated: "We care for China and, as part of the Chinese citizenry, we have the rights and obligations to participate in and comment on the affairs of China."[88] Subsequently, the Democratic Party called for the condemnation of the 1989 Tiananmen Incident as well as an amendment of the Basic Law before 1997 to allow full direct election of the SAR Chief Executive and the Legco in Hong Kong.[89]

The victory of service professionals in the 1991 elections, Patten's welfare and electoral reforms, and the growing power of the service professionals in the Legco politicized big business. For those pro-big business CRC elites who were removed from the Exco by Patten in 1992, they formed a political party to reposition themselves representing business interests. Following London's footstep appropriating the democratic discourse, these pro-business CRC members called their party the "Liberal Party." The aims of the Liberal Party were to promote political stability, enhance the investment environment, and ensure a smooth transfer of sovereignty in 1997 by working with Beijing.[90]

As Patten was proposing his electoral reforms, big businesspeople felt a greater need than ever to keep up with political development in Hong Kong. Andy Ho, a political consultant, explains: "They're more aware that they can't simply ignore what's going on in the street. What the average person thinks is now likely to be reflected in the Legco. Businessmen need to become more proactive." Since December 1992, Liberal Party members reversed their previous pro-colonial regime stance in the CRC or pre-electoral eras, and acted like an opposition party in the Legco, criticizing Patten's democratic reforms and attacking government policies and voting against them in order to build up an image to rival that of the pro-democratic service professionals.[91]

Deepening of the "Unholy Alliance"

Top business figures, such as industrialist T.K. Ann, tycoons Henry Fok and Li Ka-shing, and banker David Li, were recruited to the Preliminary Working Committee. In this respect, the Preliminary Working Committee and batches of Hong Kong Affairs Advisors provided the critical institutional linkages for the "unholy alliance" of Beijing-businesspeople.

Subsequently, many businesspeople appropriated patriotism to legitimize their pro-Beijing stand. As David Chu, the director of Wah Tak Fung Development, explains: "I label myself as pro-China, but my definition is not that simple. My explanation is that I am a Chinese who wants to help China and Hong Kong, which will be a part of China as well. I do my best to help China to develop into a greater state. I want to make China better."[92] For David Chu, who used to hold a US passport, Hong Kong must have a good working relationship with China regardless of the type of regime in power. Many businesspeople remarked that Beijing was willing to listen to local views, especially on fiscal and monetary matters.[93] Even the Hong Kong General Chamber of Commerce shifted its stand from pro-British to pro-Beijing. In 1994 the Chamber membership failed to re-elect to its board pro-democratic legislator Jimmy McGregor, who was later appointed by Patten to the Exco. In 1995 the Chamber for the first time joined other business associations in celebrating the PRC National Day on October 1.[94]

Empowered by party formation and their Beijing alliance, big businesspeople began to criticize Patten's democratic reforms in public. First, they lamented that Patten's ambitious social program (such as the proposed Central Provident Fund) would sap Hong Kong's "spirit of diligence" and turn it into a "welfare society." They feared Patten's ambitious proposals would increase government spending and impose higher taxes — dark clouds that could spoil the territory's favorable business climate. Second, Patten's electoral proposals were seen as seriously undermining of Hong Kong's stability and prosperity. Patten's democracy-widening efforts would ensure that the Legco elected in 1995 would be dominated by the populist, pro-grassroots politicians.[95] Third, big businesspeople were worried about Patten's confrontational approach toward Beijing. The Business and Professional Federation (BPF), a conservative pressure group of 150 invited corporate members and business professional elites, issued a statement in favor of "convergence" with Beijing's Basic Law: "BPF strongly believes a smooth transition in 1997 and convergence with the Basic Law is in the best interests of the territory. Our future lies in a sound working relationship with China."[96]

The 1995 Elections and the Consolidation of the Populist Alliance

In 1995, the appointment system in the Legco came to an end. Both the officials and appointed seats were abolished. As a result, of the 60 Legco members, 30 were to be elected by functional constituencies, 20 by geographical constituencies, and 10 by an election committee composed of directly elected District Board members.[97]

Despite its objections to Patten's reforms, Beijing had seen fit to field candidates in the coming polls. Beijing did not want unchallenged pro-democracy parties to sweep into power, enact laws and policies that could undermine Hong Kong's traditional pro-Business economic policies, and even entrench political rights that could be used to agitate against Beijing. Subsequently, Beijing devoted all resources to support its candidates. Beijing backed the DAB with money and votes. The Bank of China and other PRC State corporations in Hong Kong provided economic resources and the pro-Beijing Hong Kong Federation of Trade Unions (HKFTU) mobilized its grassroots manpower during the election campaigns.

Like the 1991 elections, two issues stood out in the 1995 Legco election campaigns. First, there were the issues of autonomy and Hong Kong's relations with Beijing. The Democratic Party invoked the "HongKongese" identity and the anti-Beijing sentiment. It presented itself as a Hong Kong party to safeguard Hong Kong's interests against Beijing's intrusion. It argued that more popularly elected members in a stronger Legco were the best guarantee for Hong Kong's autonomy after 1997. However, as memories of Tiananmen were fading by 1995, the anti-Beijing line of the Democratic Party might be less attractive to the voters than in the 1991 election. On the other hand, the DAB proposed that dialogue rather than confrontation with Beijing would best promote Hong Kong's interests. The DAB campaigned as the party best able to defend Hong Kong's interests because of its ability to work with Beijing. The DAB's slogan was, therefore, "Love Hong Kong, Love China." Beijing supporters, furthermore, suggested that if more of them won, Beijing might even be prepared to leave the legislature alone in the 1997 changeover.[98]

Second, there were the bread and butter issues of unemployment, importation of labor into Hong Kong, inadequate social security and welfare, and dilapidated public housing. With the unemployment rate rising to 3.5% (which is high by Hong Kong standard) and the property market in the doldrums in 1995, service professionals' "welfare capitalism" agenda was highly appealing to the grassroots population. According to a survey of Legco election candidates conducted by the University of Hong Kong, the Democratic Party candidates received a rating of 7 (10 representing the highest degree of support) on commitment to a welfare society, while the pro-business Liberal Party candidates registered a score of 1.75.[99] Businesspeople criticized the Democratic Party for raising populist expectations to levels that might harm Hong Kong's free-market spirit. On the other hand, pro-Beijing's DAB sought to appeal to the electorate on the same welfare and livelihood issues as the Democratic Party.[100]

With regard to election results, the Democratic Party took 19 seats out of a total of 60 seats. Ian Scott argues that the Democratic Party won because it represented the voters on both the anxiety about the Beijing's intentions and welfare and livelihood issues.[101] With support from like-minded independents, the democratic camp now commands as many as 29 votes in the Legco.[102] The pro-Beijing DAB picked up six seats, mainly in the small "functional constituencies" representing occupational groups and from the election committee. But its three well-known top party leaders, Tsang Yok-sing, Tam Yiu-chung, and Cheng Kai-nam, ran their Democratic Party opponents fairly close but still lost in the end.[103] Despite its dismay showing in direct election, the pro-business Liberal Party still managed to secure 10 seats in the Legco through indirect elections in functional constituencies and electoral college and 1 seat (Allen Lee, party chairman) through direct election. With the support of pro-Beijing forces and other "independents" in the Legco, businesspeople could master enough votes to block any radical policy proposed by the democratic camp in the Legco.

The geographical constituencies election results show the consolidation of the populist alliance between the pro-democracy forces and the grassroots population. The democratic faction attracted 739,412 votes, constituting two-thirds (63.7%) of the total number of votes in the geographical constituencies. The pro-China faction only attracted 299,996 votes, or one-third (32.9%) of the total. The conservative business faction received 15,216 votes, representing 1.7% of the total. As Jermain Lam remarks, these figures show that the grassroots population supported the democratic faction, which advocated a faster pace of democratization, a genuinely high degree of autonomy for Hong Kong without Chinese intervention, and better social welfare under a capitalist economy.[104]

London Shifted Its Position Again

Curiously, the passing of Patten's proposals in the Legco in June 1994 also signaled a new phase of the Beijing-London relationship. It seems that tense and confrontational relationship between Beijing and London gradually faded away, and the two governments were again on speaking terms on transitional matters.[105]

In July 1994, just a month after Patten's reform victory, the Sino-British Joint Liaison Group quickly produced agreements on the financial package for the new airport and the disposal of military lands. The Joint Liaison Group also made progress on some of the 200-odd unchanged laws to reflect the shift of status from British colony to PRC Special Administrative Region.[106] In June 1995, Beijing and London finally agreed on terms for setting up a Court of Final Appeal in the territory to replace Britain's Privy Council as the highest judiciary authority for Hong Kong. In October 1995, Chinese Foreign Minister Qian Qichen paid a visit to his new British counterpart Malcolm Rifkind in London, and the two reached some agreement on smoothing Hong Kong's transition to Chinese rule. The two foreign ministers agreed on several key issues: informal meetings were to be held in Hong Kong between senior civil servants and Chinese officials on transition matters, and they would form a joint committee to plan a solemn, grand, and decent handover ceremony. Furthermore, when Qian brushed aside London's demands that the new Legco serve out a full four-year term rather than be scrapped in mid-1997, Rifkind did not press the issue too strongly.[107] According to Percy Cradock, "You now have the spectacle of the incredible shrinking Governor," as Patten was supposedly being marginalized when Beijing and London could work directly together for the 1997 transition.[108]

What explains Beijing's shift of position? It may be a result of a geopolitical shift of Beijing's diplomacy in mid 1995. Dismayed by Washington's decision to allow a "private" visit by Taipei's President Lee Teng-hui to the US and what Beijing saw as escalating US efforts to hem Beijing in, Beijing did not want at the same time to confront the British over a key issue like Hong Kong. Or it may be a result of pragmatic considerations. The changeover was too near to allow declining confidence to continue hollowing out Hong Kong. Cradock explains that the Chinese "don't want a chaotic transition, for their own interests."[109] Furthermore, Hong Kong's businesspeople had been lobbying hard for Beijing's green light for various infrastructural projects straddling 1997, and the "another stove" policy was far from popular in Hong Kong society.[110]

What then explains London's adoption of a relatively more cooperative policy toward Beijing? For Martin Lee, the British had again sacrificed Hong Kong's political rights for British commercial interests.[111] As Hong Kong's businesspeople openly complained about Patten's policy, London was under pressure to maintain cooperation with Beijing to safeguard Hong Kong's economic interests. For Neville Maxwell,[112] the change of British foreign secretaries accentuated the governor's isolation. Douglas Hurd had backed Patten up to the crisis over the Court of Appeal. Hurd's replacement by Malcolm Rifkind tilt the balance within the Foreign Office, which was always divided over the wisdom of Patten's challenges to Beijing. Joseph Cheng further laments that London felt the pressure when its Western allies, such as Australia and Canada, were eager to expand economic exchange with China.[113]

Toward a Contested Democracy

The service professionals, nevertheless, were still in defiance of Beijing despite London's change in position. In June 1995, Martin Lee of the Democratic Party condemned the Court of Appeal agreement, labeling it a "sellout" and a "joint Sino-British violation of the [Sino-British] Joint Declaration."[114] As a protest, the Democratic Party in July 1995 launched an unprecedented vote of no-confidence on Governor Patten in the Legco. In September 1995, Martin Lee remarked after winning the Legco election that he would be using the 21 remaining months of British rule to pass laws buttressing the press and free speech and implement policies to end the importation of labor and to set up a mandatory provident fund for all Hong Kong employees.[115]

In January 1996, the 150-member SAR Preparatory Committee was set up which would in turn install a 400-member Selection Committee to produce the first SAR Chief Executive and a 60-member provisional Legislative Council. Of the 94 Hong Kong appointees to the Preparatory Committee, more than 50 were big businesspeople. Collectively, they controlled 21 listed companies that accounted for 36% of Hong Kong's stock market capitalization. The four pro-Beijing political groups (the New Hong Kong Alliance, the Democratic Alliance for Betterment of Hong Kong, the Hong Kong Progressive Alliance, and the Liberal Democratic Foundation) were also strongly represented in the Preparatory Committee. On the other hand, members of the Democratic Party were frozen out. A political analyst remarks, "It is a deliberately apolitical set up to lay the foundations of Hong Kong Inc. under China."[116]

In August 1996, when the Preparatory Committee sought nominations for the 400-member Selection Committee, Vice-Premier Qian Qichen made a conciliatory gesture to the Democratic Party. Qian said that even members of the Democratic Party, once deemed subversive by Beijing because of their links to the 1989 Tiananmen Movement, were welcome to apply to serve in the Selection Committee. But the Democratic Party members still refused to join the Selection Committee because the party remained opposed to Beijing's decision "to scrap Hong Kong's elected legislature and replace it with a hand-picked version."[117]

When the 400-member Selection Committee was set up by the Preparatory Committee in November, 1996, big business was again overwhelmingly represented. Selection Committee members included property tycoons Li Ka-shing, Lee Shau-kee and Walter Kwok, gambling magnate Stanley Ho, movie mogul Run Run Shaw, and infrastructure developer Gordon Wu. The Hong Kong Progressive Alliance, a pro-Beijing business and professional group, got the highest number of seats in the Selection Committee, 47.[118]

The composition of the Selection Committee thus strongly favored candidates from a pro-Beijing, business background. It was only natural that this Selection Committee on December 11, 1996, picked Tung Chee-hwa, a big businessmen, as the Chief Executive, and selected on December 21, 1996, a pro-Beijing, business-oriented provisional legislature to replace the current elected Legco. The selection of the provisional legislature particularly lacks in legitimacy; fully 70% of the candidates and 85% of those eventually selected to the provisional Legco were themselves members of the 400-member Selection Committee which claimed 51 out of the 60 seats in the SAR provisional legislature. This suggests that the Selection Committee selected its own members to serve on the provisional legislature. Furthermore, ten of the candidates selected to the provisional legislature had earlier lost in 1995's popular elections on pro-Beijing tickets. As a result, Governor Patten dismissed the creation of the provisional legislature as a "bizarre farce," while Martin Lee of the Democratic Party called December 21, 1996, "a dark day for democracy."[119]

Conclusion

In the late 1980s, London crafted a strategic alliance of Beijing and big businesspeople. They agreed on a restricted democracy that favored business interests and wrote this conservative political model into the draft Basic Law. However, the Tiananmen Incident threw this strategic alliance apart. In the early 1990s, London formally defected to the democracy camp.

Trying to craft a strategic alliance with the democratic camp, Governor Patten appointed a few service professionals to the Legco and Exco, adopted pro-welfare policies, and implemented administrative reforms. In addition, Patten proposed a controversial reform package so as to add more "populist" elements into the restricted democracy model.

However, since the Basic Law was already promulgated and received the blessing of Patten's predecessor, Patten's democratic reforms could not possibly go beyond this constitutional framework. Subsequently, Patten reinterpreted the wording and grey areas of the Basic Law to fit his purpose. Patten redefined "functional constituency" in such a way that it would broaden the voting franchise from a few thousand corporate bodies to around 2.7 million people, and he suggested those elected in local elections would elect the remaining 10 members of the Legco.

How should Patten's democratic reforms be evaluated? On the one hand, Patten's strategic alliance with the service professionals had empowered their democracy project. Patten's reforms helped to elevate the "United Democrats" to a formal "Democratic Party." Patten's policy strengthened the pro-welfare platform of the democrats and consolidated their populist alliance with the grassroots population. Through Patten's reforms, the democrats controlled almost half of the Legco seats after they won the election in 1995.

In addition, there were many indicators that the democratic project established itself in Hong Kong civil society. First, thanks to the controversy of Patten's proposals, the mass media had extensive coverage and commentary on political affairs. As a result, surveys conducted by the Hong Kong Transitions Project in August 1993 and February 1994 showed that nearly 90% of Hong Kong people considered themselves informed about government policies related to their livelihood.[120] Second, service professionals and the grassroots populations became more assertive in protests and social movements. Between 50,000 and 100,000 demonstrators met regularly in Victoria Park every June 4 and demonstrations at Legco meetings have become quite common. Third, aside from protests and demonstrations, political participation at regular channels greatly expanded. As Michael DeGolyer remarks,[121] during election time, nearly every street in Hong Kong was festooned with signs, posters, banners, and placards. Every mailbox received more than one flyer, and thousands of store owners put up, or allowed up, campaign posters. At least two published political opinion surveys appeared every week. Voting had become a socially acceptable behavior. Fourth, Patten's reforms project further enhanced the prestige of the democrats, with Martin Lee, Szeto Wah, Lau Chin-shek, and Emily Lau continuing as the most popular legislative councilors; and the Democratic Party was the most popular party in the opinion polls.[122] In sum, by the mid 1990s, the traditional image of political apathy of the Hong Kong Chinese who were only interested in economic well-being could no longer be an accurate description of the rising tide of heated debate, active participation, and the widespread democracy movement regarding community issues, public affairs, and the prospect of the future SAR.

On the other hand, Patten's reforms did promote a contested democracy in Hong Kong. In response to Patten's reforms, Beijing deepened its "unholy alliance" with big business through appointing the latter as Hong Kong Affairs Advisors and as members of the Preliminary Working Committee, Preparatory Committee, Selection Committee, and provisional legislature. Arguing that the new electoral rules violated the Basic Law, Patten's reforms provided Beijing with an excellent opportunity to purge democratic activists out of the Legco. On June 30, 1997, popularly elected members of the Legco would be forced to step down; there would be no "through train" of the Legco from 1995 to 1999. A new SAR provisional legislature, which was pro-Beijing and favored business interests, was set up in December 1996, one which will discard or amend laws protecting human rights and permitting peaceful demonstrations.

Had Patten's reforms not been proposed and carried out, Hong Kong would still have a restricted democracy. But perhaps it would have been a more, yet stable, restricted democracy because all the political actors, including the service professionals, were forced to accept, to a certain extent, the electoral rules of the Basic Law. Short of Patten's reforms, the democrats would still win landslide elections at the ballot box because of the populist alliance, though the democrats would remain a minority in the Legco for at least 15 more years after 1997 due to the structural limitations set up by the Basic Law. Nevertheless, the political transition in 1997 might have been less turbulent without Patten's reforms.

However, Patten's reforms, through manipulating and reinterpreting the Basic Law, had greatly undermined the Basic Law's legitimacy. The Basic Law would not be "sacred" anymore, and its electoral rules were now subject to negotiation. Furthermore, Patten's reforms had created a group of Legco members (elected to office in 1995) who would see Beijing as usurping their rights with popular mandate from the Hong Kong people to serve their terms from 1995 to 1999. As Emily Lau, an outspoken Legco member, remarked: "We have been elected for four years. I don't see why we should be thrown out by the Chinese government in 1997."[123] Naturally, these Legco members would condemn the provisional Legco in 1997 as illegitimate and unconstitutional — this body was not even written into the Basic Law!

What made the matter worse was that London suddenly shifted its position again in 1995 and tried to amend its differences with Beijing. Since then, London tuned down its support for Patten's reforms and no longer declared that the provisional Legislature was illegitimate (only as unnecessary and unjustified), thus leaving the service professionals to fight their lonely democratic battle with Beijing.

In sum, as July 1, 1997 approaches, Hong Kong society is divided into two big camps: an "unholy alliance" between Beijing and big business and the traditional leftist organs, and a populist alliance between the service professionals and the grassroots population. Instead of focusing on winning elections and working through electoral rules, these two camps debated and reinterpreted the Basic Law, laying the foundation for a contested democracy in 1997 and beyond.

Notes

1. Reported in hknews@ahkcus.org (electronic news), December 11, 1996; forum@ahkcus.org (e-mail listing), December 14, 1996.

2. See hknews@ahkcus.org, December 16, 1997.

3. See hknews@ahkcus.org, December 20, 1996 and December 22, 1996.

4. See hknews@ahkcus.org, January 20, 1997.

5. Hsin-Chi Kuan, "Power Dependence and Democratic Transition: The Case of Hong Kong," *China Quarterly* 128 (1991), 775–793; Lau Siu-kai, "Hong Kong's Path of Democratization," *Asiatische Studien Etudes Asiatiques* 49 (1995), 71–90.

6. Samuel Huntington, *The Third Wave: Democratization in Late Twentieth Century* (Norman: University of Oklahoma Press, 1991); Shin Doh Chull, "On the Third Wave of Democratization: A Synthesis of Recent Theory and Research," *World Politics* 47 (1994), 135–170.

7. The terms "big businesspeople" and "big capitalists" are used interchangeably throughout the text. These terms refer to a small group of business tycoons who own or direct the transnational corporations of Hong Kong, such as the Bank of East Asia, Worldwide Shipping Group and Kowloon Wharf, Jardine and Matheson, etc. Before the 1980s, the British *hongs* (large traditional trading companies) were key players in Hong Kong politics. However, after the 1997 issue arose, the power center gradually shifted from the British *hongs* to the Hong Kong Chinese tycoons who were under Beijing's patronage.

8. Instead of using the term "new middle class," this chapter uses the term "service professionals." This is because Hong Kong's new middle class is deeply divided into two contradictory segments: service professionals and corporate professionals. These two new middle class segments have different class interests and life styles, different linkages to big business, the grassroots population, and Beijing, and different orientations and commitment towards the democracy project.

"Corporate professionals" include salaried employees working for such occupations as managers, technicians, engineers, architects, and accountants in banking, real estate, and manufacture industries. Employed by capitalists and working in the business world, corporate professionals want to perpetuate the capitalist system, and they share with capitalist concerns for capital accumulation, profit maximization, commodification, and technical efficiency. As a result, corporate professionals have a closer social relationship with the capitalists than with the working class. Similar to the capitalist, corporate professionals prefer a state that imposes little taxes on corporations, that sets up less regulations on business, and that allow business to exert influence on state policies. With respect to culture, corporate professionals embrace consumerism wholeheartedly because they can afford expensive commodities; they also strive for status symbols, become calculative and utilitarian in human relationship, and enjoy the existing status quo. Although corporate professionals are not against democracy, they are much less enthusiastic in supporting the democracy movement. Many corporate professionals calculate that since the democracy movement may fail, it is better for them to invest their energy in career development or in seeking emigration to the advanced capitalist nations. Some corporate professionals even turn into "agents" of the big capitalist class because of their business ties and social networks.

In contrast to the corporate professionals, "service professionals" are located in the state and the non-profit sectors. Service professionals include salaried employees in such occupations as teachers and college professors, social workers, lawyers, journalist, state administrators, and so forth. Since service professionals do not work in the profit sector, they have shown little interests in perpetuating and strengthening the capitalist system. Instead, service professionals are more concern with the expansion of needs and services (e.g., welfare, education, health care, and housing) to the grassroots population. Due to their daily contact with their clients, service professionals are socially closer to the grassroots population than to the capitalists. Service professionals also have developed more linkage with state administrators because they depend upon the state for jobs, funding, and other facilities. Consequently, the ideal state for service professionals is a welfare state which redistributes resources from the rich to the poor through a progressive taxation system. Service professionals also advocate stricter regulations on business because of environmental concerns, consumer frauds, and tax evasions. With respect to culture, service professionals have a reflective, critical mentality towards consumerism and hedonism in capitalism. They also value egalitarianism, social justice, and reformism. As such, service professionals tend to be highly critical toward the PRC because they worry about the political repression of the Beijing government and the possible erosion of their professional privileges under the Chinese rule. Thus, service professionals strongly advocate the democratization of Hong Kong government and they provide leaders and followers to the democracy movement.

Therefore, lumping the two contradictory groups of corporate professionals and service professionals together into a single category of "middle class" would cause confusion. For more discussion of this issue, see Alvin Y. So, "Western Sociological Theories and Hong Kong's New Middle Class," in *Discovery of the Middle Classes in East Asia*, Hsin-Huang Michael Hsiao, ed., (Taipei: Institute of Ethnology, Academia Sinica, 1993), 219–245.

9. This chapter uses the term "grassroots population" to describe the urban masses of Hong Kong. The term "working class" is avoided because Hong Kong's population are more interested in raising grassroots, livelihood issues than fighting for workplace or class issues. While no shortage of community protests exists, large-scale workers' strikes and violence were almost non-existent in Hong Kong.

10. This chapter distinguishes two kinds of alliances. An "institutional alliance" is based on sharing common class interests and values, is formalized through institutional channels, and is therefore highly stable. In the 1990s, the unholy alliance was institutionalized through Hong Kong businesspeople's investment in mainland China and through Beijing's appointment of businesspeople into such political organizations as the Preliminary Working Committee and the Preparatory Committee. The popular alliance was institutionalized as the result of direct elections to the Legislative Council. In contrast, a "strategic alliance" is based on political convenience at critical historical conjunctures. It has no institutional basis. Thus, a strategic alliance easily falls apart when the political situation changes.

11. Joseph Man Chan and Chin-Chuan Lee, *Mass Media and Political Transition: The Hong Kong Press in China's Orbit* (New York: Guilford Press, 1991), 131.

12. *Far Eastern Economic Review,* June 1, 1989, 17; *Far Eastern Economic Review,* July 20, 1989, 20.

13. Mark Roberti, *The Fall of Hong Kong* (New York: John Wiley & Sons, 1994), 256–258.

14. Sai-Wing Leung, "The 'China Factor' in the 1991 Legislative Council Election," in *Hong Kong Tried Democracy: The 1991 Elections in Hong Kong*, Siu-Kai Lau and Kin-Shuen Louie, eds., (Hong Kong: Hong Kong Institute of Asia-Pacific Studies, The Chinese University of Hong Kong,1993), p. 201.

15. Stephen Lung-Wai Tang, "Political Markets, Competition, and the Return to Monopoly: Evolution amidst a Historical Tragedy," in *Hong Kong Tried Democracy: The 1991 Elections in Hong Kong*, Siu-kai Lau and Kin-shuen Louie, eds., (Hong Kong: Hong Kong Institute of Asia-Pacific Studies, The Chinese University of Hong Kong, 1993), 293.

16. Ming K. Chan and Tuen-yu Lau, "Dilemma of the Communist Press in a Pluralistic Society: Hong Kong in the Transition to Chinese Sovereignty, 1988–1989," *Asian Survey* 30 (1990): 731–747.

17. Ming-Kwan Lee, "Community and Identity in Transition in Hong Kong," in *The Hong Kong Guangdong Link: Partnership in Flux*, Reginald Yin-Wang Kwok and Alvin Y. So, eds. (Armonk: M.E. Sharpe, 1995), 125.

18. Siumi Maria Tam, "Youth in Hong Kong: Re-Rooting of an Identity," Paper presented at the Annual Meeting of the Association for Asian Studies, Honolulu, April 1996, p. 9.

19. *Far Eastern Economic Review*, June 8, 1989, 18.

20. Stephen Tang, 1993, 281.

21. *Hong Kong Engineer*, July 1989, 11.

22. *Far Eastern Economic Review*, July 13, 1989, 11.

23. *Far Eastern Economic Review,* July 13, 1989, 10; Roberti, 1994, 264–265.

24. Chan and Lee, 1991, 132–133; Shiu-hing Lo, "The Politics of Cooptation in Hong Kong: A Study of the Basic Law Drafting Process," *Asian Journal of Public Administration* 14 (1992): 3–24.

25. Ming K. Chan, "Democracy Derailed," in *The Hong Kong Basic Law: Blueprint for "Stability and Prosperity" Under Chinese Sovereignty?*, Ming K. Chan and David J. Clark, eds., (Armonk: M.E. Sharpe, 1991), 22.

26. Ronald Skeldon, "Emigration and the Future of Hong Kong," *Pacific Affairs* 63 (1990–91): 500–523.

27. Shiu-Hing Lo, "The Problem of Perception and Sino-British Relations Over Hong Kong," *Contemporary Southeast Asia* 13 (1991): 200–219.

28. *SCMP,* October 26, 1989, 1; quoted in Shiu-hing Lo, 1991, 209.

29. Frank Ching, "Toward Colonial Sunset: The Wilson Regime, 1987–92," in *Precarious Balance: Hong Kong Between China and Britain, 1842–1992*, Ming K. Chan, ed., (Armonk: M.E. Sharpe, 1994), 182.

30. *Far Eastern Economic Review,* February 1, 1990, 16.

31. Roberti, 1994, 277.

32. Ian Scott, "An Overview of the Hong Kong Legislative Council Elections of 1991," in *Votes Without Power: The Hong Kong Legislative Council Elections*, Rowena Kwok, Joan Leung, and Ian Scott, eds. (Hong Kong: Hong Kong University Press, 1992), 10.

33. Ian Scott, "Political Transformation in Hong Kong: From Colony to Colony," in *The Hong Kong Guangdong Link: Partnership in Flux*, Reginald Yin-wang Kwok and Alvin Y. So, eds. (Armonk: M.E. Sharpe, 1995), 202.

34. Ian Scott, 1992, 11.

35. Ian Scott, 1995, 203.

36. Shiu-Hing Lo, "The Politics of Cooptation in Hong Kong: A Study of the Basic Law Drafting Process," *Asian Journal of Public Administration* 14 (1992): 3–24.

37. Roberti 1994, 275.

38. Jiefeng Zhang, et al., *Bubian, Wushi Nian? Zhongyinggang Jiaoli Jibenfa* (No Change, Fifty Years? China, Britain, and Hong Kong Wrestle with the Basic Law). (Hong Kong: Langchao Chubanse, 1991), 241.

39. Roberti, 1994, 287–288.

40. Jane Lee, "The Emergence of Party Politics in Hong Kong, 1982–92," in *25 Years of Social and Economic Development in Hong Kong*, Benjamin K.P. Leung and Teresa Y.C. Wong, eds. (Hong Kong: Centre of Asian Studies, the University of Hong Kong, 1994), 280,283.

41. Jane Lee, 1994, 279.

42. Jane Lee, 1994, 279–280.

43. Ming K. Chan, "Under China's Shadow: Realpolitik of Hong Kong Labour Unionism Toward 1997," in *Politics and Society in Hong Kong Towards 1997*, Charles Burton, ed. (Toronto: University of Toronto-York University Joint Centre for Asia Pacific Studies, 1992), 27.

44. Sai-wing Leung, "The 'China Factor' in the 1991 Legislative Council Election," in *Hong Kong Tried Democracy: The 1991 Elections in Hong Kong*, Siu-kai Lau and Kin-shuen Louie, eds.(Hong Kong: Hong Kong Institute of Asia-Pacific Studies, The Chinese University of Hong Kong, 1993), 223.

45. Ta-lok Lui, "Two Logics of Community Politics: Residents' Organizations and the 1991 Election," in *Hong Kong Tried Democracy: The 1991 Elections in Hong Kong*, Siu-Kai Lau and Kin-Shuen Louie, eds. (Hong Kong: Hong Kong Institute of Asia-Pacific Studies, The Chinese University of Hong Kong, 1993), 341.

46. Ming-kwan Lee, "Issue-Positions in the 1991 Legislative Council Election," in *Hong Kong Tried Democracy: The 1991 Elections in Hong Kong*, Siu-kai Lau and Kin-shuen Louie, eds. (Hong Kong: Hong Kong Institute of Asia-Pacific Studies, The Chinese University of Hong Kong, 1993), 240-241.

47. Jane Lee, "Campaigning Themes of the Candidates in the 1991 Legislative Council Election," in *Hong Kong Tried Democracy: The 1991 Elections in Hong Kong*, Siu-kai Lau and Kin-shuen Louie, eds. (Hong Kong: Hong Kong Institute of Asia-Pacific Studies, The Chinese University of Hong Kong, 1993), 300.

48. Stephen Tang, 1993, 149.

49. Ming K. Chan, "Decolonization Without Democracy: The Birth of Pluralistic Politics in Hong Kong," in *The Politics of Democratization: Generalizing East Asian Experience*, Edward Friedman, ed. (Boulder: Westview Press, 1994), 174.

50. Ian Scott, 1992, 5–6.

51. Sai-Wing Leung, 1993.

52. Jermain T.M. Lam and Jane C.Y. Lee, *The Political Culture of the Voters in Hong Kong: Part Two, A Study of the Geographical Constituencies of the Legislative Council* (Hong Kong: City Polytechnic of Hong Kong, 1992), 88–105.

53. Ian Scott, 1992, 23.

54. Siu-lun Wong, "Business and Politics in Hong Kong During the Transition," in *25 Years of Social and Economic Development in Hong Kong*, Benjamin K.P. Leung and Teresa Y.C. Wong, eds. (Hong Kong: Centre of Asian Studies, the University of Hong Kong, 1994), 217–235.

55. Ming-kwan Lee 1995, 129.

56. Jermain T.M. Lam, "From a Submissive to an Adversarial Legislature: The Changing Role of the Hong Kong Legislative Council in the Political Transition," *Asian Profile* 22 (1994): 21–32.

57. Ngai-ling Sum, "More than a 'War of Words': Identity, Politics and the Struggle for Dominance During the Recent 'Political Reform' Period in Hong Kong," *Economy and Society* 24 (1995): 67–100.

58. Norman Miners, "Constitution and Administration," in *The Other Hong Kong Report 1993*, Po-King Choi and Lok-sang Ho, eds. (Hong Kong: The Chinese University Press, 1993), 1–37.

59. Ngai-ling Sum, 1995, p. 81.

60. House of Commons, Foreign Affairs Committee, *Relations Between the United Kingdom and China in the Period up to and Beyond 1997* (London: Her Majesty's Stationery Office, March 23, 1994).

61. Suzanne Pepper, "Hong Kong in 1994." *Asian Survey* 35 (1995): 48–60.

62. *Asiaweek,* December 7, 1994, 28.

63. Norman Miners, "The Transformation of the Hong Kong Legislative Council 1970–1994: From Consensus to Confrontation," *The Asian Journal of Public Administration* 16 (1994): 224–248.

64. Frank Ching, "Politics, Politicians and Political Parties," in *The Other Hong Kong Report 1993*, Po-King Choi and Lok-sang Ho, eds. (Hong Kong: The Chinese University Press, 1993), 23–37.

65. Ngai-ling Sum, 1995.

66. Christopher Patten, "Governor Patten's Policy Speech to Legco," *Canada and Hong Kong Update* 8 (1992), 30. See also in *Our Next Five Years: The Agenda for Hong Kong* (Address by Governor Chris Patten to the opening session of the Legislative Council on October 7, 1992) (Hong Kong: Government Printer, 1992).

67. Christopher Patten, 1992.

68. Christopher Patten, 1992.

69. Bernard Luk, "Reactions to Patten's Constitutional Proposals," *Canada and Hong Kong Update* 8 (1992), 1–4.

70. Percy Cradock, *Experiences of China* (London: John Murray, 1994); Jermain T.M. Lam, "Chris Patten's Constitutional Reform Package: Implications for Hong Kong's Political Transition," *Issues and Studies* 29:7 (1993): 55–72.

71. Percy Cradock, 1994; Pang-kwong Li, "Elections, Politicians, and Electoral Politics," in *The Other Hong Kong Report 1995*, Stephen Y.L. Cheung and Stephen M.H. Sze, eds. (Hong Kong: The Chinese University Press, 1995), 51–65; Ming K. Chan, "Global Dimensions of Hong Kong's Transition Toward 1997" (University of Wisconsin-Milwaukee and Marquette University Center for International Studies, Occasional Paper, 1995).

72. Ngai-ling Sum, 1995.

73. Jermain Lam, 1993; K.K. Leung, "The Basic Law and the Problem of Political Transition," in *The Other Hong Kong Report 1995*, Stephen Y.L. Cheung and Stephen M.H. Sze, eds. (Hong Kong: The Chinese University Press, 1995), 33–49.

74. *Beijing Review*, February 7–20, 1994, 33.

75. Ngai-ling Sum, 1995, 74.

76. *South China Morning Post*, October 11, 1992, 2.

77. Bernard Luk, 1992.

78. John P. Burns, "Hong Kong in 1993: The Struggle for Authority Intensifies," *Asian Survey* 34 (1994), 55–63.

79. Jermain T.M. Lam, "Failure of Sino-British Talks over Hong Kong: Consequences and Implications," *Issues and Studies* 30 (1994), 95–115.

80. Percy Cradock, 1994.

81. Economist Intelligence Unit, *Country Report: Hong Kong, Macau* (London: Economic Intelligence Unit, 1994).

82. Sonny Shiu-hing Lo and Donald Hugh McMillen, "A Profile of the 'Pro-China Hong Kong Elites': Images and Perceptions," *Issues and Studies* 31:6 (1995): 98–127.

83. Economist Intelligence Unit, 1994.

84. Michael DeGolyer, "Politics, Politicians, and Political Parties," in *The Other Hong Kong Report 1993*, Donald H. McMillen and Si-Wai Man, eds. (Hong Kong: The Chinese University Press), 75–101.

85. Pang-kwong Li, "Elections, Politicians, and Electoral Politics," in *The Other Hong Kong Report 1995*, Stephen Y.L. Cheung and Stephen M.H. Sze, eds. (Hong Kong: The Chinese University Press, 1995), 51–65.

86. Yu-ying Liang, "Beijing Set on Establishing a Provisional Legislature in Hong Kong," *Issues and Studies* 31 (1995, #1): 101–102.

87. Chi-kin Lo, "Constitution and Administration," in *The Other Hong Kong Report*

1995, Stephen Y.L. Cheung and Stephen M.H. Sze, eds. (Hong Kong: The Chinese University Press, 1995), 1–12.

88. *South China Morning Post,* April 19, 1994, 6.

89. *Ming Pao,* October 3, 1994.

90. The Liberal Party was based on the CRC (Cooperative Research Center) core group. For the CRC's anti-democratic maneuvers, see Ming K. Chan, "Decolonization Without Democracy: The Birth of Pluralistic Politics in Hong Kong," in *The Politics of Democratization: Generalizing East Asian Experience*, Edward Friedman ed. (Boulder: Westview Press, 1994), 161–181.

91. Norman Miners, "The Transformation of the Hong Kong Legislative Council 1970–1994: From Consensus to Confrontation," *The Asian Journal of Public Administration* 16 (1994): 224–248.

92. Lo and McMillen, 1995, p. 111.

93. *Far Eastern Economic Review*, December 7, 1995, 74.

94. *Far Eastern Economic Review*, December 7, 1995, 73.

95. *Asiaweek*, December 7, 1994, 22–26.

96. *South China Morning Post,* November 22, 1992, 1.

97. Lo, 1995.

98. *Far Eastern Economic Review*, September 14, 1995, 26–27.

99. Jermain T.M. Lam, "The Last Legislative Council Election in Hong Kong: Implications and Consequences," *Issues and Studies*, 31:12 (1995): 68–82.

100. *Far Eastern Economic Review,* April 20, 1995, 29.

101. Ian Scott, "Party Politics and Elections in Transitional Hong Kong," Paper presented to the Annual Meeting of the Association for Asian Studies, Honolulu, Hawaii, April 11–14, 1996.

102. *Asiaweek,* September 29, 1995, 34; *Far Eastern Economic Review*, November 9, 1995, 36.

103. *Far Eastern Economic Review*, September 28, 1995, 16–17.

104. See Jermain Lam, 1995, 73.

105. Joseph Cheng, "Sino-British Negotiations and Problems of the British Administration," Paper presented to the conference on Hong Kong and its Pearl River Delta Hinterland: Links to China, Links to the World, at the University of British Columbia, Vancouver, May 1995.

106. Michael DeGolyer, "Politics, Politicians, and Political Parties," in *The Other Hong Kong Report 1993*, Donald H. McMillen and Si-Wai Man, eds. (Hong Kong: The Chinese University Press, 1994), 75–101.

107. *Asiaweek,* October 20, 1995, 35.

108. *Asiaweek*, October 20, 1995, 35; *Far Eastern Economic Review*, October 26, 1995, 20.

109. J.S. Adams, "Interview with Sir Percy Cradock," *Asian Affairs: Journal of the Royal Society for Asian Affairs* 26 (1995), 9.

110. Joseph Cheng, 1995.

111. *Asiaweek*, June 30, 1995, 38.

112. Neville Maxwell, "Britain Backs Off," *Far Eastern Economic Review*, November 9 1995, 39.

113. Joseph Cheng, 1995.

114. *Asiaweek*, June 30, 1995, 38.

115. *Asiaweek*, September 29, 1995, 39.

116. *Asiaweek*, January 12, 1996, p. 27; Liang Yu-ying, "Preparatory Committee Established for Hong Kong SAR," *Issues and Studies*, 32:1 (1996), 122–124.

117. See *Asiaweek*, August 23, 1996, p. 19.

118. *Asiaweek*, November 15, 1996, p. 28.

119. *Asiaweek*, January 10, 1997, p. 24; *Far Eastern Economic Review*, January 9, 1997, p. 22.

120. Michael DeGolyer, 1994.

121. Michael DeGolyer, 1994.

122. Robert Chung, "Public Opinion," in *The Other Hong Kong Report 1993*, Donald H. McMillen and Si-Wai Man, eds. (Hong Kong: The Chinese University Press, 1994), 103–123.

123. *Far Eastern Economic Review*, September 28, 1995, 17.

4

Legal Institutions in Transitional Hong Kong

Alison W. Conner

By the terms of the Sino-British Joint Declaration (the Joint Declaration),[1] sovereignty over Hong Kong will revert to the People's Republic of China (the PRC) on July 1, 1997, and Hong Kong will shed its colonial status to become a Chinese special administrative region (SAR or the HKSAR). The PRC promised in the Joint Declaration that Hong Kong's legal system would remain essentially unchanged for fifty years after the 1997 transfer. Those promises were further elaborated in the Basic Law of the Hong Kong Special Administrative Region of the PRC, which China promulgated in 1990 and which will serve as Hong Kong's "mini-constitution" when it goes into effect on July 1, 1997.[2] The Basic Law reconfirms the Joint Declaration's guarantees that Hong Kong will after 1997 "exercise a high degree of autonomy and enjoy executive, legislative and independent judicial power."[3] The fundamental issue therefore is: to what extent can Hong Kong's legal system, in the form promised by the Joint Declaration, survive the 1997 handover?

Although there may be grounds for optimism in other areas, many serious issues relating to Hong Kong's future legal system remain the source of great controversy. This essay will focus on four of those key legal areas: the composition of the court of final appeal, the establishment of the initial legislature, the survival of the bill of rights, and the possible application (direct or indirect) of Chinese law to the territory. All four areas involve complex issues, but this essay will attempt to summarize them and place them in a broader context.

Court of Final Appeal

When in August 1995 the Hong Kong government finally adopted legislation to establish a new court of last resort,[4] it seemed that debate over at least one future legal institution had ended. Nevertheless, the composition of that court, the exact timing of its establishment, and even the requirements for appointment of judges may still be in doubt.

At present, the Judicial Committee of the Privy Council, which is based in London, serves as Hong Kong's highest court;[5] but when Hong Kong reverts to China, "independent judicial power, including that of final adjudication," will be vested in the Hong Kong SAR.[6] The Privy Council will therefore be replaced by a new Hong Kong-based court, to be known as the Court of Final Appeal (CFA). According to the Joint Declaration, the CFA "may as required invite judges from other common law jurisdictions to sit on the court of final appeal,"[7] and the same provision was repeated word for word in article 82 of the Basic Law.

Although the Basic Law introduced a citizenship requirement for the Chief Justice of the CFA,[8] neither it nor the Joint Declaration contained any other restrictions on the CFA's composition or structure. Those details were originally agreed upon in 1991 by Chinese and British representatives on the Joint Liaison Group (JLG), after several years of negotiation.[9] According to their agreement, the CFA was to be composed of four permanent members, including the Chief Justice and three Hong Kong judges; and a fifth judge, who might be either a serving or retired local judge, or a judge chosen from another common law jurisdiction (who would be chosen from alternating panels).[10]

The proposed CFA composition met with strong opposition in Hong Kong, particularly from the legal profession, which argued that it violated the Joint Declaration and the Basic Law by (1) adding a restriction not contemplated in either document, and (2) usurping the power of the CFA itself to determine whether any foreign judges might be required for a particular case, and if so, how many.[11] Such a court, it was also argued, would not be sufficiently distinguished in membership from the existing Court of Appeal and would be unlikely to attain sufficient prestige and expertise to replace the Privy Council.[12]

The real issue, as many commentators stressed, was not simply the number of foreign judges permitted to sit on the court but the judicial independence and autonomy promised to Hong Kong under both the Joint Declaration and the Basic Law. Because those agreements left it to the CFA to decide when foreign judges might be "required," the effect of the proposal was to limit the freedom of the Hong Kong court in a way not contemplated when the Joint Declaration was presented to Hong Kong. Left unspoken in many discussions was the fear that China viewed local judges as potentially more controllable than foreign judges, and that the CFA might ultimately be no different from — and no more independent than — courts in the PRC.[13]

Both British and Chinese officials rejected such arguments or professed not to understand them. They maintained that it was necessary to fix the number of foreign judges in order to delineate the court's composition[14] and that the language in question did not mean that the CFA could invite outside judges "whenever it pleases, but only as required" — which could be interpreted to mean only if suitable judges could not be found in Hong Kong.[15] But the strong opposition to the proposed court effectively tabled the CFA bill for three years, until the Hong Kong government revived it for comment in late 1994.[16]

Legal Department spokesmen then argued that it was essential to have the CFA in operation before the 1997 transition and that time was running out: the bill had to be introduced and passed during 1995 if the court was to be in place by the handover. Although the Hong Kong government still maintained that the proposed structure of the CFA breached no agreements, its primary argument for passage of the bill appeared to be expediency: no better deal could be obtained from the PRC, whose officials had stated repeatedly that the discussions could not be reopened on any grounds and had threatened to dismantle any court whose composition it disapproved of.[17]

In June 1995, after further rounds of discussion, the Chinese and British representatives to the JLG finally reached agreement on the proposed CFA bill. Britain made further concessions and agreed not to establish the court before July 1, 1997[18] in exchange for involvement in China's preparations for the court, which would be led by the SAR's Chief Executive designate and the principal officials-designate.[19] Although the amended bill did not adopt the controversial provisions on "post-verdict remedial mechanisms" (which would have cast doubt on the finality of the court's rulings in all but commercial matters), it did include other features strongly opposed by many members of the legal profession and representatives of Hong Kong's two largest political parties, such as the limit on overseas judges.

The CFA bill was also sharply criticized for its incorporation of the controversial article 19 of the Basic Law, which provides that Hong Kong courts have no jurisdiction over "acts of state such as defense and foreign affairs."[20] Bar representatives have argued that both provisions introduced a "limitation on the powers of the courts not previously known and extending the common law definition of acts of state."[21] They were particularly concerned that the words "such as" implied that acts of state could be extended beyond the customary interpretation of acts relating to foreign affairs and defense matters to include acts of the government in relation to its own citizens.[22] Although that language already appears in the Basic Law[23] (which Legco has no power to amend), its re-adoption in the CFA bill without objection or discussion was viewed as problematic.[24] Despite those objections, however, the expediency argument undoubtedly won supporters for the CFA bill; amendments to the government's version of the bill were rejected and it was finally passed by Legco in July and signed into law in August 1995.[25]

Many members of the legal profession were troubled by other aspects of the

Sino-British agreement on the CFA; they objected, for example, to the failure to provide a role for the Judicial Services Commission to make recommendations for appointments to the CFA. At the same time, nothing in the CFA agreement would preclude participation in the selection of judges by the government-designate (the executive branch).[26] Indeed, while the Hong Kong government was pressing for the adoption of the CFA bill in late 1994, PRC representatives were suggesting that the post-1997 government would have the right to re-appoint CFA judges, as well as all other judges in the SAR, and would necessarily do so.[27] Although article 93 of the Basic Law provides that judges serving in Hong Kong before 1997 may remain in their employment, Chinese officials argued that article 88, which provides for appointment of judges by an independent commission, required measures for the reappointment of all judges if they were to continue in office after 1997.[28] Such an approach would effectively allow the PRC to screen all Hong Kong judges and disqualify any it disapproved of.[29]

Despite the many concessions apparently made by the British to reach an agreement on the CFA, Hong Kong may still not see the court it bargained for. According to reported Chinese timetables for the transition, preparations for the CFA are scheduled to begin in early 1997 and will presumably be undertaken at least in part by the Preparatory Committee, the 150-member body appointed by the PRC to prepare for the establishment of Hong Kong's post-1997 government.[30] The result may be a court whose composition many legal experts still argue will violate the legal agreements, but which will not be sufficiently established before the transition to build confidence in its competence — and whose judges will no doubt be vetted by China, thus calling into question its independence as well.[31]

Provisional Legislature

A potentially more serious dispute has arisen over Hong Kong's post-1997 legislature, despite the detailed provisions enacted by the PRC for its establishment and composition. The PRC promised in the Joint Declaration and the Basic Law that the legislative power of the Hong Kong SAR would be vested in its legislature, which would be "constituted by elections."[32] Article 68 of the Basic Law, together with a supporting decision enacted at the same time by the National People's Congress (the 1990 Decision), provides for the selection, primarily by elections, of the first legislative council of the HKSAR.[33] By its terms the Decision allows at least some legislators elected in the 1995 elections to complete their terms and continue in office for two years after the July 1, 1997 transfer of sovereignty: they could ride the "through train" to the SAR if they met the requirements of the 1990 Decision and were reconfirmed in office.[34]

The availability of the through train, however, has always depended in part on the format of the last pre-1997 elections to the Legislative Council (Legco), Hong Kong's current legislature.[35] Although Legco was originally composed of officials or appointed members, beginning in 1985 the Hong Kong government introduced indirect elections for some Legco seats[36] and in 1991 for the first time introduced a limited number of directly elected seats.[37] After his appointment to Hong Kong in 1992 (and the failure of Sino-British negotiations on this issue), Governor Chris Patten announced a package of further reforms expanding Legco's functional constituencies, with the result that in the September 1995 elections all sixty members of Legco were elected, either directly or indirectly.[38]

From the beginning, the PRC government strongly opposed the Governor's election reforms, charging that they violated the Basic Law (and various Sino-British agreements, including the Joint Declaration, as well as the principle of "convergence" with the Basic Law), and arguing that implementation of the proposals would necessarily derail the through train.[39] Chinese officials also threatened to dissolve the entire Legco and replace it with a "provisional" legislature, which would be appointed by the PRC or its representatives and sit for as long as one year from July 1, 1997. In August 1994, the NPC Standing Committee took a first step to formalize those threats with its adoption of a decision (the 1994 Decision) providing for the termination of the current legislature (as well as the Urban and Regional Councils and the District Boards) as of June 30, 1997. The 1994 Decision also provided that the Preparatory Committee would be responsible for the establishment of the Hong Kong SAR and related matters, and that it should, in accordance with the provisions of the 1990 Decision, prescribe the specific method for forming the first legislative council of the SAR.[40]

In March 1996, the Preparatory Committee voted in Beijing to replace Legco with an appointed provisional legislature,[41] and issued a decision setting out the selection process, terms and duties of the provisional legislature.[42] According to that decision, the 60 members of the provisional legislature would be chosen by the Selection Committee, a 400-member body to be appointed by the Preparatory Committee and already charged with selecting the HKSAR's first Chief Executive.[43] Once appointed, the provisional legislature would operate until the formation of the first legislature of the HKSAR, but no later than June 30, 1998.[44] Its duties were specifically defined to include formulating or abrogating laws as necessary, adopting the SAR's budget and approving revenue measures, hearing and debating reports from the Chief Executive, confirming judicial appointments, and handling any other matters necessary before the establishment of the first legislature. Although no laws it adopted could take effect until July 1, 1997, the provisional legislature was clearly expected to start work on legislation well before the actual date of sovereignty transfer.[45]

In October 1996, the Preparatory Committee announced that the provisional legislature would be selected by the end of December and would begin work shortly thereafter.[46] At the same time, Chinese officials also indicated that they would seek financial support for the operation of the provisional legislature to be provided in the Hong Kong 1997–98 budget.[47] On December 21, 1996, despite international objections and continued local protests, the Selection Committee met in Shenzhen and selected sixty out of the 130 "candidates" to serve on the provisional legislature.[48]

Despite the Preparatory Committee's March 1996 decision and the "election" of the provisional legislature, the establishment of this appointed interim body raises serious constitutional and legal issues that cannot easily be dismissed or pronounced away. Constitutional experts in Hong Kong have argued very strongly that the provisional legislature must be in breach of the Joint Declaration and the Basic Law, essentially on two counts: (1) its composition and method of formation, and (2) its operation before July 1, 1997.

The first difficulty with the provisional legislature is the complete lack of support for a fully appointed body in either the Joint Declaration or the Basic Law. The Joint Declaration held out the promise of a high degree of autonomy for Hong Kong through an elected representative government and it was presented to the people of Hong Kong on that basis (whatever the PRC's opposition to elections).[49] Although article 68 of the Basic Law provides for the "principle of gradual and orderly progress," it also clearly states that the "ultimate aim is the election of all members of the Legislative Council by universal suffrage." But Hong Kong now faces the dissolution of an elected legislature and its replacement by a non-elected one, a move that clearly violates the spirit of the Joint Declaration and reverses more than ten years of expanded participation in elections since 1985.

The actual appointment of the provisional legislature also failed to comply with the specific method for forming the initial SAR legislature prescribed in Annex II of the Basic Law and the 1990 Decision (which it incorporates by reference).[50] The 1990 Decision provides for the election in some manner of all sixty members of Hong Kong's initial legislature (30 from functional constituencies, 20 from geographic constituencies, and 10 by an "election committee"). The provisional legislature, however, was appointed by the Selection Committee, a procedure that neither the Basic Law nor the 1990 Decision contemplated. Although that decision gives the Preparatory Committee responsibility for prescribing the concrete method of forming the first legislature, it can only do so "in accordance with this Decision"[51] and not in violation of its specific procedures.

Second, whatever its legality after the handover, the appointment and operation of a second and competing legislative body for Hong Kong before July 1, 1997 contravenes the Joint Declaration and casts doubt on the legitimacy of any actions it might take before that date. While Britain retains sovereignty over Hong Kong and the current Legco continues to exist, there is already a duly constituted legislature in Hong Kong.[52] The establishment and operation of second legislature before July 1, 1997 is an assertion of sovereignty by the PRC government over Hong Kong and therefore constitutes a breach of the Joint Declaration as well as of the laws of Hong Kong governing the establishment of one Legislative Council in the territory.[53]

Adoption of legislation by the provisional legislature also appears to violate the Basic Law, as it could not comply with the provisions relating to the passage of laws (in article 74 and Annex II.II) before that law even comes into effect. If the HKSAR government-designate operates according to those procedures as though July 1, 1997 had already arrived, any "laws" they pass must therefore be of doubtful validity. And if the provisional legislature lacks the authority to make law for Hong Kong, its legislation could not be considered as part of those laws "previously in force" in Hong Kong, which would automatically survive the transition.[54]

In the face of these arguments, the Chinese authorities have relied primarily on the doctrine of necessity to support their establishment of the provisional legislature: they had no choice but to remove all sixty current Legco members (not just those elected to the nine new functional and the ten new election committee seats created by the Patten reforms), and the appointment of a provisional legislature was therefore necessary to avoid the resulting "legal vacuum." Lu Ping, director of the Hong Kong and Macau Affairs Office, for example, has stated that without a provisional legislature Hong Kong would face a legal vacuum: "If there is no provisional legislature, how would Hong Kong operate?"[55] In this view, the NPC's 1994 Decision providing for the dissolution of Legco on June 30, 1997 and the Preparatory Committee's 1996 decision establishing the provisional legislature provide sufficient legal support for the committee's actions.[56]

The Chinese position has been echoed by Tung Chee-hwa, vice-chairman of the Preparatory Committee as well as the SAR Chief Executive-designate, in his repeated calls for support for the provisional legislature, which he stated was necessary to avoid a political vacuum and to maintain stability. To meet other objections to its operation, he also suggested that the provisional legislature should meet in China, thus "avoid[ing] the existence of parallel legislatures." But perhaps his ultimate argument was expediency: "The provisional legislature has become a necessity. These are the realities. We have to work it out."[57] For those reasons, he maintained, the Hong Kong government should "work closely with the provisional legislature and those who disagree with its establishment should drop their firm stand."[58] In his view, the interim body would gain credibility after its formation.[59]

But the 1990 Decision does not grant the Preparatory Committee the power to form a provisional legislature, nor could the committee grant itself the power to do so through its 1996 decision.[60] "Necessity," moreover, is a technical doctrine with limited application, which cannot support the creation of the provisional legislature any more than the legal documents themselves. The "through train" was only one possible option for the SAR's first legislature: even if Legco must be dissolved and no member can ride it, there are clearly less drastic alternatives to its replacement by an interim, appointed body. The PRC could, for example, arrange new elections of the full HKSAR legislature soon after the handover, which would eliminate the need for a provisional legislature entirely.[61] Or the Chinese could allow representatives from the 41 older constituencies (i.e., those established before the 1992 reforms) to serve out their full four-year term through the transition and simply elect replacements for the new constituencies they object to.[62] But neither approach would permit the removal of popular directly elected Legco members whom the PRC has refused to recognize.

Persistent doubts about the "necessity" for and the legal validity of the provisional legislature have led to proposals that some further action be taken to validate it. One suggestion is for the interim body's status to be affirmed by the NPC Standing Committee through approval of the Preparatory Committee's work report justifying its plan for the provisional legislature, a move some Preparatory Committee members argue would be sufficient.[63] A second (and more formal) option would be an elaboration or "interpretation" by the NPC Standing Committee of the 1990 Decision to specifically recognize the provisional legislature, or even the adoption by the full NPC of a supplementary resolution to confirm the legal status of the provisional legislature before the July 1 handover.[64] Even the HKSAR Chief Executive-designate, while insisting that the "legal status of the provisional legislature has been very firm already," has admitted that some such resolution would be "helpful" and has vowed to work towards its adoption.[65]

But constitutional experts in Hong Kong have argued very persuasively that a provisional legislature would require an amendment to the Basic Law, which the Chinese authorities have repeatedly said cannot be enacted at this stage.[66] In the best legal and scholarly view, therefore, a provisional legislature would violate both the Joint Declaration and the Basic Law, and would set a dangerous precedent in every respect.[67] The PRC has now disregarded specific legislation on the establishment of the initial legislature — legislation that the PRC itself enacted. Doubts about the legality of the provisional legislature and the validity of any actions it takes (whether in China or Hong Kong, whether before or after July 1, 1997) will affect confidence in the legal system of Hong Kong as a whole. Under these circumstances, any laws it adopts will be open to challenge in the courts, and its very existence poses a "threat to stability."[68]

The PRC's stance on the provisional legislature also raises broader concerns about Chinese intentions towards Hong Kong. Dissolving Legco means dismantling Hong Kong's first fully elected legislature, a body for which more than a million people voted in the most democratic elections ever held in the territory. Its replacement, by contrast, was selected by a group of 400 people already hand-picked by China — hardly a "democratic election with Hong Kong characteristics" — and the selections process came under fire for favoritism, vote-trading and factionalism, as well as for its general lack of transparency and substantive issues.[69] Pro-China politicians were placed in a strong position because many of them were already on the Preparatory Committee or even the Selection Committee itself,[70] and many pro-Beijing candidates defeated in 1995 Legco elections also applied for slots as soon as the "nominations" period opened in November 1996.[71]

The results of such an "election" could hardly be in doubt: despite Chinese claims that the new assembly was balanced and broadly based, nearly half of the sixty successful candidates were members of the Preparatory Committee and ninety percent served on the Selection Committee itself;[72] ten of those named to the provisional legislature had been defeated in the 1995 Legco elections.[73] The selection thus ensured Chinese control of the legislature during the first year of the transition, when it will adopt critical legislation,[74] including the new electoral laws, which will govern the 1998 elections, and the subversion statute required by article 23 of the Basic Law.[75]

Although 33 members of the current Legco were named to the interim body (constituting a "partial through train"), all members of the Democratic Party, who oppose serving on the provisional legislature as a matter of principle, have now been excluded.[76] This is of course the true reason for the dissolution of Legco, what has made the establishment of the provisional legislature a "necessity." There would otherwise have been no way to displace members of the Democratic Party, which won 19 seats in the 1995 Legco elections (including eleven geographical constituency seats). The Democrats are the most popular party, having won three times as many seats as the pro-Beijing group and they constitute the largest political faction in Legco.[77] But they are regarded as "subversives" by the PRC and could not be permitted to remain in Legco past July 1, 1997. The Patten election reforms were therefore only the pretext for the dissolution of Legco and the derailment of the through train — the real reason is June 4, 1989 and the role the leading Democrats are seen to have played in it by China.

The January 1997 inaugural session of the provisional legislature did little to allay Hong Kong's worst fears about the interim body. Meeting across the border in Shenzhen because of the threat of legal challenges to its formal operation in Hong Kong, the group barred representatives from the public on the pretext that the venue was too small to host a public gallery.[78] Although members of the provisional legislature have repeatedly stated that it would formulate laws for the SAR, the body began its operation without formal rules for considering or adopting legislation and had no means of gazetting them (nor is there even any policy for declassifying its documents).[79]

Many Hong Kong people and their representatives therefore continue to openly oppose the provisional legislature despite its "inevitability" and "reality."[80] They have gone to London to seek a declaration from the British Parliament that the establishment of a provisional legislature is in breach of the Joint Declaration[81] and to Geneva to present their objections to the UN Human Rights Committee,[82] and have attempted to protest the legislature in Beijing.[83] The Democratic Party, whose members have consistently refused to serve in the provisional legislature, has pledged to put its case forward both in legal courts and the court of public opinion, not ruling out "anything that is lawful."[84] The party's chairman, Martin Lee, has also suggested that the Hong Kong government should apply for an injunction blocking the provisional legislature from meeting in the territory and a court declaration stating that the provisional legislature cannot perform any functions of the current Legco.[85]

British officials, however, have not so far been prepared to state unequivocally that Legco's dissolution will contravene the Joint Declaration (the Hong Kong Governor has come very close),[86] although they have continued to oppose the creation of the provisional legislature, describing it, for example, as a "thoroughly bad idea" and stressing "not just the undesirability of it but also the practical difficulties" it creates.[87] They do oppose its operation before July 1, 1997: it would "have no constitutional basis,"[88] and its early establishment "would seriously call into question China's commitment to its obligations under the Joint Declaration."[89] For that reason, the Hong Kong government has consistently stated it would refuse to recognize or cooperate with the provisional legislature if it was established or help it withstand legal challenges if it tried to start operations and begin voting on laws before July 1, 1997.[90]

But for more than two years, the Chinese authorities have remained adamant that the Legco elected in 1995 would be dissolved on July 1, 1997. The Chinese have, moreover, clearly rejected diplomatic attempts to reopen the issue, informing the British foreign secretary in early 1996 that there was no room for negotiation;[91] they continue to reject his calls to submit the question of the provisional legislature's legality to the International Court of Justice for independent legal settlement.[92] Despite its shaky legal status and lack of credibility, and the strong opposition from Hong Kong, therefore, the provisional legislature has been established and already operates as a rival or shadow legislature well before the change of sovereignty in Hong Kong.

Bill of Rights Ordinance

An equally troubling issue is the survival past July 1, 1997 of Hong Kong's current legislation, particularly more recently adopted ordinances of which the Chinese disapprove. According to the Joint Declaration, the laws previously in force in Hong Kong "shall be maintained," so long as they do not contravene the Basic Law (and subject to amendment by the SAR legislature),[93] and that guarantee is repeated in article 8 of the Basic Law. But will these provisions be sufficient to preserve the Hong Kong Bill of Rights in its present form?

In June 1991, the Hong Kong government enacted the Bill of Rights Ordinance (BOR), which in essence adopted as part of Hong Kong's domestic law the United Nations International Covenant on Civil and Political Rights (ICCPR).[94] At the same time the Hong Kong Letters Patent were also amended to prevent the Hong Kong legislature from enacting any laws inconsistent with the ICCPR.[95] The introduction into Hong Kong of some form of a bill of rights had been discussed since the mid-1980s, but the official announcement that it would indeed be drafted only came in October 1989.[96] Although the ICCPR has applied to the territory since 1976, the BOR was intended to provide further reassurance to the people of Hong Kong — who were badly shaken by the events of June 4, 1989 — that their rights would be protected even after the 1997 return to Chinese sovereignty.[97]

The PRC strongly opposed the introduction of the BOR and continues to protest its adoption, on several somewhat contradictory grounds.[98] Chinese officials argued generally that its enactment worked a fundamental change in Hong Kong's legal system and therefore contravened the provisions of 3(3) of the Joint Declaration that Hong Kong's laws were to "remain basically unchanged." They have also claimed that the BOR's "entrenched" position and special status inevitably place it in conflict with the Basic Law, which as Hong Kong's "mini-constitution" may alone have superior or overriding status after 1997. Finally, the Chinese argued that the BOR is redundant, since the Basic Law will provide sufficient protection for individual rights and freedoms, and at the same time, that some provisions of the BOR conflict with the Basic Law and must therefore become void when the Basic Law goes into effect.[99]

During the latter part of 1995, the BOR came under increasing attack, in particular for its "special status," by the SAR Preliminary Working Committee (PWC), which had been appointed by the PRC in 1993 to begin preparations for the HKSAR government. According to some PWC spokesmen, the BOR would have to be repealed after the 1997 handover and any laws struck down because of it would necessarily be reinstated.[100] The PWC argued specifically that section 2(3) on the principles and purposes of the BOR, section 3 on the effect of pre-existing law and section 4 on interpretation of subsequent legislation were all inconsistent with articles 8, 11, and 39 of the Basic Law. Consequently in October 1995 they made a formal recommendation to the PRC government that sections 2(3), 3 and 4 not be adopted as laws by the HKSAR.[101]

The PWC further declared that the amendment of six Hong Kong ordinances relating to public order to bring them into line with the BOR also violated the Joint Declaration provisions that the laws previously in force in Hong Kong should remain basically unchanged.[102] They charged that allowing such statutes to be struck down or amended would not only weaken the administration of Hong Kong but also failed to be "conducive to the maintenance of stability in Hong Kong." The PWC therefore recommended that those six laws be readopted by the SAR after 1997 in their unamended version — perhaps indicating that their greatest concern lay with the retention of outdated colonial public order statutes for the use of Hong Kong's future Chief Executive.

The Hong Kong government defended the BOR, maintaining that nothing in either the BOR ordinance itself or the Letters Patent gave it special status superior to other ordinances, and rejecting charges that the enactment of the BOR altered the legal system of Hong Kong or that it has overriding power over the Basic Law.[104] According to BOR supporters, an analysis of the actual application of the ordinance fails to support Beijing's contention that the BOR has seriously harmed the legal system or made it easier for criminals to be freed, even though it has had its major impact on criminal cases.[105]

Moreover, Hong Kong legal experts also strongly argued that the Chinese characterizations of the BOR were technically incorrect. Thus, it is not the BOR itself that has been entrenched, but the provisions of the ICCPR, which already applied to Hong Kong and will continue to do so after 1997 (by virtue of articles 8 and 18 of the Basic Law as well as the Joint Declaration).[106] Potential conflicts between the BOR and the Basic Law are limited and can be harmonized through interpretation, and since the two laws have little overlap, there is no reason to view the BOR as redundant. Nor does the BOR upset the legal and political system that existed either in 1984 when the Joint Declaration was signed or in 1990 when the Basic Law was enacted, since the ICCPR has applied to Hong Kong from the mid-seventies.[107] On the contrary, the proposed repeal of the BOR provisions, if implemented, would constitute a breach of both the Joint Declaration and the Basic Law, since these provisions are central to incorporating the ICCPR into Hong Kong legislation.[108]

Late in 1995 Legco voted to adopt a motion "strongly objecting" to the PWC proposals to repeal key provisions of the BOR and reinstate the six ordinances it struck down,[109] and members of Hong Kong's legal professional bodies also overwhelmingly opposed the proposals.[110] The continued Hong Kong opposition together with international criticism of the proposals led many to hope that the full Preparatory Committee might rethink the PWC's recommendations to dismantle the BOR and restore old colonial ordinances.

But those hopes were dashed in early 1997, when the Preparatory Committee passed a resolution adopting virtually all of the PWC's (and its own legal subgroup's) recommendations and listed twenty-five pieces of legislation to be repealed in full or in part on the grounds of inconsistency with the Basic Law.[111] Laws slated for repeal included the BOR provisions relating to its status (sections 2(3), 3 and 4), and the Public Order Ordinance and Societies Ordinance,[112] which were amended in 1992 and 1995 respectively to restrict police powers and allow societies to have overseas links, in order to bring them into line with the BOR.[113]

Justifications for the Preparatory Committee's decision differed little from those offered by the PWC several years ago and remained weak in legal terms. PRC officials continued to argue that the enactment of the BOR and the amendment of the two ordinances breached the Joint Declaration and the Basic Law by introducing major changes to the legal system without Chinese consent. More specifically, the Chinese argued that the Societies Ordinance was inconsistent with article 23 of the Basic Law, which banned local groups from having links with foreign political groups. PRC officials also denied that the earlier versions of those ordinances violated international human rights covenants.[114] But other Chinese statements suggested that the real reasons for the proposed repeal were political rather than legal: according to one PRC spokesman, for example, there is "no such thing as absolute rights and freedoms. There are limits."[115]

The Preparatory Committee's legal subgroup proposed the full reinstatement of the original versions of the two ordinances, apparently assuming that the earlier laws would automatically be revived if the NPC accepted their proposals for repeal. Even the Chief Executive-designate initially stated that the original versions of the ordinances would once again become law in Hong Kong on July 1, 1997 (although he implied that they would be reexamined by the first elected legislature in 1998).[116] But those assumptions were roundly criticized by the legal community: the NPC Standing Committee might find Hong Kong laws to be in contravention of the Basic Law but there was no provision in the Basic Law allowing them to reinstate old versions of ordinances or to revive legislation already repealed.[117] In the event, perhaps as a result of legal objections from Hong Kong,[118] Lu Ping declared that the NPC Standing Committee would declare the two laws in contravention of the Basic Law but leave it to the Hong Kong SAR to replace or amend them.[119]

Unfortunately, despite continuing popular support for the BOR and the amended versions of the Public Order and Societies Ordinances,[120] it seems likely that the future application of the BOR will indeed be limited and that restrictive versions of both ordinances will be reinstated by the provisional legislature in 1997. Not only will this revive a repressive colonial order clearly in breach of international human rights standards — it must also create legal confusion, as these attempts to restrict the BOR or to reinstate the old legislation will undoubtedly be subject to legal challenge in the SAR courts after the transition.

Application of Chinese Law

The formal documents not only provide for the continuation of Hong Kong's laws after 1997[121] but also exclude, with very limited exceptions, the application of Chinese law in the Hong Kong SAR. According to article 18 of the Basic Law, "National laws shall not be applied in the Hong Kong Special Administrative Region," except for the six specifically listed in Annex III, the most important of which is the PRC's Nationality Law.[122] Article 18 also provides that the NPC Standing Committee may add to this list, but only those laws "relating to defense and foreign affairs as well as other matters outside the limits of" the HKSAR's autonomy. Chinese law experts have themselves repeatedly (if not consistently) acknowledged those restrictions, stating, for example, that China's martial law would not be applied to Hong Kong, nor could it be, under the Basic Law.[123]

Despite the clear language of the Basic Law and various official pronouncements, however, the PRC's actions have already raised the possibility that Chinese law — its concepts or method of interpretation — could nevertheless "spill over" into Hong Kong, applying indirectly where direct application was prohibited. Law in Hong Kong would thus become — like law in the PRC — soft rather than hard law, and Chinese legal approaches would be introduced into Hong Kong's legal system, with the same effect as if the laws themselves had been adopted. One might argue that such a process has already begun, through, for example, the introduction of further restrictions not originally contemplated for the CFA, or by the loose interpretations of the Basic Law put forward in support of the provisional legislature.[124]

One of the greatest areas of concern is the application, even indirectly, of the PRC's criminal law or procedure to Hong Kong people.[125] The James Peng case, for example, was closely followed in Hong Kong since his abduction from Macau in 1993 by Chinese security personnel and his removal across the border to stand trial in Guangdong province. Peng was eventually convicted on corruption and embezzlement charges and sentenced to eighteen years of imprisonment under a statute that had not yet been enacted at the time of his alleged offenses.[126] Despite a host of procedural irregularities in the case, his conviction was upheld and he remains in custody in China.[127]

Many Hong Kong people were also shaken by the December 1995 sentencing of Chinese dissident Wei Jingsheng to 14 years' imprisonment on charges of plotting to overthrow the PRC government[128] for doing little more than establish a company and criticize the government — actions taken by Hong Kong people every day.[129] The October 1996 conviction of the former student leader Wang Dan and his 11-year prison sentence dealt a further blow to confidence on this issue, and thousands of people demonstrated in Hong Kong for Wang Dan's release.[130] The main charge against Wang was that he conspired to subvert the government and endangered state security; his articles, some written for Hong Kong publications, "attacked and slandered the Chinese government."[131] Could the same result be reached in Hong Kong after 1997? The answer will depend in large part on the legal definition of "subversion" enacted in the HKSAR and the interpretation of the free speech provision of the Basic Law, which by all signs now will have pride of place over the BOR.

Both Wei Jingsheng and Wang Dan were convicted under Chinese laws on "counterrevolution" (i.e., subversion or sedition), which as part of China's criminal law will technically not apply to Hong Kong. Instead, the SAR is required under article 23 of the Basic Law to enact its own laws prohibiting any "act of treason, secession, sedition, subversion against the Central People's Government, or theft of state secrets . . . " Such vague language, however, arguably introduces Chinese criminal law concepts, and the form that Hong Kong's legislation might take has long been a matter of concern to human rights groups in the territory.[132]

Hong Kong commentators have also speculated that the provisional legislature would enact the HKSAR's subversion law, and that its drafting process would coincide with — and be influenced by — the reformulation of the PRC's criminal law, which is expected to include tough new provisions on violations of state security.[133] Such fears find confirmation in Tung Chee-hwa's remarks that the legal group of the Preparatory Committee (whose members were handpicked by China) would "forward recommendations to the provisional legislature" on this matter and that "[b]ecause no legal vacuum should be allowed, the law concerned must be in effect on" July 1, 1997. The provisional legislature, in other words, would draft the subversion law on the basis of Chinese suggestions rather than genuine consultations in Hong Kong.[134]

The convictions of Wei Jingsheng and Wang Dan withstood appeal despite the protections ostensibly provided by article 35 of the Chinese Constitution,[135] which states that PRC citizens "enjoy freedom of speech, of the press, of assembly, of association . . . " The language of the comparable Basic Law provision, article 27, is virtually identical to that of the PRC Constitution, which provided them no protection against prosecution despite the nonviolent and routine nature of their activities. Although the detailed provisions of the Hong Kong BOR have a concrete meaning developed through interpretation and broader ICCPR jurisprudence, the PRC has argued that the BOR protections for individual rights are at best redundant, and they may not survive the transition.

Instead, PRC officials have shown a marked preference for the vaguer language of the Basic Law — and at the same time imply that further restrictions on speech and assembly will be put in place after the transition. The PRC Constitution itself greatly limits its apparently broad freedoms (in article 51, for example, which has no Basic Law equivalent),[136] and those freedoms are also restricted by the Criminal Law and regulations governing assembly and demonstrations. PRC representatives have already (as discussed earlier) announced their intention of reinstating in Hong Kong the old colonial public order statutes, and their frequent statements that "all freedoms must be within the limits allowed by law"[137] imply that further restrictions are definitely being considered.

Of course, the PRC has long put Hong Kong people on notice that they have nothing to fear so long as their actions are "patriotic." Hong Kong publishers already had before them the example of Xi Yang, the China-born Hong Kong journalist who received a 12-year sentence in 1994 for leaking state secrets after he reported information relating to interest rates and gold prices.[138] During 1996, however, as the transition drew nearer, PRC officials stepped up their warnings about future limits on permissible reporting and demonstrations in Hong Kong. In his May 1996 CNN interview, Lu Ping stressed that "freedom of the press has to be regulated by laws" and implied that Hong Kong might have to abide by some national laws, including prohibitions on suggesting independence for Taiwan or Hong Kong. It would also be illegal, he said, for anyone to advocate the overthrow of the central government.[139] Moreover, although people could disagree, "opinion is one thing, putting it into action is another." "It's all right if reporters objectively report. But if they advocate, it is an action. It has nothing to do with press freedom."[140]

Chinese Foreign Minister (and Preparatory Committee chairman) Qian Qichen's October 1996 interview with the *Asian Wall Street Journal* also caused an uproar in Hong Kong. According to Qian, the media could "put forward criticism but not rumors or lies," and "personal attacks" on Chinese leaders would not be allowed after 1997. Nor could Hong Kong people hold "political activities which directly interfere in the affairs of the mainland"— implying that local activities to commemorate the June 4 crackdown would be banned in Hong Kong after the transition.[141] The New China News Agency has issued even more ominous warnings against dissent. Commenting on Hong Kong's June 4 demonstrations, the deputy director said, "It's up to the laws passed by the post-1997 government to determine if these events continue. But I tell you one thing: This is certainly not a patriotic activity . . . It also disturbs public order."[142]

A related area of concern is Hong Kong's continued access to the free flow of information, including even financial news, since the PRC appears to draw no sharp distinctions between political and financial reporting. In spring 1996, the PRC issued regulations controlling access to the internet and later in the year to control access to internet Web sites.[143] It also adopted regulations restricting the distribution of on-line economic news in China. Under those tough new rules, foreign economic news agencies were ordered to submit to control by the New China News Agency and threatened with punishment if they released any information that "slanders or jeopardizes the national interest of China."[144] Although these regulations now apply to China only, some Hong Kong commentators have expressed the fear that, if the PRC remains obsessed with stability and control, similar regulations might also be applied, at least indirectly, to Hong Kong after 1997.

The depth of Hong Kong concern over these issues,[145] together with the uncertainty caused by a 16-month deadlock in the JLG over the legal definition of subversion, no doubt prompted the Hong Kong government to announce the introduction of its own legislation in late 1996.[146] Introduction of the bill was defended by the Hong Kong government as enabling public consultation without usurping the SAR's power, providing workable proposals requiring minimal change to survive the transition. Under the draft bill (an amendment to the Criminal Ordinance), mere expression of opinions or criticism would not constitute subversion; according to a government official, subversion and sedition would constitute crimes in Hong Kong only if they involved "force or a violent act," and the definition of "force" would be left to the courts.[147]

But PRC representatives denounced the bill, claiming it would bring "instability and disruption" to Hong Kong and insisting that only the post-handover government had the right to enact such legislation.[148] They argued that any attempts by the Hong Kong government to preempt the enactment of more restrictive legislation by the provisional legislature would be an infringement of the HKSAR's jurisdiction and contravene article 23 of the Basic Law.[149] The Preparatory Committee therefore endorsed a proposal that any such laws passed before the handover should be repealed.[150] More ominously, one member of the Preparatory Committee suggested that article 23 was intended to curb all activities that threatened the Chinese government, not just those involving force; he also found the proposed ten-year prison term too lenient.[151]

The Hong Kong government's draft bill faced opposition from other quarters, moreover, as legal professionals argued that the "violence" clause might fail to provide sufficient protections for speech and demonstrations or even that new laws on subversion and sedition were unnecessary in Hong Kong.[152] Some lawmakers also called on the government to qualify the two proposed offences further[153] and it was uncertain whether the bill would be passed by Legco. Despite the Hong Kong government's attempt to introduce a potentially more definite and liberal statute, therefore, the scope of subversion and other such laws that will apply to Hong Kong people after July 1, 1997 must remain unclear — though it seems likely that nonviolent demonstrations or other expressions of dissent will be greatly restricted.

Conclusion

Many factors have contributed to Hong Kong's past success, but a critical component has doubtless been the territory's legal system and framework of laws, which have provided stability and certainty to support Hong Kong's development. This essay has raised for consideration four areas of that legal system during the final stages of its transition from British colony to Chinese special administrative region. But perhaps only one fundamental issue underlies all four: will Hong Kong's legal system be allowed the autonomy promised by both the Joint Declaration and the Basic Law? Without such autonomy, Hong Kong is unlikely to preserve its separate values and way of life, regardless of official PRC pronouncements.

How the underlying issue of autonomy will be resolved, unfortunately, has depended not on Hong Kong's efforts alone, but also on larger factors far beyond its control, including the state of Sino-British relations, which deteriorated after the events of June 4, 1989 and the subsequent introduction of political reforms in Hong Kong by Governor Patten. Even more important is the PRC's leadership transition, which remains unresolved despite the offical line that the reins have passed to the next generation. The PRC's own state of uncertainty and potential instability has meant a return to "politics in command" (reformulated as "attaching the utmost importance to politics"), when economic considerations appear less important to the Chinese leadership than political posturing, and they have seemingly opted for a tough nationalistic line on all issues — including Hong Kong.

Thus, although most of the issues discussed in this essay now appear settled (they are "cooked rice," in the words of mainland officials), the results are not encouraging. Hong Kong will have neither the court of last resort nor the initial elected legislature it was promised by both the British and Chinese governments under the terms of the Joint Declaration and by the Chinese government under the Basic Law. Chinese law will not apply directly to the SAR, but a much-restricted bill of rights and new versions of the old public order statutes will weaken civil liberties protections. In the end, Beijing has been able — with or without British cooperation[154] — to put in place the legal institutions it may always have been determined to see in Hong Kong. But its methods have called into question the rule of law and the system is unlikely to provide the stability and order Beijing requires. For Hong Kong will have a final court lacking in prestige and independence and a legislature whose legislation and very existence will be subject to legal challenge — and the early days of the HKSAR will necessarily be dominated by legal arguments.

Notes

1. The Joint Declaration of the Government of the United Kingdom of Great Britain and Northern Ireland and the Government of the People's Republic of China on the Question of Hong Kong (signed on December 19, 1984 and entered into force on May 27, 1985). For the text see Andrew Byrnes and Johannes Chan, eds., *Public Law and Human Rights: A Hong Kong Sourcebook* (Hong Kong: Butterworths, 1993), pp. 45 ff.

2. The Basic Law was enacted by the National People's Congress of the PRC on April 4, 1990. For an English version, see Ming K. Chan and David J. Clark, eds., *The Hong Kong Basic Law: Blueprint for 'Stability and Prosperity'?* (Hong Kong: Hong Kong University Press, 1991), pp. 165 ff.

3. In article 2.

4. Hong Kong Court of Final Appeal Ordinance, Ord. No. 79 of 1995, signed into law on August 3, 1995 (the CFA Ordinance).

5. See Peter Wesley-Smith, *Constitutional and Administrative Law in Hong Kong* (Hong Kong: Longman Asia Limited, 1994) pp. 138 ff.

6. According to Annex III of the Joint Declaration.

7. Article 3(3) of the Joint Declaration.

8. According to article 90, both the CFA Chief Justice and the chief judge of the High Court must be "Chinese citizens who are permanent residents of the Region with no right of abode in any foreign country."

9. For a discussion of these issues and the background to the earlier dispute, see Alison W. Conner, "Final Appeal Court Proposal Stirs Controversy in Hong Kong," *East Asian Executive Reports,* November 1991, pp. 8, 10–11.

10. Ibid. Often referred to as the "4+1 composition."

11. For an analysis — and refutation — of the arguments that the agreement on the 4+1 composition was (1) merely a "subsequent elaboration of a general principle" contained in the Joint Declaration or (2) an "agreement between the parties regarding the

interpretation or the application of its provisions" see Roda Mushkat, *One Country, Two International Legal Personalities: The Case of Hong Kong* (Hong Kong: Hong Kong University Press, 1997) pp. 157–58.

12. *South China Morning Post,* October 29, 1991, p. 1.

13. PRC courts are subject not only to Communist Party direction but to pressures from administrative units at the same or higher level of government. See the discussion in Donald C. Clarke, "Dispute Resolution in China," 5 *Journal of Chinese Law* (1991), pp. 245 ff. Foreign judges, of course, would not necessarily be immune from pressure, especially if they wished to be reinvited to sit on the CFA.

14. *South China Morning Post,* October 2, 1991, p. 6.

15. *South China Morning Post,* September 28, 1991, p. 1.

16. Legco voted against the 4+1 CFA composition by a wide margin in 1991, and no bill was introduced then. *South China Morning Post,* October 26, 1991, p. A-1.

17. *South China Morning Post,* October 25, 1991, p. 6; October 23, 1991, p. 1; October 31, 1991, p. 1. "Clarifying the Court of Final Appeal Bill," (letter to editor from the Director of Administration), *South China Morning Post* (Int. Weekly), July 8, 1995, p. 10.

18. The CFA is therefore intended to begin formal operation on July 1, 1997. Indeed the CFA Ordinance specifically provides in section 1(2) that it "shall not come into operation on or before 30 June 1997 and the following day shall be the day for the coming into operation of the Ordinance . . . " For a discussion of whether the CFA Ordinance as drafted can constitutionally come into operation, see Peter Wesley-Smith, "Legal Institutions in Flux" (conference paper), pp. 7–9.

19. *South China Morning Post* (Int. Weekly), May 27, 1995, p. 1; June 17, 1995, p. 1. Agreement on the Question of the Court of Final Appeal in Hong Kong, signed on June 9, 1995.

20. In article 4(2) of the CFA Ordinance.

21. *South China Morning Post* (Int. Weekly), July 1, 1995, p. 2. Although the Bar Council continued its earlier opposition to the CFA proposal, the Law Society voted (858–746) not to oppose the 4+1 composition when the government revived it. *South China Morning Post* (Int. Weekly), January 21–22, 1995, p. 1.

22. Christine Loh, "Chance to discuss the basic problems," *South China Morning Post* (Int. Weekly), June 24, 1995, p. 10.

23. And reflects the Chinese view that there may be other limits to the jurisdiction of the SAR courts. See for example, Wu Jianfan, "Several Issues Concerning the Relationship between the Central Government of the People's Republic of China and the Hong Kong Special Administrative Region," 2 *Journal of Chinese Law* (1988) pp. 67–69; and Xiao Weiyun, "A Study of the Political System of the Hong Kong Special Administrative Region Under the Basic Law," 2 *Journal of Chinese Law* (1988) pp. 111–12.

24. And still difficult to reconcile with the Joint Declaration's promise to vest the Court with the "power of final adjudication." Mushkat, *One Country, Two International Legal Personalities*, p. 159.

25. *South China Morning Post* (Int. Weekly), July 29, 1995, p. 1; CFA Ordinance.

26. *South China Morning Post* (Int. Weekly), July 1, 1995, p. 1.

27. According to Lu Ping, the Director of the Hong Kong and Macau Affairs Office. *South China Morning Post,* December 13, 1994, p. 2.

28. Ibid. But a closer reading of the two provisions suggests that Lu Ping's interpretation must be wrong. See Peter Wesley-Smith, "Judges and the Through Train," 25 *Hong Kong Law Journal* (1995), p. 1.

29. That process has been made easier by the failure of attempts to ensure a through train for members of the Judicial Services Commission, which appoints Hong Kong's

judges. In early 1997, the Hong Kong government announced that appointments to the commission would end on June 30, 1997; at the same time, Chinese officials stated that it was for the Chief Executive-designate to name his own appointments to the SAR's Judicial Services Commission. *South China Morning Post,* February 1, 1997, p. 1.

30. The Decision of the NPC on the Method for the Formation of the First Government and the First Legislative Council of the HKSAR (adopted on April 4, 1990 with the Basic Law) [hereinafter the 1990 Decision] provides that the NPC will establish a "Preparatory Committee" for the HKSAR, which will be responsible for preparing the establishment of the SAR's first government. See Chan and Clark, *The Hong Kong Basic Law,* pp. 207–208 for the text of the Decision. The Preparatory Committee was formally appointed by the NPC Standing Committee in January 1996. Its 150 members include fifty-six mainland officials and ninety-four Hong Kong members, most of them long-time pro-Beijing figures and big-business tycoons. *South China Morning Post* (Int. Weekly), January 6, 1996, p. 1.

31. The Privy Council's announcement of a March 1, 1997 cut-off for appeals led to a rush by Hong Kong lawyers to file applications for appeals to that court. "Lawyers want their cases heard in London because they have no faith in the Court of Final Appeal," according to one barrister. *Hong Kong Standard,* January 16, 1997, p. 4.

32. In Annex I.I of the Joint Declaration and article 68 of the Basic Law.

33. In Annex III of the Basic Law (Method for the Formation of the Legislative Council of the Hong Kong Special Administrative Region and its Voting Procedures) and in the 1990 Decision.

34. International Commission of Jurists, *Countdown to 1997* (Geneva, 1992), pp. 72–73.

35. Technically, the Governor and the Legislative Council together constitute the territory's legislature: the Governor "by and with the advice and consent of" Legco is empowered to make law for Hong Kong. Wesley-Smith, *Constitutional and Administrative Law in Hong Kong,* p. 154.

36. In 1985 indirect elections were held for twelve functional constituency and twelve district seats in the then 57-seat Legco. Ming K. Chan, ed., *Precarious Balance: Hong Kong Between China and Britain,* 1842–1992 (Hong Kong University Press, 1994), p. 206.

37. When 39 of the 60 members were elected, 18 of them directly elected from geographical constituencies. Peter Wesley-Smith, *An Introduction to the Hong Kong Legal System* (Hong Kong: Oxford University Press, 1993), pp. 84–5.

38. See Wesley-Smith, *Constitutional and Administrative Law,* pp. 155–57 for a summary of the reform proposals, which were enacted into law in 1994. *South China Morning Post* (Int. Weekly), September 23, 1995, p. 1.

39. A clearer "through train" problem, as some pro-China politicians have claimed, is that more than 20% of Legco's members have passports or foreign right of abode — but article 67 of the Basic Law restricts such membership to 20% of the total.

40. *Renmin Ribao* (People's Daily), September 1, 1994, p. 1.

41. Like its predecessor, the Preliminary Working Committee, which voted to establish a provisional legislature for one year. *South China Morning Post,* December 9, 1994, p. 2.

42. Decision of the Preparatory Committee of the HKSAR Relating to the Establishment of the HKSAR Provisional Legislature, adopted on March 24, 1996. *Fazhi Ribao* (Legal Daily), March 26, 1996, p. 2.

43. The 1990 Decision provides for the establishment of the Selection Committee and its role in the selection of the first HKSAR Chief Executive. The members of the Selection Committee were chosen by the Preparatory Committee after a period of "nomi-

nations" and the final membership was announced in November 1996. *International Herald Tribune,* November 4, 1996, p. 4.

44. *Legal Daily,* March 26, 1996, p. 2.

45. Ibid.

46. *South China Morning Post,* October 8, 1996, p. 6.

47. Expenses including allowances for its 60 members and its staff, as well as money to hire venues to host the meetings. Preparatory Committee members also supported the view that Hong Kong should fund the provisional legislature. *South China Morning Post,* October 7, 1996, p. 4. The support was refused, so the Chinese government agreed to provide funding until after the transition, and then claim back the money from Hong Kong taxpayers. *South China Morning Post,* January 4, 1997, p. 4; January 6, 1997, p. 1.

48. *South China Morning Post,* December 22, 1996, p. 1; *International Herald Tribune,* December 23, 1996, p. 4.

49. Ian Scott, *Political Change and the Crisis of Legitimacy in Hong Kong* (Hong Kong: Oxford University Press, 1989), pp. 214–215. See pp. 279–298 for a discussion of these developments and the Chinese opposition to direct elections during the 1980s.

50. In Annex III of the Basic Law (Method for the Formation of the Legislative Council of the Hong Kong Special Administrative Region and its Voting Procedures), and in the 1990 Decision.

51. Sections (2) and (6) of the 1990 Decision. Although the Preparatory Committee's decision states it was issued in accordance with the 1990 Decision, it does not explain how the two can be reconciled.

52. The only other institutions with legislative powers for Hong Kong are the Queen in Parliament and Her Majesty in Council. Gladys Li, "Must find legal and constitutional solution" (letter to the editor), *South China Morning Post,* August 21, 1996, p. 14.

53. Gladys Li, "Argument leads back to same absurd result" (letter to the editor), *South China Morning Post,* November 7, 1996, p. 18. This is the reason Lady Thatcher stated in an interview in Beijing that the provisional legislature would constitute a breach of the Joint Declaration. *International Herald Tribune,* November 16–17, 1996, p. 4.

54. *South China Morning Post,* August 21, 1996, p. 14.

55. *South China Morning Post,* October 15, 1996, p. 4.

56. Kam Lam, "Finding legal reason difficult to follow," *South China Morning Post,* December 19, 1996, p. 18.

57. Quoted in the *International Herald Tribune,* October 28, 1996, p. 4; *South China Morning Post,* October 12, 1996, p. 4.

58. *South China Morning Post,* October 12, 1996, p. 4. His statements in support of the provisional legislature if anything became stronger during his "campaign" for Chief Executive: "The provisional legislature is necessary. It must be set up and must go into operation." He also indicated that if the Chief Secretary stayed on, he would not "allow her to insist on noncooperation with the provisional legislature." News report (hknews@ahkcus.org), December 3, 1996.

59. *South China Morning Post,* October 17, 1996, p. 4.

60. For this argument, see Johannes Chan, "Representation in dispute," China Rights Forum (Winter 1996), pp. 5–6; Christine Loh, "Keeping up the fight," *South China Morning Post,* December 7, 1996, p. 19.

61. Yash Ghai, "Back to Basics: The Provisional Legislature and the Basic Law," 25 *Hong Kong Law Journal* (1995), pp. 6–7. *International Herald Tribune,* November 16–17, 1996, p. 4. Since the current Legco takes a break every year, it could stop for two months, which would allow time for elections. Emily Lau, quoted in *South China Morning Post,* December 21, 1996, p. 6. Even if one accepts the Chinese arguments, it is

difficult to argue that a full year's term is necessary for the provisional legislature: One supporter of the doctrine's application has argued that "necessity" could only justify its operation for the three months required to arrange new elections. Stephen Law Shing-yan, "The Constitutionality of the Provisional Legislature," 26 *Hong Kong Law Journal* (1996), pp. 153–154.

62. Suggested by a number of commentators, including Frank Ching, "Time for Hong Kong Conciliation," *Far Eastern Economic Review,* January 19, 1995, p. 29.

63. *South China Morning Post,* February 1, 1997, p. 6.

64. Otherwise, "[w]hen the legality of the provisional legislature is challenged in court, the court will face difficulties whatever it rules." *South China Morning Post,* October 12, 1996, p. 4. *South China Morning Post,* October 22, 1996, p. 6; January 4, 1997, p. 4; January 29, 1997, p. 1. See also Law, "The Constitutionality of the Provisional Legislature," p. 153.

65. *South China Morning Post,* December 20, 1996, p. 4; January 3, 1997, p. 1; January 4, 1997, p. 4; January 6, 1997, p. 1. At its meeting in Beijing on January 31 to February 1, 1997, the Preparatory Committee passed a resolution affirming the present status of the provisional legislature, suggesting further concerns over the legitimacy of the interim body. *South China Morning Post,* February 2, 1997, p. 1.

66. Ghai, "Back to Basics," p. 4; *South China Morning Post,* January 13, 1997, p. 18.

67. See Ghai, "Back to Basics"; Johannes Chan, "Representation in dispute" for these arguments.

68. According to a report prepared by Human Rights Monitor for submission to the United Nations Human Rights Committee. *Sunday Morning Post,* October 13, 1996, p. 2.

69. *South China Morning Post,* November 18, 1996, p. 1; November 19, 1996, p. 1; December 13, 1996, p. 7; December 21, 1996, p. 19; *Sunday Morning Post,* December 22, 1996, p. 1. The Hong Kong Governor described the selection process as a "bizarre farce" and "stomach-churning." *Sunday Morning Post,* December 22, 1996, p. 1. Lu Ping claimed that it was the Governor's failure to cooperate with the provisional legislature that made it impossible for China to make its appointment more democratic. *South China Morning Post,* January 1, 1997, p. 1.

70. *South China Morning Post,* November 23, 1996, p. 6.

71. It was reported that at least 11 of the 57 applicants on the first day of nominations were losing candidates in Legco elections. *South China Morning Post,* November 19, 1996, p. 1.

72. *South China Morning Post,* December 24, 1996, p. 17.

73. *South China Morning Post,* December 22, 1996, p. 1; December 24, 1996, p. 17; *International Herald Tribune,* December 23, 1996, p. 4.

74. Clearly recognized: the Governor has said this quite plainly. News report (hknews@ahkcus.org), March 20, 1996.

75. *South China Morning Post,* October 15, 1996, p. 4. Lu Ping has stated that the provisional legislature would probably introduce the anti-sedition or subversion laws. Beijing interview reported in the *International Herald Tribune,* November 14, 1996, p. 6.

76. *South China Morning Post,* December 22, 1996, p. 1; December 24, 1996, p. 17; *International Herald Tribune,* December 23, 1996, p. 4.

77. *South China Morning Post* (Int. Weekly), September 23, 1995, p. 1.

78. *South China Morning Post,* January 20, 1997, p. 4; January 21, 1997, p. 17; January 23, 1997, p. 19.

79. *South China Morning Post,* January 10, 1997, p. 10; *Sunday Morning Post,* January 26, 1997, p. 4.

80. *South China Morning Post,* October 22, 1996, p. 6; October 17, 1996, p. 4.

81. *International Herald Tribune,* November 11, 1996, p. 6.

82. News report (hknews@ahkcus.org), October 18, 1996.

83. *South China Morning Post,* November 1, 1996, p. 1. They have won support from the International Commission of Jurists, whose most recent report concludes that the provisional legislature would breach the Basic Law and the Joint Declaration. News report (hknews@ahkcus.org), December 3, 1996.

84. *International Herald Tribune,* March 26, 1996, p. 4.

85. News report (hknews@ahkcus.org), May 7, 1996.

86. *South China Morning Post* (Int. Weekly), March 9, 1996, p. 1; *Wall Street Journal,* March 25, 1996, p. 1. The Governor was commenting on the Preparatory Committee's decision to dissolve Legco and establish the provisional legislature when he noted that the Joint Declaration did not include any mention of an interim body.

87. According to Minister for Hong Kong Affairs, Jeremy Hanley, quoted in the *South China Morning Post* (Int. Weekly), September 21, 1996, p. 1.

88. Government House spokesman, quoted in *South China Morning Post,* October 8, 1996, p. 6.

89. According to Foreign Secretary Malcolm Rifkind. *South China Morning Post,* November 15, 1996, p. 7.

90. For example, *International Herald Tribune,* October 3, 1996, p. 1.

91. *International Herald Tribune,* January 12, 1996, p. 4.

92. *South China Morning Post,* December 21, 1996, p. 1; news report (hknews@ahkcus.org), December 26, 1996.

93. In Annex I.

94. See Byrnes and Chan, *Public Law and Human Rights,* pp. 215 ff.

95. Philip Dykes, "The Hong Kong Bill of Rights 1991: Its Origin, Content and Impact," in Johannes Chan and Yash Ghai, eds., *The Hong Kong Bill of Rights: A Comparative Approach* (Hong Kong: Butterworths, 1993), pp. 40–41.

96. Nihal Jayawickrama, "Public Law," in Raymond Wacks, ed., *The Law In Hong Kong, 1969–1989* (Hong Kong: Oxford University Press, 1990), pp. 107–08; Nihal Jayawickrama, "The Bill of Rights," in Raymond Wacks, ed., *Human Rights in Hong Kong* (Hong Kong: Oxford University Press, 1992), pp. 65–71; Philip Dykes, "The Hong Kong Bill of Rights," p. 40.

97. Jayawickrama, "The Bill of Rights," pp. 69 ff.

98. Made in many forums. See for example, News reports (hknews@ahkcus.com), October 21, 1995; October 30, 1995; November 2, 1995; November 14, 1995.

99. For a full discussion and analysis of these arguments see Yash Ghai, "The Hong Kong Bill of Rights Ordinance and the Basic Law of the Hong Kong Special Administrative Region: Complementarities and Conflicts," 1 *Journal of Chinese and Comparative Law* 30; Yash Ghai, "The Bill of Rights and the Basic Law: Inconsistent or Complementary?," in George Edwards and Andrew Byrnes, eds., *Hong Kong's Bill of Rights: 1991–1994 and Beyond* (Hong Kong: University of Hong Kong Faculty of Law, 1995), pp. 53–67.

100. News report (hknews@ahkcus.com), November 2, 1995.

101. "Statement of the Legal Sub-Group of the Preliminary Working Committee concerning the Bill of Rights Ordinance (Press Release)," October 17, 1995, in George Edwards and Johannes Chan, eds., *Hong Kong's Bill of Rights: Two Years Before 1997,* pp. 163–165.

102. They called for the reinstatement of the emergency regulations ordinance, including provisions that allowed the government to censor and suppress publications; of the Governor's power of censorship; and of the former ban on societies not registered with the police. Ibid.

103. "Statement of the Legal Sub-Group of the Preliminary Working Committee." *South China Morning Post* (Int. Weekly), October 21, 1995, p. 1.

104. *South China Morning Post* (Int. Weekly), November 25, 1995, p. 1; November 18, 1995, p. 2; January 20, 1997, p. 1; January 22, 1997, p. 1. See also the "Statement of the Hong Kong Government in Response to the Statement of the Chief Justice on the Hong Kong Bill of Rights," in *Hong Kong's Bill of Rights: Two Years Before*, pp. 171–81.

105. *South China Morning Post* (Int. Weekly), November 25, 1995, p. 1. The then Chief Justice unleashed a storm of controversy when he suggested in a conversation with Chinese officials that the BOR had "undermined the Hong Kong legal system." *South China Morning Post* (Int. Weekly), November 18, 1995, p. 1; Wesley-Smith, "Legal Institutions in Flux," pp. 18–19.

106. Ghai, "The Hong Kong Bill of Rights Ordinance," p. 58; Wesley-Smith, "Legal Institutions in Flux," pp. 14 ff.; Roda Mushkat, "The wrong course over the Bill of Rights," *South China Morning Post*, January 30, 1997, p. 17.

107. Ghai, "The Hong Kong Bill of Rights Ordinance," pp. 54–55.

108. Mushkat, "The wrong course over the Bill of Rights," p. 17. Professor Ghai also argues that article 39 of the Basic Law can be read as granting entrenched status to the ICCPR after 1997 and therefore also to the BOR, so that its proposed repeal — not its continuation — would contravene the Basic Law. Ghai, "The Hong Kong Bill of Rights," pp. 59–60.

109. *South China Morning Post* (Int. Weekly), November 18, 1995, p. 1; *International Herald Tribune*, November 16, 1996, p. 7.

110. "Lawyers Speak Out against PWC Proposals," *The New Gazette* (November 1995), p. 19.

111. *South China Morning Post*, January 20, 1997, p. 1. The group reviewed all of Hong Kong's 624 laws at its two-day meeting. Ibid. *Sunday Morning Post*, February 2, 1997, p. 1.

112. The Preparatory Committee decided on the full repeal of sixteen ordinances, also including the Application of English Law Ordinance and Hong Kong's election laws, and the partial repeal of nine additional ordinances. See *South China Morning Post*, January 20, 1997, p. 4; and January 21, 1997, p. 6 for a complete list of the laws and the effects of repeal. One effect of the repeal of the Application of English Law Ordinance would be the disappearance of Hong Kong's habeas corpus law from the SAR's statute books, since habeas corpus provisions are now applied to Hong Kong through the Application of English Law Ordinance. It has yet to be localized, although the Hong Kong government has declared it on a priority list of bills to be introduced to Legco before July 1, 1997. *South China Morning Post*, January 24, 1997, p. 22; February 5, 1997, p. 14 (letter from Director of Administration).

113. *South China Morning Post*, January 20, 1997, p. 1; January 22, 1997, p. 1.

114. *South China Morning Post*, January 30, 1997, p. 4. These arguments have been repeated by the Chief Executive-designate, who supports the proposals. *South China Morning Post*, January 22, 1997, p. 1; February 5, 1997, p. 6. At one point he also described the proposed changes as "legalistic and technical in nature." *South China Morning Post*, January 24, 1997, p. 1.

115. *South China Morning Post*, January 30, 1997, p. 4.

116. *South China Morning Post*, January 24, 1997, p. 1.

117. *South China Morning Post*, January 22, 1997, p. 6; January 25, 1997, p. 4; news report (hknews@ahkcus.org), January 24, 1997.

118. See for example Albert H.Y. Chen, "Questions of law and order," *South China Morning Post*, January 30, 1997, p. 17.

119. *South China Morning Post*, January 31, 1997, p. 1. But the new laws could still

be prepared by the provisional legislature and might therefore differ little from the original versions.

120. Shown even a year after the PWC's vote. In an October 1996 poll conducted by the *South China Morning Post,* more than 84% of the respondents were opposed to any repeal of human rights legislation by the provisional legislature; only 5% thought such laws should be repealed. *South China Morning Post,* October 8, 1996, p. 6. Even after the Preparatory Committee's decision, a majority of those polled (55%) opposed Chinese moves to repeal sections of the Public Order and Societies Ordinances. *South China Morning Post,* February 3, 1997, p. 1.

121. The Joint Declaration provides in 3(3) that "The laws currently in force in Hong Kong will remain basically unchanged." In Annex I.II of the Joint Declaration, the PRC declared that "the laws previously in force in Hong Kong (ie the common law, rules of equity, ordinances, subordinate legislation and customary law) shall be maintained, save for any that contravene the Basic Law and subject to any amendment by the Hong Kong Special Administrative Region legislature." Article 8 of the Basic Law repeated that promise almost word for word.

122. The other laws relate to the PRC capital, national day and national emblem; also the Declaration of the Government of the PRC on the Territorial Sea, and the Regulations of the PRC concerning Diplomatic Privileges and Immunities.

123. *South China Morning Post* (Int. Weekly), December 30, 1995, p. 2. But article 18 also provides that if the NPC Standing Committee "by reason of turmoil within the Hong Kong Special Administrative Region which endangers national unity or security and is beyond the control of the government of the Region" decides that the SAR is in a "state of emergency" the central government may issue an order applying the "relevant national laws" (e.g., martial law) to the SAR.

124. Ghai, "Back to Basics," p. 10.

125. Despite the March 1996 amendments to the procedure law and criminal law revisions proposed for 1997. The Criminal Law of the PRC was enacted by the NPC on July 1, 1979 and went into effect on January 1, 1980; the PRC's Criminal Procedure Law, originally adopted at the same time as the Criminal Law, was amended by the NPC on March 17, 1996. Legal Daily, March 25, 1996, p. 2. Matt Forney, "Coming to Get You," *Far Eastern Economic Review,* October 31, 1996.

126. *South China Morning Post* (Int. Weekly), October 7, 1995, p. 11.

127. *South China Morning Post* (Int. Weekly), December 2, 1995, p. 2.

128. *South China Morning Post* (Int. Weekly), December 16, 1995, p. 1. Margaret Ng, "Spirit of the law must be preserved," *South China Morning Post,* January 19, 1996, p. 11.

129. *International Herald Tribune,* December 19, 1995, p. 4.

130. *International Herald Tribune,* November 4, 1996, p. 4. Legco also passed a motion (29–26) urging China to release Wang Dan. "Today Wang, tomorrow you and me." (Democratic Party chairman Martin Lee Chu-ming.) *South China Morning Post,* November 7, 1996, p. 1.

131. *New York Times* (Int.), October 31, 1996, p. 1; *Washington Post,* October 31, 1996, p. A23. A series of articles Wang wrote for the Hong Kong Chinese-language newspaper *Ming Pao* formed part of the "evidence" of Wang's subversion, a point not lost on Hong Kong journalists. *South China Morning Post,* October 19, 1996, p. 19.

132. This article introduces vaguely worded crimes from the PRC's own criminal law (subversion and theft of state secrets) unknown to common law; it was revised in this fashion only after June 4, 1989 and Hong Kong's enthusiastic support for the Tiananmen demonstrators. See the discussion in Nihal Jayawickrama, "'One Country, Two Systems' and the Law: Illusion or Reality," in Donald H. McMillen and Michael E. Degolyer, eds.,

One Culture, Many Systems (Hong Kong: The Chinese University Press, 1993), pp. 46–47.

133. Bruce Gilley, "Shoe-In's Challenge," *Far Eastern Economic Review,* November 28, 1996, p. 24.

134. News report (hknews@ahkcus.org), December 3, 1996 (article from the *Hong Kong Standard*).

135. Constitution of the PRC, adopted by the National People's Congress on December 4, 1982 (as amended in 1988 and 1993).

136. Article 51 provides that "The exercise by citizens of the People's Republic of China of their freedoms and rights may not infringe upon the interests of the state, of society and of the collective . . ."

137. For example, by Foreign Ministry spokesman Shen Guofang. *South China Morning Post* (Int. Weekly), Oct 26, 1996, p. 4. News report (hknews@ahkcus.org), October 18, 1996.

138. Kevin Kwong, "High price for telling the truth," *South China Morning Post* (Int. Weekly), February 17, 1996, p. 11. Xi Yang was charged with "stealing and prying into state secrets" for having illegally obtained confidential information and passing it on for publication to a "Hong Kong publication." Amnesty International, *State Secrets — A tool of Repression* (May 1996 report), pp. 23–25. Although Xi Yang was given early release on parole in January 1997, he is far from the only journalist to have been punished in this fashion. *South China Morning Post,* January 26, 1997, pp. 1, 2. See, for example, the case of Gao Yu, also convicted for disclosing state secrets involving economic information and leaking them to a Hong Kong magazine. "State Secrets," pp. 26–7.

139. *International Herald Tribune,* June 6, 1996, p. 8; "Anniversary Blues," *Far Eastern Economic Review,* June 13, 1996, p. 18.

140. Quoted in *South China Morning Post* (Int. Weekly), June 8, 1996, p. 1.

141. *South China Morning Post* (Int. Weekly), October 19, 1996, p. 1. *South China Morning Post*, November 13, 1996, p. 6.

142. *Far Eastern Economic Review,* June 13, 1996, p. 18. The same official, commenting on demonstrations in support of Wang Dan, was reported as saying, "If you keep on using public opinion or organizing protest demonstrations, this is interfering in China's judicial process and is not permitted." News report (hknews@ahkcus.org), October 22, 1996.

143. *International Herald Tribune,* January 24, 1996, p. 15; *Wall Street Journal,* September 5, 1996, p. B5.

144. *International Herald Tribune,* January 17, 1996, p. 1; January 19, 1996, p. 13; April 17, 1996, p. 13; April 25, 1996, p. 4. In January 1997 the State Council released regulations on publishing that were clearly aimed at increasing control over the industry: the spreading of ideas detrimental to "state and public interests" is forbidden and the release of materials containing state secrets is also banned. *South China Morning Post,* January 16, 1997, p. 11; *Hong Kong Standard,* January 16, 1997, p. 7.

· 145. People were "most worried about whether article 23 of the Basic Law will become a tool to curb their freedom of speech after the handover." According to Democrat Szeto Wah. News report (hknews@ahckus.org), November 1, 1996.

146. *South China Morning Post,* November 27, 1996, p. 1.

147. Ibid. There must be an "intention of causing violence or creating public disorder or a public disturbance." *South China Morning Post,* January 27, 1997, p. 4.

148. News report (hknews@ahkcus.org), December 3, 1996.

149. *South China Morning Post,* November 29, 1996, p. 7; November 30, 1996, p. 6; December 13, 1996, p. 7.

150. *South China Morning Post,* December 14, 1996, p. 6.

151. *South China Morning Post,* November 27, 1996, p. 4.

152. *South China Morning Post,* January 18, 1997, p. 4; January 19, 1997, p. 2.

153. *South China Morning Post,* January 22, 1997, p. 6.

154. It seems that British cooperation or non-cooperation has made little difference to the outcome. The Chinese have achieved their goals through agreement (on the CFA) and through unilateral action despite British opposition (the provisional legislature).

5

Media Structure and Regime Change in Hong Kong

*Chin-Chuan Lee**

"Rights and freedoms, including those of the person, of speech, of the press, of assembly, of . . . will be ensured by law in the Hong Kong Administrative Region." — *Sino-British Joint Declaration, 1984*

"There should be no problem [for the foreign press to exist in Hong Kong] so long as your reports are accurate and objective. [By being objective] I mean in line with the objectives of the government of the People's Republic of China." — *Zhou Nan, director of Xinhua in Hong Kong, to foreign journalists.*[1]

"Why are the privileged [Hong Kong] people kowtowing to Beijing? They wouldn't be doing it if most of them didn't have foreign passports in their back pockets." — *Chris Patten, Governor of Hong Kong*[2]

"A confident wine maker would choose to be minimally interventionist, allowing the wine to make itself. After all, there is no way for the wine to escape the bottle." — *Raymond Chien, Executive Council Member, an economist and managing director of a food-and-beverage conglomerate, to the Preparatory Committee*[3]

* Earlier versions of this paper were presented at the annual convention of the Association for Asian Studies, Honolulu, Hawaii, April 1996, and at the Conference on "Chinese Communication in the Age of Modern Media" held under the auspices of the China Times Center for Media and Social Studies at the University of Minnesota, Minneapolis, June 29–30, 1996. The able research assistance of Anthony Fung is cordially acknowledged. This paper is part of a larger project entitled "Mass Media and Political Transition in Hong Kong," of which I am the principal investigator, supported with funds from the Universities Grants Committee in Hong Kong.

As Hong Kong is being rebonded with the People's Republic of China (PRC), mass media — major cultural arms and agencies of symbolic control in modern capitalism — bear the brunt of the momentous sociopolitical transformation. They are seen at once as a site of ideological struggle and as a cultural commodity in the market economy. Absorbing political and economic pressure from dominant power blocks on the one hand, the media also define issues, focus public attention, expand or narrow the range of social debate and imagination. However, they must compete fiercely with other information goods in circulation by satisfying consumers' needs. Linguistically and culturally grounded, the media cannot be as easily uprooted to an alien environment as other financial institutions or manufacturing plants. They must ultimately cater to stratified taste cultures of the audience and advertiser, some of which may not be holy or even decent. But no media organizations — whether those of downright vulgarity or those of serious purpose and high instinct — can survive the critical test in the market if their reportage or commentary should be seen as seriously lacking credibility or consistency. It is precisely this dual role that requires the media to attend not only to state legitimation but also to their own legitimation in a market economy.

Mass media reflect unevenly the perspectives of the power structure and thus react unevenly to the changing power relations in society. Should there be a collapse of elite consensus or should the power structure face a legitimacy crisis, the media may construct conflicting realities. Reconfiguring the power structure significantly affects the media's political realignment, which results in changes in organizational routines and cultural production. Once the political order is restored, the media may be brought back in line with the resettled consensus, thus returning from a strayed trajectory to their normal (perhaps narrower) range of latitude.[4] In a similar vein, Donohue, Tichenor and Olien propose a "guard dog" hypothesis: "Media perform as a sentry not for the community as a whole, but for groups having sufficient power and influence to create and control their own security systems."[5] Despite their notable differences, many have developed important insights on the media's substantial, but not total, dependence on the power structure.[6] For example, Bennett argues that the media "index" legitimate voices in the news according to the range of views expressed by prominent officials and members of institutional power blocs likely to influence the outcome of a situation.[7] Voices falling outside the official range of debate can be admitted occasionally, but they are largely marginalized. This important insight should not, however, fall into the reductive trap. As Raymond Williams persuasively argues,[8] the media uphold the dominant reality and weaken alternative or oppositional realities by incorporating, marginalizing, or directly opposing them, but this dominance is continually contested.

What challenges face Hong Kong's media? As the new sovereign, authoritarian in nature, takes over a mature capitalism that may have a different inner logic, there will be a series of ongoing struggles involving the mediation "between civil society and the market economy" as well as the mediation between "civil society and the bureaucratic state."[9] These struggles represent the dialectic between the political and the economical. In this chapter, I am taking a broadly defined political economy approach[10] to examine — and speculate on — the conditions of Hong Kong's press change and the limits to that freedom in an historical context.

While promising to maintain Hong Kong's autonomy, the PRC has issued threatening conditions on the supposedly guaranteed "freedom of the press."[11] How would citizen rights and freedoms be defined in ways that may intrude on and restrict media expression in civil society? Moreover, Beijing has much at stake to protect Hong Kong's capitalistic economy that accounts for 21% of China's domestic gross product, while two-thirds of foreign investment in the mainland pass through Hong Kong as a gateway. Can Hong Kong remain economically viable without a free press, and can the market forces withstand or countervail political intervention? As the capitalistic logic pursues "profit rationality," how does the economic environment in which the media operate enhance the media's own calculations? Will information, as a "public good,"[12] give the media needed prestige and legitimacy while putting state controllers on the defensive? But, then, as the capital accumulation may sacrifice non-economic values, how does it distort cultural production? Finally, how does this economic calculation interact with political pressure, both positively and negatively?

I shall first account historically for the rise and fall of what Seymour-Ure calls "press-party parallelism"[13] — a system in which the press is aligned organizationally, financially or ideologically with political parties — in relation to the stages of political transition. Press-party parallelism can be seen as the way in which the colonial regime has tried to position itself — and to walk a fine line — between two opposing Chinese forces in the past five decades. The rise and fall of this parallelism also signifies the rise and fall of these contending camps, besides acting as a barometer of the legitimacy of British rule. The political transition means reconstituting the power structure and power relationships — from British dominance, to Sino-British dual power centers, and to China's final supremacy — thus radically redistributing resources and realigning social forces. While under British rule the Hong Kong media could criticize the PRC and Taiwan, it becomes much more testy for them to criticize Beijing under Chinese jurisdiction.

To cope with the political transformation, the media have had to revamp what Gaye Tuchman calls the "news net" according to new patterns of authority configuration,[14] but they will continue to operate in a market economy. Inasmuch as the political logic and the economic logic have a dialectical relationship, economic concerns have resulted in media mergers and takeovers that limit the diversity of opinions expressed. Paradoxically, economic and professional concerns may also provide a political space for some media workers to deflect and resist state stricture, even to fight it at the margins in some circumscribed ways.

Media organizations are indeed developing a set of institutional strategies in the name of media professionalism to relieve themselves of undue cross-pressure.[15]

Press-Party Parallelism and Stages of Political Transition

Hong Kong's press system consists of party, partisan, and popular-centrist orientations, which have coexisted uneasily to span the entire ideological spectrum. It stands for an anomalous case of what Seymour-Ure calls "party-press parallelism."[16] This parallelism is an enduring historical legacy in many European countries and much of the Third World, applying more strongly to press editorials than to broadcast media.[17] In contrast, the US media system prides itself on being "professional" and "non-partisan," albeit predicated on an unarticulated commitment to the established order and mainstream values.[18]

The Hong Kong case is considered anomalous because its press has until recently been linked to exogenous Chinese parties — the PRC and Taiwan — rather than indigenous parties operating within the territory.[19] While the broadcast media and cable tend to identify with the center of the political spectrum, the print media are more ideologically divided. The party press was traditionally run by two rival Chinese regimes, the partisan press displayed a high degree of belief consonance with either regime, and the popular-centrist press was oriented toward the political and economic markets of Hong Kong.

This press-party parallelism changes in tandem with the three stages of political transition that have characterized Hong Kong since 1949. The first stage began with the founding of the People's Republic and ended with the conclusion of the Sino-British Joint Declaration in 1984. In its interim, the party and partisan presses dominated in the 1950s and 1960s, only to be eclipsed by the rise of the popular-centrist press in the subsequent decades. The second stage extended from 1984 to 1989, and the third and current stage covers the aftermath of the Tiananmen Incident. While the prospect of Britain's handing Hong Kong over to China has further weakened the old press-party parallelism, it should be noted that the three local parties that did emerge in the 1990s (the Democratic Party, the Liberal Party, and the Democratic Alliance for Betterment of Hong Kong) have received prominent press coverage but not given rise to a new parallelism.

First Stage (1949–84)

During the first stage, the colonial regime held the unchallenged power, subjugating external Chinese forces to subservient — if not marginal — positions. Local political parties were banned. The pattern of electoral representation, as a commentator noted, hardly progressed beyond the nineteenth century as far as franchise extension was concerned.[20] Minimally integrated with the local Chinese civil society,[21] the British-dominated state implements what Ambrose King calls "administrative absorption of politics."[22] A tiny minority of local Chinese elite (primarily businessmen and professionals, including some media owners) were coopted into the governing bodies in substantive or advisory capacities. The media, linking the weak state-society ties, acted as a means to fine-tune administrative bureaucracy and to forestall popular discontent, rather than to initiate change.[23]

At the height of the Cold War, Beijing was diplomatically ostracized. The PRC used Hong Kong as a major window to the Western world and to generate some 40% of China's much-needed foreign exchanges. In the 1950s and early 1960s Premier Zhou Enlai instructed Xinhua (the New China News Agency) to assume a low profile in the British colony and told the local communist press to be ideologically flexible in order to win the support of non-communists.[24] While controlling the rules of the game, the British allowed different Chinese interests to operate their propaganda bases against each other. The much celebrated "press freedom" in Hong Kong — the degree of which is undoubtedly among the highest in Asia — should be understood as the latitude allowed for the press to criticize the PRC and Taiwan, but the press — except the pro-PRC organs — was conspicuous by its absence of strong criticism of the British colonial regime.[25]

Viewing Hong Kong as a temporary refuge, much of the Chinese-language press was primarily preoccupied with Chinese politics and, by comparison, remained relatively unconcerned with local political affairs in the 1950s and 1960s. During the Cultural Revolution (1967–76) all non-communist media supported the British against Beijing, the colonial regime broke up local communist organizations, and the communist press hit its all-time low in circulation and fared not much better afterwards.[26] Although the press-party alignment continued abated, a group of popular-centrist newspapers began to emerge around 1970 — in the aftermath of the 1967 leftist riots — and quickly established a centrifugal place in the market. They owed much of their success to the rapid economic growth that provided a strong advertising revenue base and to the demographic transformation with the local-born population outnumbering mainland immigrants. Pursuit of the market logic necessitated them to pledge their primary allegiance to local interests while being more detached from the PRC-Taiwan rivalry.

Media criticisms of the colonial government remained docile, while social movements were sporadic and often narrowly based. The government maintains a huge and sophisticated apparatus — i.e., the Government Information Services (GIS) with staff officers attached to all departments — to manage its public relations and, to borrow a Gramscian language, manufacture social consent conducive to maintaining colonial hegemony.[27] The generally pro-British and pro-status quo media were highlighted as a trump "public opinion card" to play against China's "sovereignty card" before, during, and after the 1982–84 negotiations. All but the communist media supported the British efforts to extend the lease of the New Territories beyond June 30, 1997 and, having failed that, to seek Beijing's approval for continued British administration under Chinese sovereignty. But they felt disheartened and even betrayed by one result after another from the talks.

Second Stage (1984–89)

The second stage commenced with the conclusion of the Sino-British Joint Declaration in 1984 — which engendered a dualistic power structure shared by the colonial authorities and the PRC — and ended with the Tiananmen crackdown in 1989. The Joint Declaration thrust both power centers into profound legitimacy crises. The British could no longer justify colonial rule, much less to defend their failure in fulfilling repeated promises to gain China's concession for de jure or de facto British rule over Hong Kong after 1997. They had to retain public trust by projecting the image of an active, positive, and "accessible" government. The PRC's resumption of sovereignty over Hong Kong was, however, an act of fait accompli forced upon the people of Hong Kong without their prior consent, so China also must overcome a doubting population by making optimistic promises and improving its public image.[28] Meanwhile, the British must prepare for an honorable exit in due course. China, now a transformed "insider" rather than an "outside" critic, should share with the British a guardian responsibility toward Hong Kong. As a result, both regimes competed fiercely to bolster their own legitimacy while cooperating to foster a smooth transition. Situated at the center of a struggle that was full of twists and turns, the media had a confusing and often contradictory role to play.

The media, first of all, tried to play duplicity with the twin authority structures, which sought to woo their support through the politics of cooptation rather than coercion. Both regimes provided the media with tangible (advertising, news) or intangible (status, attention and access) rewards. The colonial regime sharpened its traditional politics of entitlement and elite absorption that they had practiced with skills and effect for decades.[29] It continued to confer British titles and honors on socioeconomic elite (including selected media owners) and to incorporate them into multilayered advisory boards. The government was, suddenly, more media-friendly. In what Ambrose King characterized as the "political absorption of economics,"[30] the PRC also took pains to emulate the same political style by recruiting members of the same socioeconomic elite circle into the power circle, as conspicuously symbolized by the Drafting Committee and the Consultative Committee of the Basic Law. Many of the elite had been strongly pro-British. China was, however, tolerant enough at this time to enlist some prominent journalists and media owners into these committees even if their stand was not known to be pro-communist.[31] Chinese leaders, including Deng Xiaoping, listened to various prominent leaders from Hong Kong and pledged a commitment to continued stability and prosperity after 1997.[32] Many elites, including some media owners and "star" writers, were simultaneously wooed by both regimes. Cooptation enabled the PRC to form cordial institutional ties with many media, fueled by warm feelings among media owners, editors and writers toward Xinhua's amicable head, Xu Jiatun.[33]

The media were, however, also energized by their new-found duty and opportunities to report about — and in the process, galvanize — the activities of pressure groups and political activists that had surged since the mid-1980s. Given the indeterminacy of the transition, the media became at once a uncertain "looking glass mirror" (using a metaphor borrowed from Lang and Lang[34]) through which both power structures tried to tentatively gauge each other's intention and actions. Owing to the ambiguities involved in concretizing the Basic Law, the media also came to the forefront of public forum in which various interest groups, including power holders and challengers, exchanged views, traded insults, and tried to garner support. The mounting political activism partly grew out of Britain's decolonization policy aimed to accord local people with greater autonomy, as in Hong Kong and elsewhere, before extricating itself from the colonies.[35] The media were emboldened to criticize the colonial regime, while becoming more calculating toward criticizing China. Many once taciturn officials now urged the media not to censor themselves. The British were obviously intent on harnessing local media voices against China's making rapid inroads into the political market in Hong Kong.[36] Against China's preference, this new activism also paradoxically drew a latent impetus from China's rhetoric of "letting Hong Kong people run Hong Kong" — by which both the British and the Chinese governments meant their business and professional allies rather than democratic activists or their "proletarian comrades."[37]

Despite their lack of faith in China's promises, the media could do no better than acquiesce to the inevitability of Chinese sovereignty retrocession and struggle to obtain the most favorable conditions within the parameter of the Basic Law. Meanwhile, the media turned their new target to the colonial regime. In 1984 the government issued a white paper intended to develop a more representative polity, with measured steps to increase the number of elected members and to decrease the number of appointed members in the District Boards and the Legislative Council.[38] Democratic representation had eluded the British colony for nearly a century and a half, and Britain's sudden change of mind was clearly an attempt to introduce a system that would curtail Beijing's arbitrary power after 1997. Such proposal, however, provoked China's objection, particularly vehemently in 1987–88 over the direct election issue. On the other hand, the British wanted to install democratic reform only at a pace they could control, and this half-hearted measure ended up frustrating many of their democratic critics and their media allies, who openly accused the colonial government of being too accommodating and excessively timid toward Beijing. Little in the way of democratic development was accomplished in those years. After the Tiananmen crackdown and the subsequent purges in 1989, the media had no alternatives but to acknowledge that China's "one country, two systems" policy should be fully carried out to the letter and spirit, which was the very concept they had criticized since 1984.[39]

Third Stage (since 1990)

The third and final stage, entered in 1990, is still unfolding — a period marking the "fading out" of British power and the "ushering in" of the PRC's dominance. The Sino-British relations have taken the worst turn as Beijing fumes at Hong Kong and its media for the outpouring of vital support given to the Beijing student protesters in the pro-democracy movement of 1989. In contrast to China's influence in Hong Kong that has grown in proportion to proximity to July 1, 1997, surveys have registered declining trust in the Hong Kong government from 76.4% in 1986 to 48.5% in 1988 to 42.9% in 1990. The approval ratings seem to have hovered around 40% since then.[40] Cooptation by the colonial administration is less important for political advancement than seeking China's endorsement and recruitment.[41] Now with the sovereignty issue effectively closed, cooptation was less pertinent, and the PRC has hardened its position toward Hong Kong. The renewed belligerence belies Beijing's own succession crisis, in which no Chinese party-state leaders could afford to appear weak vis-a-vis foreign power or international pressure. In communist politics, to err on the right is seen as a fatal mistake in the fundamental "political line" whereas to err on the left only involves a much less grave problem of incorrect understanding. Feeling much less inhibited to lash out at the lame-duck British regime, the press became increasingly apprehensive about offending the new sovereign.[42]

In 1992, Christopher Patten — a professional politician, rather than a conventional bureaucrat from the Colonial Office or a "China hand" diplomat from the Foreign Office — became the Governor who saw his term in office as a last British opportunity to broaden electoral participation on the eve of China's takeover. He presided over a series of elections during 1994–95, culminating in the formation of a new Legislative Council in 1995 with one-thirds of its members directly elected. China's intimidation could not prevent the Democratic Party from triumphing over the pro-Beijing party (DAB) and the bourgeois-elitist Liberal Party in such elections. The PRC repudiated these elections as violating the Joint Declaration, the Basic Law and the agreements exchanged between Beijing and London, while castigating Patten as "sinner of a millennium" (*qiangu zuiren*). Refusing to negotiate with Patten, Beijing has installed its own power organ: the Hong Kong Affairs Advisers and the Preliminary Working Committee (PWC) of the Special Administrative Region (SAR) Preparatory Committee, neither of which was provided by the Basic Law. Only the pro-China elite was recruited while critics of China, including former media cooptees in the 1980s, have been excluded.[43] On July 1, 1997, a Beijing appointed "provisional legislature" will come into office to replace the 1995 fully elected Legislative Council.[44]

During this stage, reflecting self-interest and public concerns, the media have thoroughly covered various sets of controversies developed between Britain and China, between Governor Patten and Xinhua, and among different political groups in Hong Kong. In view of the media's structural dependence on the power structure to make news, as Daniel Hallin argues, "legitimate controversies" over the definition of situation and distribution of interests allow the media to expand their editorial boundary by presenting the various sides of opinion.[45] But this time the media exhibit no enthusiasm to reestablish a parallelism with the three newly emerged and precarious local parties, thus sending old press-party parallelism into bygone history. As shall be seen, this stage has seen the diminishing of the party press and the toning down of the partisan press, while the popular-centrist press is experiencing significant changes in ownership and content — with important implications for press freedom after 1997.

The Party Press

An immediate impact of the political transition has been the marginalization — and eventual demise — of the pro-Guomindang (GMD) newspapers in rapid succession. The pro-GMD press had a substantial anti-communist following in the 1950s, only to become gradually weakened in the subsequent decades. When it appeared more certain that Chiang Kai-shek was not to recover the mainland, the GMD's influence in Hong Kong began to wane and finally became marginalized. The colonial regime also came under Beijing's pressure to suppress pro-GMD activities, including denial of entry visas to Taiwan officials and the banning of sensitive Taiwan-made films. This decline of the GMD's influence was coterminous with the attrition of its supporters due to aging, death or departure, whereas the rising tide of the post-war generation grew increasingly impatient with the traditional CCP versus GMD partisan polemics.[46]

As part of the gestures to placate public anxiety when vying with the British for public support, Deng Xiaoping made a big point in the early 1980s by urging the GMD elements to remain in Hong Kong after 1997, though on conditions that they abide by the "one China" policy and do not create unrest. Once the Joint Declaration was concluded in 1984, however, the GMD institutions became increasingly irrelevant to the political life of Hong Kong. Having wavered its positions several times, the Taiwan authorities have decided not only to stay put but also to heighten its profile in Hong Kong, not as an anti-Communist beachhead but as a cultural and commercial bridge to mainland China.[47] Since the line between legal, legitimate activities and the "one China" policy is unclear, Taipei's role is precariously conditioned on Beijing's whim and will. Taiwan has had little to say or do to influence the transition process.

The first pro-GMD newspaper to take its toll was *Kung Sheung Yat Pao* (Industrial-Commercial Daily) owned by the Hotung family. Founded in 1925 at the time of the anti-colonial Canton-Hong Kong General Strike-Boycott, the paper warned in its inaugural editorial that the burgeoning tide of communism would spell a "disaster" for China.[48] Robert Hotung was part of the local pro-British establishment elite, while his heir, General Ho Shili, had served as Chiang Kai-shek's deputy defense minister. Having altered little of its strident anti-communism despite the sea change surrounding the demographic and political environments, this once influential paper saw its readership base continually eroded away in the 1970s by upstart centrist competitors. At the decade's end, it was already reduced to marginal influence and would never regain its vitality. With its prospect further dimmed by the political transition, the paper bid fare-well to its readers in November 1984, two months after the Joint Declaration was initiated.

The GMD's official mouthpiece, *Hong Kong Times* (Xianggang Shibao) — whose finance, staff and ideology was directly controlled by Taipei — continued to operate for one more decade, but a serious internal rift erupted over whether it should adopt a more flexible editorial policy to suit the new political ecology.[49] Despite its small circulation and marginal public influence, it symbolized the presence of Taiwan's GMD, significant enough to warrant a close watch by the colonial regime.[50] As Taiwan lifted its martial law in 1987, however, the paper's staunch conservatism was anachronistically out of step with both Taiwan's vast democratic change and its increasing detente with mainland China. The GMD could not draw as freely on the national treasury as in the past to subsidize unprofitable and self-serving operations, including that of the *Hong Kong Times* (which was having an annual deficit of HK$20 million) and the *China Youth Morning Post* (Shaonian Zhongguo Chengbao) which was founded by Sun Yat-sen in San Francisco. The GMD was eager to shift the paper from party to state sponsorship in order to subsidize it with public funds, only to be firmly rejected by the opposition Democratic Progressive Party (DPP). Under such circum-stances the paper's closure became inevitable in February 1993, causing bitter resentment among the local GMD old guards.

In 1992, the two largest newspaper chains in Taiwan tried to test the waters in the Hong Kong market by publishing a Hong Kong edition of the *United Daily News* and *China Times Weekly*. Having reached market saturation in Taiwan with two-thirds of the island's newspaper circulation and advertising revenues, they were waiting to reach over into mainland China — a false prospect obviously inspired by the sudden collapse of the Soviet Union and the growing economic and social rapprochement between Beijing and Taipei. Both were based in Hong Kong, reflecting Taiwan's political orientations but were not necessarily antago-nistic to the PRC. The *United Daily News*'s parent company in Taipei, often playing up Beijing's denouncement of Taiwan's aspirations for independence, was the target of a boycott campaign in 1992 for its alleged pro-Beijing and pro-unification stance.[51] Its Hong Kong edition was editorially serious, specializing in China reporting and highly critical of Taiwan's President Lee Teng-hui. Its circulation briefly soared to 20,000 copies when it serialized an exclusive memoirs of Xu Jiatun, former director of Xinhua's Hong Kong branch who has taken refuge in the United States since 1990, but then settled down to meager 3,000 copies.[52] Though respected by media professionals, the paper was largely ignored by the local market.

Emulating the US *Time* magazine and proclaiming to serve global Chinese communities, *China Times Weekly* started out playing up the tune of "Chinese unification" and promoting closer ties between mainland China and Taiwan. It experimented with various formats, adopted the usage of mainland terminology (different from that used in Taiwan) which was of considerable political import, and said to have arranged an informal and semi-underground team of freelance writers in various mainland cities. The political approach did not seem to pay off, so the magazine was briefly renamed *China Times Economic Weekly* championing an integrated Chinese economic system. Contents relating to Taiwan were kept to a minimum. Nor did the economic emphasis seem to catch on, so it then reverted to its original name, dropping "economic" from the title.

With a "foreign" or "external" origin and flavor, neither outlet managed to gain a viable stronghold in the already crowded Hong Kong market. They held talks with mainland media for establishing joint ventures; contracts were reached but broken, all hinging on Beijing's insistence of retaining final and complete editorial control. Even when taking the softened "let economy takes command" approach, *China Times Weekly* could not ease Beijing's restrictions. The mainland market not only proved illusory, this seemingly pro-China approach was beginning to sound controversial in Taiwan. Beijing began to verbally vilify Governor Patten's political reform in Hong Kong in late 1992 and launched military threats against Taiwan in 1995 and 1996. The deteriorated relation across the Taiwan Strait caused an adverse effect on Taiwan's economy. The *United Daily News* had invested HK$100–200 million in Hong Kong but lost $5–6 million in 1994 alone. Partly triggered by a price war at the end of 1995, both Taiwan outlets decided to retreat from Hong Kong. Media voices representing Taiwan have been virtually extricated, thus substantially narrowing Hong Kong's pluralistic ideological field.

On the opposite side, the PRC has tightened its control since 1989 of such press organs as *Ta Kung Pao* and *Wen Wei Po*. In the 1980s both papers undertook localization programs, and Xinhua also imposed less rigid control of their work as part of the overall gestures to show Beijing's commitment to the "one country, two systems" policy. However, when the Tiananmen protests broke out in 1989, both papers joined the rank of other Hong Kong papers to condemn the hardline Chinese authorities, pressuring top leaders to resign and be punished. Bitter purges resulted in the ouster of publisher Lee Tze-chung of *Wen Wei Po* and his top assistants, who together founded the *Contemporary* news magazine, only to be folded down in 1995 due to financial hardship.[54]

Embittered by the 1989 episode, Beijing has appointed ideologically more rigid officials to take charge of the State Council's Hong Kong and Macau Affairs Office as well as refurbished hardliners to manage Xinhua's local branch. To ensure the party line, Xinhua has staffed many top editorial positions at both papers with mainland appointees (rather than local recruits) on a rotation basis. These mainlanders are less likely to empathize with the local views because of their lack of cognitive and emotional ties to Hong Kong.[55]

Despite their low credibility and dismal circulation in Hong Kong, these mouthpieces are well-financed by advertising revenues from the PRC companies, thanks to the windows of opportunity opened up by China's economic change. The once rebellious *Wen Wei Po* has received more funds from the PRC to "repair the image of June 4." Since 1992 it has reaped considerable advertising revenues from mainland real-estate interests. In 1995, its circulation ranked twelfth and advertising revenues fifth in Hong Kong. *Ta Kung Pao*, playing a second ideological fiddle to *Wen Wei Po,* has tried to develop its mainland market through the networks of formal and informal ties with provincial party secretaries.[56] Half of its advertising revenues came from advertisers aiming to reach mainland consumers. Both papers print many Xinhua-initiated commentaries under pseudonym aimed to criticize and intimidate China's critics. Both papers have tried to strengthen their China reporting — for example, *Wen Wei Po* has 12 reporting stations inside the PRC staffed primarily by mainland reporters of Hong Kong origin — but rigid party control has prevented them from providing authoritative accounts about the PRC.[57] Competing for the same small pool of readers and revenues, the two ideological siblings have subtly sniped at each other. The *Hong Kong Commercial Daily,* one of the second-tier pro-Beijing publications, is now controlled by the PRC-owned Joint Publishing Group. Instead of continuing to subsidize some of its more fringe papers, China has had to let *Ching Pao* (Crystal Daily) meet its natural fate.

The Partisan Press

The other major impact on the press structure has been a progressive blurring of boundaries between the centrist (popular) and rightist (partisan) newspapers. Both catered to the market and allied with the colonial regime. But there is a crucial difference in their respective histories: the rightist newspapers had been founded long before the communists took power in China, thus historically supportive of the GMD, whereas the popular-centrist press did not arise until 1970 and owes no binding loyalty to the GMD. The two most significant rightist daily papers were *Wah Kiu Yat Pao* (Overseas Chinese Daily) and *Sing Tao Jih Pao* (Star Island Daily), founded in 1925 and 1939 respectively. Until the late 1980s both had borne in their mastheads the official "Republic of China" chronological designation and celebrated October 10 as the national day of the Nationalist government. Registered in both Hong Kong and Taiwan, they mirrored Hong

Kong's prevailing popular sentiment in being mildly critical of the mainland communist regime.[58]

Xinhua began to coopt these two papers in the mid-1980s. *Wah Kiu Yat Pao*'s family owners responded positively and participated in the Consultative Committee of the Basic Law, which would serve as Hong Kong's mini-constitution after 1997. *Sing Tao Jih Pao*'s reaction was much more circumspect, simply sending a Taiwan-educated editor to represent the publisher to join the committee. In any case, both papers tried hard to play a balance game with the Beijing and Hong Kong authorities, while managing not to alienate their GMD friends.[59] But their loosening of traditionally pro-Taiwan ties was facilitated by continued erosion of the GMD's base in Hong Kong and the gradual warming of the relationship across the Taiwan Strait. Meanwhile, local-born Taiwanese have wrested the GMD's leadership from the traditional mainlander core on the island.

Keen market competition — along with political uncertainty — has not been particularly kind to the weaker of the two: *Wah Kiu Yat Pao*. Losing HK$40 million per year in the 1980s, the family owners were eager to dislodge it. Eyeing the tantalizing China market, Rupert Murdoch, having taken control of the prestigious English-language *South China Morning Post*, acquired *Wah Kiu Yat Pao* in 1992 for HK$46 million, presumably as a first step to set foot in the Chinese press market.[60] The paper's traditional tilt toward the GMD was severed. Before long, however, Murdoch left the local press business and moved over to run the Hong Kong-based STAR satellite television whose signal reaches the whole of Asia, including the Chinese mainland where official bans on satellite reception have been sporadic and ineffective. Robert Kuok, a Malaysian-Chinese business tycoon with strong business ties to mainland China, took a controlling interest of the *South China Morning Post*. *Wah Kiu Yat Pao* continued to struggle unsuccessfully under different hands until its closure in January 1995.

Beijing had long extended an olive branch to *Sing Tao Jih Pao*, offering to return confiscated family properties to its publisher, Sally Aw, and to treat her with high honor if she would accept an invitation to visit the mainland. Expressing a vote of little confidence in the communists, however, she relocated her business empire's headquarters to Australia in 1985 and then invested heavily in its overseas editions published in Europe, North America and Australia. Sing Tao became publicly incorporated in the following year. Aw was seeking ways to diversify her investments and gain legal protection as a foreign company.[61] Aw earned HK$300 million from real estate investments in Hong Kong from 1985 to 1989, and plunged more deeply into short-term speculations.[62] In late 1989 Aw had incurred a mountain of debt totaling HK$1.96 billion as overseas property markets started to tumble and Hong Kong's market was devastated by the Tiananmen crackdown. She was pressured by major bank creditors to reorganize her board of directors and to refocus on the core publishing business.[63]

Beijing extended its olive branch again, to which Aw responded with enthusiasm this time, presumably in hopes of pursuing market opportunities in China. She visited Beijing in 1992 and was warmly received by President Jiang Zemin and Premier Li Peng. (Other publishers, including Ho Man Fat of *Sing Pao* and Ma Ching-kuan of the *Oriental Daily News,* followed suit and visited mainland China soon afterwards.) She hired a new chief editor from Singapore to distance herself from what was perceived to be a somewhat critical stance toward the PRC, and dropped the "Republic of China" chronological designation from the paper's masthead. She instructed her staff to de-emphasize politics by "taking a neutral course" in reporting because it was "infeasible to hold political views in Hong Kong."[64] By 1995 she had reportedly invested a total of HK$250 million in mainland China. One of the investments was the joint publication of the non-political *Xingguang* (Starlight Monthly) with the *People's Daily,* China's chief party organ. Aw secured a government approval to publish a financial paper (*Shenggang Economic Times*) in Shenzhen in 1993, which is neither profitable nor influential. *Huanan Jingji Ribao* (South China Economic Daily), briefly available to mainland subscribers, ceased operation when a price war struck the local Hong Kong press in 1995.[65] In October 1994, her English-language *Hong Kong Standard* became the first and only overseas newspaper allowed to be printed inside China, under an agreement with the *China Daily,* for distribution to Beijing's major tourist hotels. (The *Standard*'s business section carried a weekly page provided by the *China Daily.*) The contract, supposedly good for three years, was abruptly terminated on short notice after only four months of printing.[66] *Xingguang* was also closed in 1995 on account of "reorganization of the editorial department." Since April 1995 *Sing Tao Jih Pao* has printed a weekly economic news section produced by Shanghai's *Liberation Daily,* but *Sing Tao*'s news cannot appear in the latter. Despite Aw's futile ventures in mainland China, *Sing Tao* now resembles *Ming Pao* in editorial orientations, effectively obfuscating traditional distinctions between the rightist and centrist newspapers. Meanwhile, at the end of 1996 Aw decided to close down the once popular but now highly unprofitable *Sing Tao Evening News,* whose circulation had seriously eroded since the 1970s due in part to challenges from television and cable news. This paper, along with the weekly *Qingxiu* (Delicate and Pretty) *Magazine* was also a partial victim of a price war that undermined the Sing Tao group's profit base.

The Popular-Centrist Press

This group of newspapers has ascended since the late 1960s to bring about a weakening of the partisan press and to mark a progressive delinking of the traditional press-party ties. This group is composed of intellectual taste culture (notably, *Ming Pao* and the *Hong Kong Economic Journal*) and mass taste culture (notably, the *Oriental Daily News*, the *Apple Daily, Sing Pao* and the *Tin Tin Daily News*), controlling two-thirds of newspaper circulation and advertising.[67] As is typical of the "professional" press in the United States,[68] they are deeply oriented toward market economy, middle-class liberalism, and the centrally legitimated institutions to the exclusion of views that fall outside the boundary of social consensus. They support the current system that benefits them, and interpret the PRC-Taiwan conflict from Hong Kong's vantage point.

International capital has flowed into Hong Kong as a springboard to get into mainland China. The prime example is the *South China Morning Post (SCMP)*. Akin to the power stratification in the colony, the press has perpetuated a two-tier structure in which an overwhelming majority of the local populace read the Chinese-language press, while the English-language *SCMP* serves a small but powerful constituency consisting of the expatriate community and elite Chinese. The *SCMP* came closest to what Ithiel de sola Pool calls a "prestige paper" in that it "functions to express the views of the (British and Chinese) elite and to disseminate to the elite information and judgments needed by them to function as an elite in society."[69] With a circulation of 115,000 copies (which is 87% of the English-language press market but only 4% of the total readership), the *SCMP* enjoys high respect among journalists in surveys[70] and provides an essential forum for elite discourse. Xu Jiatun, former director of Xinhua's Hong Kong branch, disclosed in his memoirs that China made a failed attempt to acquire the *SCMP* in the mid-1980s.[71] Now the paper's ownership was transferred through Murdoch to Kuok in 1993. Kuok holds a controlling interest of the paper (34.9% of the stocks worth HK$349 million) and also owns 33% of TVB, the largest television station. Appointed by Xinhua as a Hong Kong Affairs Advisor, he also sat on the SAR Preparatory Committee and Selection Committee.[72]

Kuok's close business ties with China prompted the *Eastern Express,* newly published by the Oriental Daily News group, to advertise itself as "*the only* independent English-language newspaper in Hong Kong." Some share similar concerns by noting that the *SCMP* constitutes only a small fraction of Kuok's total assets and that the paper has diluted its political reporting about China since his takeover.[73] The attack on *SCMP*'s integrity might have actually caused its staff and readers to stand more vigilantly against editorial interference. It should be noted that the *SCMP* hired a senior Beijing journalist as "editorial consultant" in 1997. No matter how unsympathetic the new sovereign may be toward the press, the *SCMP* can be expected to enjoy a freer rein than its Chinese-language peers. Most authoritarian regimes are more tolerant of the English-language press within their countries because it appeals to a more sophisticated audience and has a direct bearing on their external image. The *Eastern Express,* which never seriously threatened the *SCMP*, ceased publication in 1996, after only two years of operation. Neither can the *Hong Kong Standard* (owned by the Sing Tao group) menace the *SCMP*'s leading role. But the SCMP is not — and will never be — as dominant as it was.

In addition, Murdoch's bold foray into satellite television is motivated not so much by journalistic merits as by the elusive aim of breaking into China's market.[74] It was no accident that his New York-based publishing firm, HarperCollins, sponsored a much publicized trip to the United States in 1995 for Deng Rong to promote her inauspiciously received biography of her powerful father, Deng Xiaoping. Furthermore, Murdoch dropped the BBC World Service, at which Beijing takes offense, from the northern part of STAR satellite TV's footprint covering East Asia. Symbolizing a strange marriage of money and politics, the Phoenix TV satellite channel, of which he owns 45%, provides entertainment fare to China's state-owned cable system, while leaving its news to strict official control.

Most significant change of ownership on the Chinese-language press side has been that of the intellectual-oriented *Ming Pao* (Enlightenment Daily). Under the mantle of its founder, Louis Cha, a renowned editorialist and novelist, the paper was widely acclaimed for its expertise on China watching and insightful political analysis during the Cold War era. Having been scathingly critical of China's radical-left leadership faction during the Cultural Revolution, Cha entered the 1980s as a firm supporter of Deng's economic reform policy, even forbidding his paper to criticize Deng by name. As an influential local figure in the Basic Law drafting process he authored a conservative proposal in 1988 that would delay the pace and extent of direct legislative elections, on grounds that any hasty elections would put the well-organized Communist Party at an advantage.[75] He even used his paper to promote his proposal, provoking angry protesters to burn *Ming Pao* in front of its premises. Cha had ignored the Hong Kong Journalists Association's admonition not to take part in the Basic Law Drafting and Consultative Committees to avoid a serious conflict of interest, but finally resigned from these bodies in protest against Beijing's brutal crackdown in 1989.[76]

Cha sold his paper to Yu Pun-hoi in December 1991. Fancying himself to be a Chinese media empire builder, Yu ventured to set up a global Chinese Television Network (CTN) with a capital of HK$312 million. Yu proceeded his venture against Cha's counsel that under no circumstances would communist China yield the control of the media, the military and the Party to the outsiders.[77] Not allowed to operate in China, CTN became a financial drain. In November 1993 Yu also initiated a tabloid paper (*Hong Kong Today*) in Hong Kong and another daily (*Modern Mankind*) in Guangzhou; both were abruptly closed down after heavy losses. Press revelations of Yu's criminal record while studying in Canada did further damage to his credibility, status, and financial standing, and forced him to resign as chairman of the Hong Kong Newspapers Association. Yu's real estate investment in mainland China was a debacle, and his heavy investment in printing facilities added to *Ming Pao*'s financial problems.[78] Debt commitments compelled Yu to sell 10% of the paper's share to Oei Hong Leong in 1994, an Indonesian-Chinese publisher of the pro-China *Wide Angle* magazine with close business ties with China.[79] Oei was made *Ming Pao*'s chairman of the board, but the move was too late to reverse Yu's fortune. Yu had no choice but relinquish his short reign over *Ming Pao* in 1995 to the Malaysian-Chinese publisher, Tiong Hiew King, also known to have significant business investment in China. The implications of this ownership change for the paper's editorial independence are not entirely certain. Yu retained the control of the unprofitable CTN until 1996 when it was finally sold to Taiwanese interests.

Ming Pao boasts of the most comprehensive China coverage, with 11 of its 14 China Page editors being former mainland journalists. Its editorial position, written by some of the same people and usually printed on the second page, tends to be rigidly nationalistic — in fact, far more critical of Taiwan than several inside-page columns written by Luo Fu (a former deputy chief editor of the communist-controlled *Ta Kung Pao* who was once detained in Beijing for several years on "spying" charges) and Huang Wenfang (former deputy secretary-general of the local Xinhua branch in charge of the Taiwan affairs).[80] *Ming Pao* wrote several long editorials (for example, February 17–18, 1995) advocating the notion of "running a Chinese paper" which would view the questions of Tibet and other world affairs "through a Chinese prism." To be a paper for Hong Kong was not good enough, it said, it must be a paper for all Chinese — a point that invited heated rebuttals from some readers as "hegemonic."

Even so, the paper had a strained relationship with Beijing. It was repeatedly singled out by Xinhua for blame on account of lapses in facts or interpretations, even when other papers committed similar errors. The tension culminated in the arrest of the reporter Xi Yang in September 1993 under provisions of the Chinese state security law. Having migrated from his native Beijing just two months earlier, Xi returned there on a reporting assignment and wrote about an expected policy change in interest rates and international gold sale. He was charged with the alleged crime of "probing and stealing state secrets," even though the same information had been covered by many other papers, including the PRC-controlled *Wen Wei Po*. Publisher Yu yielded to his staff's pressure and took measures toward openly applying pressure on Beijing. The paper argued that Xi broke no laws and that China did not try him openly and fairly. The staff led by the chief editor took part in protesting rallies. The paper printed interviews with experts and postcard letters from readers denouncing Beijing's transgression of human rights and press freedom, and further suggesting that this case would produce a chilling effect on Hong Kong people and damage China's international image.[81]

No offense was thought to be more serious than an open defiance that in effect accused Beijing's paternal-authoritarian leaders of wrong-doing. Through personal connections Yu unsuccessfully pleaded with Beijing for Xi Yang's leniency. Finally he had to apologize, in person and in the paper, to the already agitated Chinese authorities, but all in vain. Xi earned a stiff 12-year imprisonment in March 1994, sending an ominous sign to Hong Kong journalists who must cover news on the mainland.[82] Earlier, a female reporter from the *Express*

Daily was similarly detained in Beijing for conspiring to "steal" an advance copy of President Jiang's speech. Her low-key boss rushed up to Beijing to make an apology, and the reporter was released within days. But Yu did not have the option to remain silent, for he was pressured by his staff to protect the reputation of Hong Kong's premier Chinese language paper. China showed little signs of conciliation toward Yu. In recent years the paper's avoidance of strident criticisms of the PRC in the editorials has been notable.[83] Now that Yu has relinquished his control of *Ming Pao*, how China will treat the paper under Tiong is still too early to tell. But Xi Yang, the imprisoned reporter, was suddenly released on parole and returned to Hong Kong in January 1997 — two weeks before the Chinese New Year — due partly to the new owner's plea to Beijing. Xi's release is also viewed as part of Beijing's effort to create a more favorable climate for the incoming Chief Executive Tung.

The mass-circulated press field has been led by the *Oriental Daily News* and *Sing Pao* (Success Daily) — until the *Apple Daily* entered the fray — pampering the audience with vivid, vulgar and sensational accounts of crime stories, mixed with a large dosage of entertainment gossip, and daily tidbits of soft pornography. These papers copy and outwit each other in an effort to offer new variations on the same theme. The *Oriental Daily News* boasts of a contingent of 80 spot-news reporters and 30 others covering "societal news," with reporting vehicles and devices to eavesdrop police radio communication, priding itself on the ability to beat the police in speed to arrive at spots of crime or accidents. By contrast, the paper only has 10 political reporters and 20 economic reporters. Deliberately apolitical, these papers cultivate a pro-underdog image befitting their grassroots readers. Their relationship with the Chinese authorities is more ambiguous: not wanting to offend Beijing on the one hand, while feeling less pressured to ingratiate themselves with China on the other.[84] As long as they are not too critical of China, these culturally tasteless dailies may offend the sensibilities of the morally puritan Beijing regime but pose little direct threat to its hegemonic power. Beijing's officials (among them, Liao Chengzhi, Lu Ping, and Deng himself) have repeatedly chided that Hong Kong people will be allowed to keep the trappings of their decadent way of life such as horseracing, pornography and other capitalistic trifles.

The market equilibrium was upset when Jimmy Lai, who had made a fortune in the garment business, decided to found the *Next* magazine. *Next*'s surprising market success provoked the *Oriental Daily News* to publish a similar *Eastweek*, both thriving on pushing the "sex and violence" themes beyond the present state of the "art." These outlets either shun political affairs or unfailingly sensationalize them for commercial exploitation. Inspired by his own success, Lai set out to launch the highly publicized HK$700-million *Apple Daily* in mid-1995, preparing to lose a lot of money before it would turn profitable. Modeling itself after *USA Today* in colorful, eye-catching graphic design and its brisk, brief writing, the *Apple Daily* was sold at a 60% discount for the first month and bolstered by

HK$100 million promotional campaigns. Lai lured 10 managers and 235 reporters from other papers with higher salaries to embellish the crime-gossip-sex formulas. The paper displays nude pictures of female bodies on a daily basis and even advises its readers where and how to obtain sex service, all written in lively and highly personable Cantonese vernacular. In the name of "muckraking," moreover, the paper relentlessly exposes personal secrets and dark underside of entertainment celebrities to satisfy the reader's peeping curiosity. Reporters were sent out as "doggy teams" to follow and record every move of some targeted personalities, causing the frustrated Hong Kong Performers Association to stage a 72-hour boycott on media interviews.[85] Within months, the paper climbed quickly to near the top of the pack by amassing a circulation of 300,000 copies among the mass readers, cutting into the commanding lead of the *Oriental Daily News*.[86] Accused of not playing fair, Lai retorted that he was entitled to advance his own best interests rather than look after his competitors' weak spots.[87]

Lai defied popular wisdom when he entered the fiercely competitive newspaper market against the backdrop of enormous political and market uncertainties. The PRC had then just suspended Lai's Giordano garment store in Beijing (resulting in his resignation from the company's board of directors and, later, liquidation of all his shares) to retaliate against his personalized editorial in the *Next* magazine calling Premier Li Peng a "bastard idiot." In spite of his well-publicized anti-communist attitude, Lai has been steering the expensively invested and commercially successful *Apple Daily* away from political trouble. Seemingly eager to establish a new image, Lai said that his paper "would no longer be anti-Communist."[88] Even so, Beijing has not lessened its intense hostility toward Lai and continued to bar the entry of his reporters to the mainland. Beijing's hostility has failed to prevent the paper from leading others in what media sociologists have called "domesticating"[89] China news by applying traditional "crime news" formulas — highlighting the themes of "yellowism (eroticism), gambling, drug, darkness, and deviousness" — to mainland stories. China news is thus a taken-for-granted extension of Hong Kong news; familiar crime stories are now being "scripted" by mainland characters, and even political news is treated as a variation on the same "crime news" themes.[90] Also most responsive to audience interest, the paper pays readers for providing news tips that have market appeal. Though highly controversial and often ethically dubious, the *Apple Daily* has compelled its rivals to rethink their own practices and to compete innovatively for the lowest cultural common denominator.

Most papers had at this time been suffering from the slack economy and depressed advertising revenues, made worse by the doubling of newsprint price in one year due to a global shortage.[91] These papers put aside whatever differences that might have divided them, and agreed to comply to a price set by the newspaper cartel instead of matching Lai's action. As the newspaper industry was nervously taking respite from a temporary truce, the cash-rich *Oriental Daily News* saw its peers' vulnerability as perfect timing for revenge and sharply cut the cartel-imposed price from HK$5 to $2 per copy in early 1996. This time most papers had no alternative but to join the price war. In a manner akin to what a Chinese proverb describes as "drinking poison to quench thirst" (*yin zhen zhi ke*), they competed to cut prices and offer raffle tickets that could win such grand prizes as an automobile or an apartment. But it took only two weeks to claim the lives of those less fit to survive: the *Express* (which reappeared in late 1996 with a dubious future), the *United Daily News*, the *Television Daily* and the *South China Economic Daily*. Other papers (including, ironically, the *Apple Daily* itself) were downsized. A total of 600 news workers lost their jobs.

The price war lasted for six months and ended only with Lai negotiating with Ma in person. Most outlets suffered huge losses. Thanks to market segmentation, only the two English-language newspapers (the *SCMP* and the *Hong Kong Standard*) and the two specialized newspapers (*Hong Kong Economic Journal* and *Hong Kong Economic Daily*) were relatively unharmed. But overall press stocks were significantly devalued. Even though the newspaper price was restored to HK$5 per copy in July 1996, an advertising war was intensified. Because of the economic downturn the Hong Kong press industry has been hard hit by a sharp decline in advertising revenues (which, for example, totaled only HK$4.37 billion in 1995, a 12% drop from the previous year). To fill up the advertising space, many newspapers offered deep discounts — in the depressed real estate areas, advertisers paid as low as 30% of the regular prices — and some even were willing to provide free service. The combined factors of a high inflation rate, low advertising revenues, the rising newsprint price, and the growth in salaries (10%) — on top of the price war and a strong competition posed by the *Apple Daily* — reduced the profit of the Oriental Press group and the Sing Tao group each by two-thirds, while turning *Ming Pao*'s profit into a net loss.[92] Most other papers did not fare any better. The unfavorable profit structure was directly or indirectly responsible for the closure of the *Eastern Express*, *Sing Tao Evening News* and *Qingxiu Magazine* by their parent companies. The press market having been saturated, the fact that the *Apple Daily* posted a total circulation of 360,000 copies at the end of 1996 means an average loss of 10% in circulation for its peers. Promising to turn in a profit of HK$100 million by the end of 1997, with its *Next* magazine due to become a public corporation, the *Apple Daily* is potentially the most profitable paper in Hong Kong.[93] *Next* magazine has spawned other imitators, including *Surprise Weekly*, while more papers will follow the *Apple Daily*'s lead to pursue junk infotainment as the prevailing order of the day. Press ownership will be further consolidated. Concentration of press ownership in the hands of a few large corporations will not only make family-owned papers difficult to survive but also restrict the diversity of views and opinion.[94]

Discussion

I have tried to analyze how political transition has so far exerted an impact on Hong Kong's press-party parallelism. The GMD-controlled party press has declined and finally demised, thus depriving Hong Kong of a major voice. On the opposite side, the Beijing-controlled party press faces a far more intriguing challenge: theoretically it should gain a more central place under Chinese rule, but it has a long way to go toward making itself accepted in Hong Kong's marketplace of opinions. To shore up its badly needed credibility, a loosening of party control is a prerequisite, which is a dubious proposition to begin with. It is important to observe how the leftist press will differ from the party organ in China. In Hong Kong's new political ecology and marketplace, will the leftist press continue to serve as a transmission belt of China's policy pronouncements and as a reluctant instrument of hurling insults at democratic activists, critics, and dissidents? I hypothesize that China will eventually return to Xu Jiatun's old way of coopting the popular-centrist press's support rather than set its own mouthpieces free.[95] Xu made no apology for mistreating those media and journalists under his control, and there is little reason to anticipate that they will receive a significantly improved treatment.[96] The leftist press may nonetheless continue to cultivate its market penetration in the adjoining south China where people are starved for information.

The partisan press has tried to lessen its partisanship by accommodating the market forces, leading to a clear convergence between the partisan press and the popular-centrist press. The pertinent distinction to be made now is between the pro-China press and the pro-Hong Kong press,[97] and within the latter there are the mass press and the serious press. Market forces have intensified merger and takeover activities by international and pro-PRC capitalists, and have also produced certain blatantly anti-democratic and anti-journalistic tendencies. As a group, the generally apolitical and sensational mass press has been gaining ground in the market to enclose the "public sphere." Making no pretense about political purposes or moral highmindedness, it unashamedly pursues crass commercialism with China's implicit approval.

The popular-centrist press is most volatile, oscillating and thus interesting to observe. If the mass press uses the market forces to defuse political forces, the journalistically serious press must seek to balance political demands with economic interests in an intertwined and paradoxical way. Professional reputation is a legitimizing source of their economic interests. To protect their economic interests, they have to make peace with the authorities that dispense vital rewards and punishments, but to be seen as fair, bold and trustworthy, they must risk irking the power that be. Insofar as this tug of war may make the media highly vulnerable, it is interesting to watch how media owners with heavy business ties with China would behave differently from those who devote themselves to media interests in Hong Kong. Their shifting positions may also be tied to specific issues, conditions, and situations. Since the Chinese-language press will bear the brunt of more direct assault, it is also likely that the elite English-language press (such as the *SCMP* and *Far Eastern Economic Review*), along with the many international media that have recently chosen to establish bureaus in Hong Kong, will exert huge influence — as they do in Singapore, Malaysia and Indonesia — despite their relatively small circulation.

In "indexing" legitimate voices, the popular-centrist press may appeal to professionalism which is rooted in social consensus.[98] The marketplace of opinions is assumed to be normally distributed, with the center covering the widest segment of the population. It can thus be argued that the official view overlaps with a substantial area of social consensus that forms the media's point of departure (and often, a point of return) to anchor their news perspectives. Media sociologists have argued that the media focus their "news net" on the centrally legitimated institutions, hence the rhythm of newswork is in tandem with the cycle of such institutions, where "facts" can be gathered.[99] Hallin maintains that the media will follow the institutionalized agendas rather than propose new or innovative approaches to the problem.[100] No doubt that the media have been shifting their focus from the Hong Kong colonial government to the SAR government, and from Britain to the PRC, as primary news sources and reality definers.

What about those social groups, notably the democrats, which have been severely denounced by the PRC but have so far enjoyed the most popular support in Hong Kong's electorate (with a 64% vote in the 1995 direct election)? Will they be tolerated as legitimate players in Hong Kong's political life? How will the popular-centrist press lend moral support to these activists without annoying Chinese authorities? Or how will the press toe the official line to marginalize these activists as "deviants" without injuring its own integrity? Further, will the activities of foreign human rights organizations be curtailed or restricted as provided by article 23 of the Basic Law? To what extent can the press report or support their criticisms of China's record? In an interview that caused public anxiety, repercussions and criticisms, Chinese Vice-Premier Qian Qichen has warned local pro-democracy activists not to hold political activities after 1997 (such as those to commemorate the June 4 crackdown) which would "directly interfere in the affairs of the mainland." He also warned the press not to launch "personal attacks" on top Chinese leaders.[101] Earlier, Lu Ping, another senior Chinese official, also made an unclear demarcation between "reporting" and "advocacy"; he ruled out advocating Taiwan's and Tibet's independence or "two Chinas" as part of press freedom after 1997. It seems that political space of the democrats is being quickly narrowed, and their legitimacy has come under increasing challenges.

The Democratic Party has refused to take part in the "provisional legislature" which they condemned as "illegal," while the pro-PRC forces have become more visible and more vocal both in the political arena and in media coverage.

As the public along with the media acquiesce to the choice of Tung Chee-hwa as the SAR Chief Executive, there arises a latent (and paradoxical) concern about the democrats taking a radical road which may disrupt Hong Kong's stability, to the extent that the democrats have complained about their receiving insufficient media attention.[102] Insofar as the democrats remain as a significant political force, however, I hypothesize that media coverage of them will be highly inconsistent and even contradictory, depending on the strength of the pressure and on various issues at a given moment. But it seems inevitable that the Democratic Party will be weakened.

History has a different side other than the one written from the top. It would be self defeating to assume that external forces, imposed from above, are so overwhelming as to render the agency and voices of Hong Kong people totally impotent. At many key moments, Hong Kong people and media have actively deflected China's pressure on issues ranging from Patten's reforms, party formation, elections, to the implementation of the Basic Law. In the mid-1980s the media also supported a groundswell of popular protest against China's construction of a nuclear power plant in the Daya Bay near the border, albeit to no avail.[103] To cope with the new situation, media organizations have developed different strategies to absorb or defuse political pressure on professional grounds. Professionalism has provided some political space for rank-and-file journalists, daily columnists, and professional editors to struggle over various meanings of reality. I doubt that China can succeed in manipulating all media owners to dismiss all critical writers if these columns touch Hong Kong's nerve and command strong popularity.[104]

From the cultural point of view — one that is born in a unique political-economic context — the 1997 issue has bred a new Hong Kong identity to differentiate from the pan-Chinese identity, for it means a test of will to defend one's way of life.[105] This stands in stark contrast to the "refugee mentality" of the 1950s and 1960s in which the grandiose Chineseness subsumed everything that was about Hong Kong. Nowadays the press is filled with discussions about how to nurture this emerging ethnic identity, and politicians of all colors boast of their "pro-Hong Kong" positions — so much so that even the pro-China party calls itself Democratic Alliance for Betterment of Hong Kong (DAB) and pro-China candidates, too, present themselves as "pro-Hong Kong" and "pro-democracy." Its leader, Tsang Yok-shing, proclaimed his party as "pro-China, but even more pro-Hong Kong," complaining that the public did not appreciate this point and the media often distort it. The party also packages itself as party for grassroots services, not as a "yes-party" to China.[106]

Holding the Hong Kong identity to heart is a constituent part of media credibility. It was small wonder that *Ming Pao*'s editorials (February 17–18, 1995) presenting itself as a paper for all Chinese rather than Hong Kong people were negatively received. The pro-China columnist, Ai Fan (Liu Naiqiang), has taken pains to urge Beijing to display greater sensitivity toward the local interests, values, and viewpoints of the Hong Kong people. He also assured his readers that Beijing is capable of rationally modifying its behaviors even though it may not openly acknowledge such a change. This ethnic identity, fueled by the "one country, two systems" rhetoric, may accomplish what political and economic factors have failed: to put the ball in Beijing's court. Despite its control of the party press and enormous influence on the partisan and popular-centrist presses, China simply cannot impose ideological hegemony on Hong Kong people who have a deep-seated distrust of the Beijing regime — a sentiment to which the media contribute mightily. Seen in this light, Governor Patten was perhaps not entirely unjustified in saying: "You can dismantle institutions, but I don't think you can destroy the values that have helped make Hong Kong such a special place."[107]

Press freedom is plainly written in the Sino-British Joint Declaration and the Basic Law. Laws being not self-protective, even the PRC's constitution formally guarantees freedom of speech and the press. Law is also an inherently political process; even the interpretations and enforcement of the First Amendment in the United States are found to have fluctuated significantly in correspondence to periods in which popular movements demanded speech rights.[108] Struggle to protect press freedom is a struggle between the state and the civil society, and a struggle between the political and the economical; in Hong Kong it will depend substantially on the integrity of the "free market" system, social pluralism, citizen vigilance and public demands.

On the legal front, the democrats have criticized the British for being too late and too slow in abolishing draconian colonial laws and in revising other illiberal instruments.[109] China, however, regards British's late conversion to the cause of democracy in the colony as hypocritical, vowing to dismantle Patten's political reform. In the mid-1980s the British aborted an attempt, under China's pressure, to turn Radio and Television Hong Kong from a government unit to an autonomous public corporation like the BBC.[110] The British have liberalized more than 40 ordinances in recent years. Of them, six ordinances were revised to restrict the arbitrary executive power over such areas as freedom of assembly, emergency situations, public order, broadcasting and telecommunications.[111] The PRC is highly suspicious of British motive to modify these ordinances. At least, the National People's Congress has in early 1997 decided to repeal the current versions of the Public Order Ordinance and the Societies Ordinance (which were created in the mid-1990s) in order to give police greater power over the control of protests and to prevent political groups from forging foreign links.

The future of the Bill of Rights and the Freedom of Information Act is dubious. Most ominous is article 23 of the Basic Law that authorizes the SAR government to enact laws to prohibit acts of "treason, secession, sedition and subversion against the Central People's Government or theft of state secrets." The Hong Kong government introduced a preemptive amendment to the Public Order Ordinance in late 1996 that defined those four anti-state crimes specifically in terms of acts involving the "use of force" rather than speech. The PRC was enraged by such an amendment and will not recognize it. But on the question of theft of state secrets, the Hong Kong government contradicted itself when it transplanted — with the PRC's consent but contrary to public demand — the highly inhibiting Official Secrets Act from Britain to Hong Kong without modification, a law that may have serious negative implications for press freedom.

Viewing the process of struggles dynamically, I believe that the multiplicity of political and economic pressures may trigger media reactions in highly situational, erratic, uneven, partial and even contradictory patterns. The media will be cyclically bold and tame. They will also be concurrently public-spirited and self-serving. Being practically minded and lacking a grand conception about the world, editors may deal with the external pressure on an ad hoc and piecemeal basis. It should be underscored that as long as there happens to be a journalist, an editor or a media organization bold enough at a particular moment to defy the authorities by breaking a sensitive story, other competitors are bound to pick up and expand it irrespective of political pressure. As "public goods," information is not exclusively enjoyed by its producers or purchasers, and once a story is broken it enters into the public domain for widespread dissemination that may then give rise to public attention.[112] Market competition demands and legitimizes media outlets to pursue the story once it is broken. In the end, journalists and their organizations have to constantly juggle various sets of pressure against their professional standards and their peers' behaviors. They may oscillate between opposing tendencies but would return to a balanced point. Media owners may *sometimes* "bend the conscience" of working journalists, but not all the time. In sum, I hypothesize that *Hong Kong's vaunted press freedom might abate under Chinese rule, but the degree of its societal transparency promises to remain relatively high.*

The Sino-British conflict is being transformed into the conflict between the PRC's central government and Hong Kong's local governance. Beijing has chosen to emphasize "one country" while Hong Kong prefers to highlight its promised "high degree of autonomy" allowed by the unique "two systems,"[113] thus foretelling some of the potential rifts in the years ahead. The PRC had hoped to use Hong Kong as a peaceful demonstration station to woo Taiwan into reunification, but its military threats against Taiwan in 1995 and 1996 has departed from this stated goal. Whether the aim of courting Taiwan will moderate Beijing's attitude toward Hong Kong is uncertain. In sum, the media are expected to defend Hong Kong's local interests against Beijing's encroachments by offering alternative and sometimes opposing interpretations of reality. Technical issues, such as the building of a new airport, may be negotiable. But the basic "one country, two systems" policy — which will constitute the outer limits of press freedom — is not.

One can argue that social and political freedoms are the indispensable "software" to the "hardware" of Hong Kong's economic miracle, and that if the PRC truly values Hong Kong's economic and functional contributions to its modernization, then freedom of the press and free flow of economic information will be a cherished pillar of the Hong Kong success story not to be eroded after 1997. It can be expected that flow of economic and cultural information will not be severely hampered; in many respects the Hong Kong media may improve their interaction with the mainland economic and cultural institutions. The right of the press to report freely about the political authorities and even criticize them is, however, much more precarious, as several Chinese leaders have displayed strong propensities toward tighter press control in their public pronouncements.[114] It is on the political front that Hong Kong has sometimes been compared to Singapore to underscore the point that economic prosperity can be maintained at the sacrifice of press freedom. This argument seems reminiscent of the theme that economic development serves to consolidate what O'Donnell calls "bureaucratic authoritarianism" rather than to advance democracy.[115] This comparison, however, grossly obscures the differences in specific historical conditions. If Hong Kong's press freedom may be curtailed from "more" to "less," Singapore will move from having "little" to "some" freedom. Hong Kong is too complex and contradictory to be sanitized, the bud of political activism inspired by the political transition cannot be nipped, and those who have tasted first fruits of elementary democracy may need more, not less, to satisfy their appetite. As an increasingly pluralistic society with diverse interests, competing ideologies and different power bases, Hong Kong cannot be pushed back to what it was 30 years ago. It is also doubtful if Singapore's current authoritarian paternalism will survive beyond the strong father figure of Lee Kuan Yew. Furthermore, unless the unthinkable martial law (armed with huge and complex coercive apparatuses) is imposed, neither will Hong Kong's press be as restrictive as its counterparts in Taiwan or South Korea when they were under authoritarian control.[116] Finally, unless there is a total collapse of the "one country, two systems" policy, no matter how narrowly interpreted it may be, Hong Kong's press freedom will never be allowed to degenerate to the level existing in mainland China.

The ultimate guarantee of press freedom in Hong Kong lies in China's continued liberalization and democratization and its determination to carry out faithfully the "one country, two systems" policy. Economic reform has transformed China's totalitarian regime into an authoritarian regime that allows for greater scope of what Isaiah Berlin calls "negative freedom" and tolerates more media diversity in non-political areas, a phenomenon resembling Taiwan under martial law in many ways.[117] But "positive freedom" for democratization is nowhere yet to be seen in China. It should not be overlooked that Hong Kong has begun to set agendas for south China and other coastal provinces in the areas of popular culture and media tastes, along with Hong Kong-sponsored trade, financial, and economic undertakings.[118] A "Greater China" is said to be taking shape, in which, as Tu Wei-ming maintains, a geographically and politically peripheral Hong Kong may act as a center of cultural, economic, and technological innovations.[119] Beijing's influence on Hong Kong is not a rigidly one-way street, and its implementation of the "one country, two systems" policy is fraught with tensions and contradictions liable to sway with a host of conditions and issues. Since a crisis also presents an opportunity, these tensions and contradictions will be fertile ground for the struggle against state control, while the glaring incongruity between Beijing's public commitment to Hong Kong and its vacillating policy whims will provide unsettling leakage in ideological control. To end on a rather positive note, China cannot, in the final analysis, fully close off the public space from liberal struggle.

References

Bennett, Lance (1990), "Toward a Theory of Press-State Relations in the United States," *Journal of Communication*, 40, 2: 103–125.

Berlin, Isaiah (1969), *Four Essays on Liberty*. Oxford: Oxford University Press.

Caporaso, James A. and David P. Levine (1992), *Theories of Political Economy*. New York: Cambridge University Press.

Chan, Joseph Man and Chin-Chuan Lee (1991), *Mass Media and Political Transition: The Hong Kong Press in China's Orbit*. New York: Guilford Press.

Chan, Joseph Man, Paul Siu-nam Lee, and Chin-Chuan Lee (1996), *Hong Kong Journalists in Transition*. Hong Kong: Chinese University of Hong Kong, Hong Kong Center of Asia-Pacific Studies.

Chan, Ming K. and David Clark, eds. (1991), *The Hong Kong Basic Law: Blueprint for "Stability and Prosperity" Under Chinese Sovereignty?* Hong Kong: Hong Kong University Press.

Chan, Ming K. and Tuen-yu Lau (1990), "Dilemma of the Communist Press in a Pluralistic Society," *Asian Survey*, 30, 8: 731–747.

Chen, Jiakang (1995), "Louis Cha on Yu Pun-hoi," *Eastweek*.

Ching, Frank (1991), "Implementation of the Sino-British Joint Declaration," in Joseph Y.S. Cheng and Paul C. K. Kwong, eds., *The Other Hong Kong Report, 1992*. Hong Kong: Chinese University Press.

Chomsky, Noam (1989), *Necessary Illusions*. Boston: South End Press.

Cohen, Stanley and Jock Young, eds. (1981), *The Manufacture of News*. Beverly Hills, CA: Sage.

Dahlgren, Peter (1995), *Television and the Public Space*. London: Sage.

Davies, Simon T. (1993), "Hong Kong Broadcasting," in Po-King Choi and Lik-sang Ho, eds., *The Other Hong Kong Report, 1993*. Hong Kong: Chinese University Press.

Dittmer, Lowell (1994), "The Politics of Publicity in Reform China," in Chin-Chuan Lee, ed., *China's Media, Media's China*. Boulder, CO: Westview Press.

Donohue, George A., Phillip Tichenor and Clarice Olien (1995), "A Guard Dog Perspective on the Role of Media," *Journal of Communication*, 45, 2: 115–132.

Donsbach, Wolfang and Bettina Kleft (1993), "Subjective Objectivity. How Journalists in Four Countries Define a Key Term of their Profession," *Gazette*, 51: 53–83.

Dreier, Peter (1982), "The Position of the Press in the US Power Structure," *Social Forces*, 29: 298–310.

Elliot, Dorinda (1996), "Betrayed?" *Newsweek*, May 13: 37–38.

Entman, Robert M. (1989), *Democracy without Citizens: Media and the Decay of American Politics*. New York: Oxford University Press.

Fan Zhongliu (1997), "A Rugged Road for the Democratic Party After 1997," *Hong Kong Economic Journal,* January 10, p. 23.

Fishman, Mark (1980), *Manufacturing the News*. Austin: University of Texas Press.

Frieberg, J. W. (1981), *The French Press: Class, State and Ideology*. New York: Praeger.

Fung, Anthony and Chin-Chuan Lee (1994), "Hong Kong's Changing Media Ownership: Uncertainty and Dilemma," *Gazette* 53: 127–133.

Gans, Herbert (1979), *Deciding What's News*. New York: Pantheon.

Gargan, Edward (1996), "New Jitters from Hong Kong: In Economics, as in Politics, China Exerts Control," *New York Times,* May 18, pp. Y17–18.

Gitlin, Todd (1980), *The Whole World Is Watching*. Berkeley: University of California Press.

Gold, Thomas (1993), "Go with Your Feelings: Hong Kong and Taiwan Popular Culture in Greater China," *China Quarterly*, pp. 907–925.

Goldstein, Carl (1996), "Hong Kong Past and Future," text of speech given at St. Johns University, Minnesota, May 1.

Hallin, Daniel (1986), *The 'Uncensored' War*. New York: Oxford University Press.

Harding, Harry (1993), "The Concept of Greater China: Themes, Variations and Reservations," *China Quarterly*, pp. 660–686.

Harris, Peter (1978), *Hong Kong: A Study in Bureaucratic Politics*. Hong Kong: Heinemann Asia.

Herman, Edward and Noam Chomsky (1988), *Manufacturing Consent*. New York: Pantheon.

Ho, Leung-mou (1996), "China News in the Hong Kong Press," Unpublished M. Phil thesis, Chinese University of Hong Kong.

HKEJ (1995), "Jimmy Lai: 'I Have no Obligation to Take Care of My Opponents," *Hong Kong Economic Journal,* June 20.

Hong Kong Journalists Association (1996), "China's Challenge: Freedom of Expression in Hong Kong," annual report.

Huang, Wenfang (1995), "To Secure the Confidence of Hong Kong People," *Ming Pao*, May 2.

Ji, Wen (1995), "Hong Kong Media," *Nineties Monthly,* Feb.: 94–95.

Journalist (1995), "From a Cold-War Outpost to a Bridge for Mutual Flow Across the Strait," *Open,* May, pp. 42–43.

Ju, Zhong (1995), "Listen to the Voices of People on Taiwan," *Hong Kong Economic Journal,* June 20–21.

Ju, Zhong (1995), "Assumptions Behind Commentaries on Taiwan," *Hong Kong Economic Journal,* July 13–14.

Kairys, David (1982), "Freedom of Speech," in David Kairys, ed., *The Politics of Law: A Progressive View*. New York: Pantheon.

King, Ambrose Y. C. (1975), "Administrative Absorption of Politics: Emphasis on the Grass Roots Level," *Asian Survey*, 15: 422–439.

King, Ambrose Y. C. (1988), "The Hong Kong Talks and Hong Kong Politics," in Jurgen Domes and Yu-ming Shaw, eds., *Hong Kong: A Chinese and International Concern*. Boulder, CO: Westview Press.

Kocher, R. (1986), "Bloodhounds or Missionaries: Role Definitions of German and British Journalists," *European Journal of Communication,* 1: 46–65.

Lang, Kurt and Gladys Lang (1981), *Batting for Public Opinion*. New York: Columbia University Press.

Lau, Siu-kai (1982), *Society and Politics in Hong Kong*. Hong Kong: Chinese University Press.

Lau, Siu-kai (1992), "Hong Kong People's View of the Government," *Wide Angle*, no. 238.

Lee, Chin-Chuan (1985), "Partisan Press Coverage of Government News in Hong Kong," *Journalism Quarterly*, 62: 770–776.

Lee, Chin-Chuan (1993), "Sparking a Fire: The Press and the Ferment of Democratic Change in Taiwan," *Journalism Monographs*, No. 138.

Lee, Chin-Chuan (1994), "Ambiguities and Contradictions: Issues in China's Changing Political Communication," in Chin-Chuan Lee, ed., *China's Media, Media's China.* Boulder, CO: Westview Press.

Lee, Chin-Chuan (in preparation), "Conglomeration, Professionalism, and Strategic Rituals: The Hong Kong Press and Political Transition," in Chin-Chuan Lee, ed., *Power, Money, and Media: Communication Patterns in Greater China.*

Lee, Chin-Chuan and Joseph Man Chan (1990), "Government Management of the Press in Hong Kong," *Gazette*, 46: 125–139.

Lee, Chin-Chuan and Joseph Man Chan (1990), "The Hong Kong Press in China's Orbit: Thunder of Tiananmen," in Chin-Chuan Lee, ed., *Voices of China: The Interplay of Politics and Journalism.* New York: Guilford Press.

Lin, You-lan (1977), *History of the Hong Kong Press.* Taipei: World.

McManus, John H. (1994), *Market-driven Journalism.* Thousand Oaks, CA: Sage.

Man, Cheuk-fei (1996), "How Did Xinhua Launch its Propaganda Work Through the Leftist Newspapers (1949–1982)?" *Hong Kong Economic Journal Monthly*, no. 226 (Jan.): 10–17.

Manoff, Robert K. and Michael Schudson, eds. (1986), *Reading the News.* New York: Pantheon.

Mitchell, Robert E. (1969), "How Hong Kong Newspapers Have Responded to 15 Years of Rapid Social Change," *Asian Survey*, 9: 673–678.

Miners, M. J. (1977), *The Government and Politics in Hong Kong.* Hong Kong: Oxford University Press.

O'Donnell, Guillermo A. (1973), *Modernization and Bureaucratic-Authoritarianism.* Berkeley: Institute of International Studies, University of California.

Patterson, Thomas E. and Wolfgang Donsbach (1993), "Press-Party Parallelism: A Cross-National Comparison," presented at the International Communication Association conference, Washington, D.C., May 28.

Pool, Ithiel de sola (1952), *Prestige Papers.* Stanford: Stanford University Press.

Qi, Xin (Lee Yee) (1993), "To the Granddaddy Up there, Yours Little Servant Confesses a Mistake," *Hong Kong Economic Journal*, October 18.

Said, Edward (1981), *Covering Islam.* New York: Pantheon.

Schlesinger, Peter (1978), *Putting 'Reality' Together.* Beverly Hills, CA: Sage.

Schudson, Michael (1978), *Discovering the News.* New York: Basic.

Seymour-Ure, Collin (1974), *The Political Impact of Mass Media.* Beverly Hills: Sage.

Shu, Yufei (1985), "The *Hong Kong Times*'s Quarrel in Taipei," *Nineties Monthly*, March.

So, Clement, Y. K. (1996), "Pre-1997 Hong Kong Press: Cut-throat Competition and the Changing Journalistic Paradigm," in Mee Kau Nyaw and Si Ming Li, eds., *The Other Hong Kong Report 1996.* Hong Kong: Chinese University Press.

So, Clement Y. K., Chin-Chuan Lee, and Anthony Fung (1996), "How Do Media Workers View Press Credibility?" *Ming Pao*, December 5, p. c5.

Song, Lingqi (1995), "The Infighting between the Two Leftist Papers," *Open,* May, pp. 74–75.

Staniland, Martin (1985), *What Is Political Economy?* New Haven: Yale University Press.

Suine, Karen (1987), "The Political Role of Mass Media in Scandinavia," *Legislative Studies Quarterly,* 12: 395–415.

Tse, Patricia Wen-sei (1995), "The Impact of 1997 on Political Apathy in Hong Kong," *Political Quarterly,* pp. 210–220.

Tu, Weiming (1991), "Cultural China: The Periphery as the Center," *Daedalus,* 120, 2: 1–32.

Tuchman, Gaye (1978), *Making News.* New York: Free Press

Walden, John (1993), "Implementation of the Sino-British Joint Declaration," in Po-king Choi and Lok-sang, eds. *The Other Hong Kong Report, 1993.* Hong Kong: Chinese University Press.

Xu Jiatun (1994), *Hong Kong Memoirs.* Hong Kong: United Daily News. 2 vols.

Yoon, Youngchul (1989), "Political Transition and Press Ideology in South Korea, 1980–1989," unpublished Ph.D. dissertation, University of Minnesota.

Weaver, David and G. Cleveland Wilhoit (1996), *The American Journalist in the 1990s.* Mahwah, N.J.: Lawrence Erlbaum.

Williams, Raymond (1977), *Marxism and Literature.* New York: Oxford University Press.

White, Lynn T. III (1990), "All the News: Structure and Politics in Shanghai's Reform Media," in Chin-Chuan Lee, ed., *Voices of China: The Interplay of Politics and Journalism.* New York: Guilford Press.

Yu, Jinglu (1990), "The Structure and Function of Chinese Television, 1979–1989," in Chin-Chuan Lee, ed., *Voices of China: The Interplay of Politics and Journalism.* New York: Guilford Press.

Zhang, Shengru (1995), "Hu Xian (Sally Aw): The Tigress Who Inherits Her Father's Fortune," *Next,* no. 257 (Feb. 10): 86–90.

Zhang, Shengru (1995), "The Tigress Who Turned the Paper Profitable," *Next,* no. 258, Feb. 17, pp. 98–104.

Zhang, Shengru (1995), "The Rise and Fall of Hu Xian," *Next,* no. 259, Feb. 24, pp. 102–108.

Notes

1. Goldstein, "Hong Kong Past and Future."

2. Elliot, "Betrayed?"

3. Gargan, "New Jitters from Hong Kong: In Economics, as in Politics, China Exerts Control."

4. Chan and Lee, *Mass Media and Political Transition: The Hong Kong Press in China's Orbit.*

5. Donohue, Tichenor and Olien, "A Guard Dog Perspective on the Role of Media," p. 115.

6. Dreier, "The Position of the Press in the US Power Structure," Tuchman, *Making News,* Gitlin, *The Whole World Is Watching,* Herman and Chomsky, *Manufacturing Consent,* Chomsky, Necessary Illusions, Hallin, *The 'Uncensored' War,* Said, *Covering Islam,* and Entman, *Democracy without Citizens: Media and the Decay of American Politics.*

7. Bennett, "Toward a Theory of Press-State Relations in the United States."

8. Williams, *Marxism and Literature.*

9. Dahlgren, *Television and the Public Space,* p. 128.

10. For a general background, see Caporaso and Levine, *Theories of Political Economy,* and Staniland, *What Is Political Economy?*

11. In the mid-1980s Deng Xiaoping, the paramount leader, boasted that the Communist Party would not be afraid of being "cursed down," but warned the opposing forces in Hong Kong (which presumably included some media outlets) not to incite disturbance or to advocate "two Chinas." After the Tiananmen crackdown, President Jiang Zemin and

other leaders lost no time in denouncing Hong Kong and its media for meddling mainland affairs. The Basic Law has subsequently outlawed "subversive" activities against socialist China, but the line between legitimate criticism and subversion is never clearly drawn. In the 1990s, Beijing has sent the same message with a different language by proclaiming that Hong Kong is, historically, an "economic city" rather than a "political center." In their midst, Beijing has sarcastically assured the Hong Kong media that they would not lose their discretion to carry pornography, horseracing, and other decadent capitalistic trappings — that is, anything but politically critical materials. Lu Ping, a senior Chinese official, warned that after 1997 "advocating" (rather than "reporting" about) two Chinas would be banned. In 1996, Foreign Minister Chen Qichen served notice that the Hong Kong media should not "create falsehood' or "personally attack national leaders" after 1997, but he did not define those terms.

12. Caporaso and Levine, *Theories of Political Economy,* pp. 93–95.

13. Seymour-Ure, *The Political Impact of Mass Media.*

14. Tuchman, *Making News,* and Gitlin, *The Whole World Is Watching.*

15. Lee, "Conglomeration, Professionalism, and Strategic Rituals: The Hong Kong Press and Political Transition."

16. Seymour-Ure, *The Political Impact of Mass Media.*

17. Patterson and Donsbach, "Press-Party Parallelism: A Cross-National Comparison," Donsbach, and Kleft, "Subjective Objectivity. How Journalists in Four Countries Define a Key Term of their Profession," Frieberg, *The French Press: Class, State and Ideology,* Hadenius, "The Rise and Possible Fall of the Swedish Party Press," Suine, "The Political Role of Mass Media in Scandinavia," and Kocher, "Bloodhounds or Missionaries: Role Definitions of German and British Journalists."

18. Tuchman, *Making News,* Gitlin, *The Whole World Is Watching,* Gans, *Deciding What's News,* Schudson, *Discovering the News,* Fishman, *Manufacturing the News,* Weaver and Wilhoit, *The American Journalist in the 1990s,* and Manoff and Schudson, *Reading the News.*

19. Lin, *History of the Hong Kong Press.*

20. Harris, *Hong Kong: A Study in Bureaucratic Politics.*

21. Lau, *Society and Politics in Hong Kong.*

22. King, "Administrative Absorption of Politics: Emphasis on the Grass Roots Level."

23. Miners, *The Government and Politics in Hong Kong.*

24. Man, "How Did Xinhua Launch its Propaganda Work Through the Leftist Newspapers (1949–1982)?"

25. Mitchell, "How Hong Kong Newspapers Have Responded to 15 Years of Rapid Social Change."

26. Xu, *Hong Kong Memoirs.*

27. Lee, "Partisan Press Coverage of Government News in Hong Kong," and Lee and Chan, "Government Management of the Press in Hong Kong."

28. Lee and Chan,"Government Management of the Press in Hong Kong."

29. King, "Administrative Absorption of Politics: Emphasis on the Grass Roots Level."

30. King, "The Hong Kong Talks and Hong Kong Politics."

31. Xu Jiatun's strategies were to "enhance mutual understanding, reduce some people's hostility, win some of the publications to be friendly publications." He established close relationships with Run Run Shaw of TVB, Yau Tak-gan of ATV, Louis Cha of *Ming Pao,* Ho Sai-chu of *Tin Tin Daily News,* Fu Chao-shu of the *Centre Daily,* and Lin Xingzhi of *Hong Kong Economic Journal.* See Xu, *Hong Kong Memoirs,* Chapter 11.

32. Huang, "To Secure the Confidence of Hong Kong People."

33. Xu, *Hong Kong Memoirs,* and Chan and Lee, *Mass Media and Political Transition,* Chapter 3.

34. Lang and Lang, *Batting for Public Opinion*.

35. King, "The Hong Kong Talks and Hong Kong Politics."

36. Lee and Chan, "Government Management of the Press in Hong Kong."

37. King, "The Hong Kong Talks and Hong Kong Politics."

38. Ching, "Implementation of the Sino-British Joint Declaration," and Walden, "Implementation of the Sino-British Joint Declaration."

39. Chan and Lee, *Mass Media and Political Transition*.

40. The cited figures were based on Lau, "Hong Kong People's View of the Government." In March 1995, the Homes Affairs Department survey indicates that 43% of the respondents were "satisfied with the (Hong Kong) government's overall performance" (*Eastern Express*, April 18, 1995).

41. Tse, "The Impact of 1997 on Political Apathy in Hong Kong."

42. Chan, Lee and Lee, *Hong Kong Journalists in Transition*.

43. Of the 96 Hong Kong members of the Preparatory Committee (the other 64 members are from the mainland), half own major companies, who got rich under the British and now need mainland ties to stay rich. It is commented that "businessmen and communist leaders share a hunger for Hong Kong's wealth, and they need each other to keep it flowing." See Elliot, "Betrayed?" In early 1996 the Preparatory Committee obligingly voted, 149–1, to scrap Hong Kong's 1995 elected Legislative Council after the handover. The lone dissenter was officially reprimanded.

44. The Preparatory Committee selected the SAR Selection Committee. All 400 Selection Committee members are Hong Kong residents; more than half of them represent commercial and industrial circles. Sixty-three percent of the members were affiliated with the PRC, including (a) deputies to the National People's Congress or the National People's Political Consultative Committee (15%); (b) representatives of the existing leftist elite organizations (23%); (c) representatives of the existing leftist grassroots organizations (16%); (d) representatives of the newly emerging leftist elite organizations (8%); and (e) representatives of the newly emerging leftist grassroots organizations (1%). Adding other pro-China politicians to this list, the PRC could effectively control 80% of the members. See *Ming Pao*, November 5, 1996.

45. Hallin, *The 'Uncensored' War*.

46. Mainland refugees increased Hong Kong's population from 1.6 million at the end of 1946 to an estimated 2.36 million by the spring of 1950. The Hong Kong born population has increased from 32.5% in 1931 to 47.7% in 1961, to 56.4% in 1971, and to 60% in 1991. See *Hong Kong 1991 Population Census: Summary Results*.

47. Journalist, "From a Cold-War Outpost to a Bridge for Mutual Flow Across the Strait."

48. Lin, *History of the Hong Kong Press*.

49. Shu, "The Hong Kong Times's Quarrel in Taipei."

50. Former Governor Edward Youde, a China expert, admitted reading five Chinese-language newspapers daily, including the *Hong Kong Times* and *Wen Wei Po*.

51. When Taiwan was under martial law, the *United Daily News* sided with the GMD's conservative faction whereas the *China Times* endorsed its liberal wing. See Lee, "Sparking a Fire." Since martial law was lifted in 1987, the *United Daily News* has supported the conservative splinter group and holdovers of the old GMD regime who are hostile to President Lee Tenghui, the first Taiwanese president, and the opposition Democratic Progressive Party (DPP) which advocates Taiwan's secession from China. The DPP's followers had been seeking revenge, and President Lee handed them a perfect opportunity by telling a group of DPP leaders that he was so disgusted with the *United Daily News* as to stop reading it. This set off a large-scale boycott campaign in 1992 on the unfair charge of the paper as "a Taiwan edition of the *People's Daily*." The paper lost

a circulation of 90,000 copies. Its chief rival, *China Times*, also an advocate of Taiwan's ultimate unification with China, has however managed to support President Lee without alienating Lee's foes and even enjoyed some trust from the DPP.

52. Xu, *Hong Kong Memoirs*. These circulation figures, as revealed to me by a top executive of the paper, were considerably lower than official claims.

53. *Hong Kong Economic Journal*, December 17, 1996.

54. Lee and Chan, "The Hong Kong Press in China's Orbit: Thunder of Tiananmen,"; and Chan and Lau, "Dilemma of the Communist Press in a Pluralistic Society."

55. Song, "The Infighting between the two Leftist Papers," and Huang, "To Secure the Confidence of Hong Kong People."

56. Song, Ibid.

57. Ho, "China News in the Hong Kong Press."

58. Lee, "Partisan Press Coverage of Government News in Hong Kong."

59. Chan and Lee, *Mass Media and Political Transition.*

60. Fung and Lee, "Hong Kong's Changing Media Ownership: Uncertainty and Dilemma."

61. Chan and Lee, *Mass Media and Political Transition*, p. 68.

62. In one single year (1988–89) she purchased properties worth HK$500–600 million in Canada, Britain, and New Zealand. In early 1989 she acquired a commercial building in Hong Kong for HK$750 million, 90% of which were bank loans, in addition to taking over Culture Communications that owned the *Tin Tin Daily News.*

63. Zhang, "Hu Xian (Sally Aw): The Tigress Who Inherits her Father's Fortune."

64. Zhang, "The Rise and Fall of Hu Xian," p. 107.

65. Zhang, "The Tigress Who Turned the Paper Profitable," and Zhang, "The Rise and Fall of Hu Xian."

66. Ji, "Hong Kong Media," p. 94.

67. According to a report by Survey Research Hong Kong (January, 1996), the *Oriental Daily News* claimed 26% of the total newspaper readership (1.4 million), followed by the *Apple Daily* (23%), *Sing Pao* (11%) and the *Tin Tin Daily News* (9%). The four popular newspapers accounted for 69% of the readership. *Ming Pao* captured 7%, by comparison. Note that readership is based on the circulation figure multiplied by a factor.

68. Tuchman, *Making News*, Gitlin, *The Whole World Is Watching*, Gans, *Deciding What's News*, Schudson, *Discovering the News*, Fishman, *Manufacturing the News*, Weaver and Wilhoit, *The American Journalist in the 1990s*, and Manoff and Schudson, *Reading the News.*

69. Pool, *Prestige Papers*, p. 120.

70. In our 1990 survey, the *SCMP* was regarded by journalists as the most credible; see Chan, Lee and Lee, *Hong Kong Journalists in Transition*, p. 98. In our 1996 survey, the *SCMP*'s credibility dropped second to the *Hong Kong Economic Journal* but ahead of the No. 3 *Ming Pao*; see So, Lee, and Fung, "How Do News Workers View Press Credibility?"

71. Xu, *Hong Kong Memoirs.*

72. Fung and Lee, "Hong Kong's Changing Media Ownership."

73. Hong Kong Journalists Association, "China's Challenge," p. 42. This report cited examples in which *Ming Pao* and *Eastern Express*, in addition to *SCMP*, have diluted their criticisms of the PRC.

74. Since Murdoch acquired the Star TV in 1994 from the real-estate tycoon Li Ka-shing for US$ 1 billion, it has not been profitable. The loss in 1996 stood at US$100 million. Advertising dollars, which were meager to begin with, generated 82% of the Star TV's revenues whereas the subscription base was so weak as to account for only 18%. This contrasts with a typical cable or satellite television which garners 80% of its revenues from subscription fees. *Hong Kong Economic Journal*, December 13, 1996.

75. Chan, "Democracy Derailed" in Chan and Clark, *The Hong Kong Basic Law.*

76. Chan and Lee, *Mass Media and Political Transition,* pp. 123–126.

77. Chen, "Louis Cha on Yu Pun-hoi."

78. *Hong Kong Economic Journal,* December 24, 1996, p. 18.

79. Born in Indonesia and educated in China during the Cultural Revolution, Oei controls China Strategic Investment with an investment of US$400 million in China which includes beer, rubber, and paper-making business. He buys China's failing state-owned enterprises and has up to 30 joint ventures in places like Shanxi, Hangzhou, Ningbo, and Dalian. Received by top Chinese leaders Jiang Zemin and Li Peng, Oei has been awarded several honorary professorships and advisorships by Chinese universities. But his wheeling and dealing has courted a sharp criticism by Beijing's *Financial Times;* Oei denied any wrongdoing and blamed the problem on China's underdeveloped legal system. See *The Nineties,* June 1996, pp. 7–8.

80. Ju, "Listen to the Voices of People on Taiwan," and Ju, "Assumptions Behind Commentaries on Taiwan."

81. Qi, "To the Granddaddy Up there, Yours Little Servant Confesses a Mistake."

82. Ibid.

83. Hong Kong Journalists Association, "China's Challenge," p. 42. Besides, the day after Wang Dan, a prominent Beijing democratic dissident, was sentenced (in 1996) to a 11-year prison term, most Hong Kong papers published editorials expressing concern. *Ming Pao* was silent on that day. It waited for one more day (and after many phone calls from the readers) to offer an ambiguously worded editorial.

84. The *Oriental Daily News* was once considered pro-Taiwan not because of its content (which was primarily apolitical) but because its owner jumped a jail bond on charges of drug trafficking and has been taking refuge in Taiwan, with which Hong Kong does not have a repatriation treaty.

85. So, "Pre-1997 Hong Kong Press: Cut-throat Competition and the Changing Journalistic Paradigm."

86. The *Apple Daily* has firmly captured one quarter of the circulation in one year, but only accounts for 10% of the total newspaper advertising revenues in Hong Kong. See *Hong Kong Economic Journal,* August 9, 1996, p. 4.

87. See HKEJ, "Jimmy Lai: 'I Have no Obligation to Take Care of My Opponents.'"

88. *China Times,* November 22, 1996. A former top assistant to Lai told me that Lai would or would not be an anti-communist publisher depending on whether anti-communism is a profitable commodity.

89. See, for example, Gans, *Deciding What's News,* Said, *Covering Islam.*

90. Ho, "China News in the Hong Kong Press."

91. The price of newsprint rose from US$300–400 to US$700–800 per ton. According to Dharmala Securities, newsprint accounts for 43% of the total cost for the *Oriental Daily News*; the corresponding figures are 20% for *SCMP,* 30% for *Ming Pao,* and 16% for *Sing Tao Jih Pao.*

92. During the six months from March to September, 1996, the Oriental Press group and the Sing Tao group posted a gain of HK$30.07 million and 4.92 million (or 78.3% and 76.2% drops from March-September, 1995), while *Ming Pao* reported a loss of $18.53 million. See *Hong Kong Economic Journal,* December 28, 1996, p. 9.

93. Ibid.

94. McManus, Market-driven Journalism, and Lee, "Conglomeration, Professionalism, and Strategic Rituals."

95. Chan and Lee, *Mass Media and Political Transition,* Chapter 3.

96. Xu, *Hong Kong Memoir,* and Ibid, p. 57.

97. During the 1995 elections the communist press actively campaigned for "patri-

otic candidates" from the Democratic Alliance for Betterment of Hong Kong (DAB) while almost completely ignoring the Democratic Party candidates. The non-communist papers invariably labeled the DAB candidates as "pro-China" and identified other candidates by their affiliation with the Democratic Party or the Liberal Party.

98. Bennett, "Toward a Theory of Press-State Relations in the United States."

99. Tuchman, *Making News*, Gans, *Deciding What's News*, Fishman, *Manufacturing the News*, Schlesinger, *Putting 'Reality' Together*, and Cohen and Young, *The Manufacture of News* .

100. Hallin, *The 'Uncensored' War*.

101. *South China Morning Post*, October 17, 1996.

102. Fan, "A Rugged Road for the Democratic Party after 1997."

103. Chan and Lee, *Mass Media and Political Transition,* Chapter 6.

104. Lee, "Conglomeration, Professionalism, and Strategic Rituals."

105. A poll by the Chinese University of Hong Kong found that 36% of Hong Kong's people see themselves as Chinese, while 49% identify themselves as "Hongkongese." See *New York Times*, June 8, 1996, p. 4.

106. *Eastweek*, August 11, 1993.

107. Quoted in Elliot, "Betrayed?"

108. Kairys, "Freedom of Speech."

109. We once wrote," Hong Kong's ordinances run into the hundreds, of which over 30 bear direct relevance to the media. Had these all been faithfully executed, Hong Kong would have written a very dark page in the history of press freedom." (Chan and Lee, *Mass Media and Political Transition*, p. 8). Many of the ordinances were enacted to cope with the leftist forces, but the British have generally refrained from invoking them. It is feared that such ordinances will assist the Chinese regime that is only too eager to control.

110. Davies, "Hong Kong Broadcasting."

111. The original version of the Broadcasting Ordinance and the Telecommunications Ordinance empowered the government to revoke licenses on security grounds and to censor films or television content prior to exhibition.

112. Caporaso and Levine, *Theories of Political Economy,* p. 93.

113. Chan and Clark, *The Hong Kong Basic Law*.

114. See Note 11.

115. O'Donnell, *Modernization and Bureaucratic-Authoritarianism.*

116. Lee, "Sparking a Fire: The Press and the Ferment of Democratic Change in Taiwan," and Yoon, "Political Transition and Press Ideology in South Korea, 1980–1988."

117. For the distinction between "negative freedom" and "positive freedom," see Berlin, *Four Essays on Liberty*. For media changes in China, see White, "All the News: Structure and Politics in Shanghai's Reform Media," Yu, "The Structure and Function of Chinese Television, 1979–1989," and Dittmer, "The Politics of Publicity in Reform China." To draw a comparison between the PRC and Taiwan, see Lee, "Ambiguities and Contradictions: Issues in China's Changing Political Communication."

118. Gold, "Go with Your Feelings: Hong Kong and Taiwan Popular Culture in Greater China."

119. Harding, "The Concept of Greater China: Themes, Variations and Reservations," and Tu, "Cultural China: The Periphery as the Center."

6

Hong Kong Families' Views of 1997

*Janet W. Salaff, Siu-lun Wong, and Mei-ling Fung**

As Hong Kong reverts to China in mid-1997, the political effects on the colony are hotly debated. To discern the local climate of opinion, surveyists poll elites and masses. Newsgroups debate the future of Hong Kong over the internet. Scholars analyze future economic and political scenarios. Looking for stability of Hong Kong, they study the inflow and outflow of resources. They study emigration and return migration and the terms emigrants use as indicators of their commitment to the new regime (Li, et al, 1994, nd.). These materials reflect widely diverse views and posit a wide range of future outcomes. In this chapter, instead of trying to predict the future, we turn to the views of the people that live in Hong Kong. How could those that have lived in Hong Kong for most of their lives arrive at such varied conclusions? The sociological contexts of people's views, what we call frames, need analysis.

There are precedents for such analyses. Isaacs (1956) described shifting Western opinions on the imperial and modern Chinese state. He found that nineteenth century French *philosophs* alternated between characterizing China as enlightened or despotic, as they projected European political struggles onto China. More

* This research was funded by the Hong Kong Research Grants Council and the Joint Centre for Asia Pacific Studies, Hong Kong Project Grant. The Department of Sociology and Centre of Asian Studies, University of Hong Kong and Centre for Urban and Community Studies, University of Toronto, gave us a helpful research environment. We thank the many respondents who generously gave their time and support.

recently, Richard Madsen (1995) finds in contemporary American views of China a projection of the West's values. In the 1980s, American opinion makers saw China as "becoming like us", interested in material goods and political expression. When the communist leadership sacrificed political expression to moral order on "June 4," Westerners were troubled by the question, "which is the 'real China'?" Madsen concludes that the "real" China is a social construction, a projection of the West's values or what he calls "cultural resources."

Jostling images of Hong Kong's reversion to China in 1997 are just as contradictory. In this chapter, we explore how people organize their stances toward 1997. We ground socially constructed popular views of "1997" held by ordinary Hong Kong Chinese in their individual social contexts. By distinguishing our own cultural frames from others' accounts, we learn more about what shapes Chinese identities.

Elements of the Social Construction of Views

There are three major sections in this paper on popular views on reversion to China. Our qualitative study first locates themes in a number of texts. Our texts are responses from people we interviewed. The texts consist of what people report they have done, their interpretations of their experiences, and their opinions on a number of issues. We organize these issues around two themes that emerge in the literature and in people's voices:
1. the economy versus the polity;
2. colonialism and nationalism.

To analyze these texts, we look at the terms people use in voicing these issues. These terms become what sociologists call "indicators" of themes. Indicators are our means of measuring how people align on issues.

Second, we group people's views to make sense of the range of perspectives of the 1997 reversion. Since the groupings or types are not logically deduced from a set of principles, we need to analyze what characterizes a version of an event, and how versions differ. We look at how twin themes of "economy versus politics," "colonialism and nationalism" cohere. We thus ask: "What attitudes are found together?"

Third, we look for an underlying structure to people's views. Naturalistic research like ours links people's opinions to their backgrounds and experiences. We believe that people make sense of their current predicament in a number of ways. People will construct their attitudes to make sense of their experiences. Political views arise from this sensemaking. To contextualize how people we met express their views toward the reversion, we locate the experiences shared by those that hold a version of events. We ask: "Which of their experiences most affect them?"

The rest of our chapter illustrates how these social contexts contribute to a number of views on Hong Kong's becoming China.

Two Major Themes

Economy Versus Polity

This is an important issue in export-oriented countries. On the "semi-periphery" of the world capitalist market, these economics survive by filling economic niches in the developed nations. Living in an entrepot, Hong Kong people are especially alert to world economic trends and to their family's place in the economy. Those in the region are said to be so alert to economic issues that they will align themselves with a strong economy at the cost of other options. It follows that if Hong Kong people perceive the HKSAR will benefit their families, they will commit themselves to working under the new regime. One indicator of people's stances on this theme is their expectations toward the economic future.

We can also look for the reasoning behind people's assessment of the Hong Kong economic engine. Some attribute Hong Kong's immense economic success to British colonial institutions. These are likely to worry about reversion to a country where legal accords and protections of contracts are in their infancy. Others, in contrast, attribute Hong Kong's spectacular growth to local and overseas Chinese businesspeople, and we would expect them to view reversion positively. We ask: "To whom do people attribute past economic growth: the colonial government, local Chinese capitalists and merchants, local labor, or international investment? Do they applaud the colonialists or appropriate Hong Kong Chinese 'ownership' of economic growth?"

Other scholars disagree that the economy comes first in this area of the Pacific Rim today. They point to an emergent Asian middle class voice that is concerned about freedom of expression (So and Kwitko, 1992; Scott, 1989). Still others disagree over whether expression is political, or an information exchange. We will explore the range of views on the newly created political institutions of the transition. Do they have faith in the Joint Accord? Are they ambivalent? Do they acquiesce because of lack of choice? Finally, do they worry that political expression will be curtailed as British institutions become Chinese?

Turning to the texts, or views we report upon, we will look for the balance of assessment of these alternative concerns of economic security versus political voice. Which of these will dominate and why? Further, to contextualize their comments, in this study our task is to understand who holds these views and how views cohere.

Colonialism and Nationalism

Ideology fuels attitudes toward independence from the colonial powers. Students of anti-colonial movements associate outbreaks of racial consciousness with decolonialization (Fanon, 1967). In Hong Kong, we expect that identification with their Chinese roots will be a central element of the views toward reversion in two ways. Resentment over the Anglo-Saxon leadership may fuel latent nationalism. Hong Kong people will consider their Chinese roots and oppose the British on this basis. Second, pride in China's world recognition and magnet of world capitalist investment boosts Hong Kong people's identification with their Chinese roots (Li, et al., n.d.). Hong Kong people feel part of the Chinese race, but not always part of the Chinese nation state. The proximity of reversion to China has prompted an interest in this identity.

In contrast, others deny that racism in cosmopolitan Hong Kong looms in people's consciousness. As evidence they point to reduced racial divisions in the colony after the Second World War. Instead, writers argue that since China did not encourage nationalism, people express attachment to Hong Kong mainly through a shared, identifiable lifestyle. Hong Kong people have a cultural identification with the territory.

The Hong Kong lifestyle is painted with broad strokes. The younger generation, born in Hong Kong and under age 35, most adhere to this lifestyle. They shared in the major social institutions, especially Hong Kong's densely concentrated housing estates, sponsored educational system, mass transit, and other public goods that shape common experiences. Some experienced political awakening, and participated in student political activities. Most powerful were cultural revolutionary outpourings in Hong Kong in the late 1960s, and ownership disputes over the Diaoyutai islands[1] both in the 1970s and in recent years. Young students join mobilization for wider enfranchisement, respond to campaigns on the greening of Hong Kong. They are sensitive to inequality in China, and help open hot lines for battered wives in China.

Apart from politics, those born and bred in Hong Kong are said to have a special local identity. This identity begins with assimilation to the local brand of culture with its Western-bias. Hong Kong locals have their "own" popular culture stars, their own slang. They scatter English phrases in their speech. They are at home with the Western based cultural "tool kits" from Windows 95, imported brand name clothing, international cuisine, and mass media. They feel "part of" Hong Kong (Tam, 1996; Cheng, 1995; Guldin, 1980; Choi, 1990; Li, et al, nd.).

But does this cultural identity serve as rallying point for political views? It has been thought that the commitment to Hong Kong culture would lead to rejection of reunification. But we can also suggest that, secure in a Hong Kong cultural identity, people may not fear unification.

In our study of themes of views toward Hong Kong's reversion to China, we will include: perceptions of colonialism and racism, and measures of a Hong

Kong identity. We will study how people articulate these issues and why they hold different stances on these themes.

Underlying Social Bases to Views About 1997

Identities are rooted in people's social experiences. By linking diverse experiences of these Hong Kong people to their social groups, we can understand sources of these views. The three key social group memberships that are likely to shape the views toward reunification of Hong Kong people are:
1. family history and networks;
2. generation or cohort which shapes cultural views; and
3. social class.

Family History and Networks

They are crucial because the family is an important group with which people align their activities and their viewpoints. Family and kinship are especially important for Hong Kong Chinese. We expect that family figures strongly in people's accounts of Hong Kong's reunification in several ways.

Views toward 1997 are likely to turn, first, on their family's experiences with China. We learn where their close members were born, grew up and currently live, whether members of the family are mainly in China, Hong Kong, or abroad. Whether the dispersion of the family has been a political or economic choice figures in their stance toward reversion to China. We need to learn the circumstances of family dispersion: did they flee politics? Poverty?

Social network theorists remind us that much behavior is "all in the family". On-going ties and connections with kin shape people's views. Some see kin often, others less. Those whose economic fates are intertwined and who see kin most often, are likely to share views. Those distant from kin are less likely to take them into account. Beyond kin, social networks of colleagues and friends that are in close contact are also likely to shape political and social attitudes.

Generational and Cohort Groups

These also contribute to the formation of political views. Studies of Hong Kong identity look first to birthplace and where people grew up. They note that most Hong Kong people are now brought up in Hong Kong. There is a strong cohort basis to the "Hong Kong identity."

Social Class

Social class position shapes access to resources, which also affects views. Business people with property view unification with the Chinese market differently from professional classes with bureaucratic careers. The working class have their own sets of resources that shape how they see the political transition. Different occupational statuses have identities that shape political views as well. (Wong, 1995; Li et al., nd.; Li et al., 1994; Ng & Cheng, 1994; Chai, 1992). Economic place in Hong Kong is critical, since the economic power of the Hong Kong-China nexus prompted the reunification (Scott, 1993).

The Sources of Our Material

Our chapter describes the range of opinions toward reversion to China of a small cohort of Hong Kong Chinese couples, whom we got to know well over the past half decade leading to 1997. They are part of a random survey of 1552 families from different social class groups living in Hong Kong in 1991 (Wong, 1995). At the time we saw emigration as a symbol of concern over 1997 (Wong, 1995) We spoke to them in detail on their views toward 1997 and intentions to emigrate.[2]

To understand more about how Hong Kong people view reversion to China, in 1992 we chose a panel of 30 people from from the survey roster. The original sample was a randomized survey, our subsample of 30 was a theoretical sample that emphasized two background features. First is social class. We chose an equal number of blue collar laborers, white collar employees and those more affluent. We call this a theoretical sampling frame because we expected that class experience would shape views toward reversion. Although they predominate in Hong Kong and in our sample, we chose relatively fewer people in working class jobs. We chose relatively more petty bourgeois and bourgeois families in order to have enough people in these groups to interview.

The second basis of selection was their intent to emigrate. Emigration has been widely taken as evidence of disaffection with Hong Kong's reversion to China. Emigration applications from Hong Kong peaked during the late 1980s. Our original random sample survey found that only 7% had taken steps to emigrate. For our in-depth study, we chose relatively more that had taken steps to emigrate. In order to study this decision-making process, we chose equal numbers of potential emigrants and those that did not intend to emigrate. Our in-depth study is not unrepresentative, since it follows the original random sample survey. It is, however, called a "theoretical sample frame," because it follows up the original survey with a sample that best answers the queries that we most needed to ask.

Our respondents were of different ages. They ranged from two unmarried men aged 30 when we met to an elderly retired ivory carver, since deceased. Twenty-eight were married and we focused on the family they formed by marriage. Two are unmarried men, and we studied the families in which they grew up. In all cases we also learned about their wider kinship units, which are relevant to their lives.

In all but one case, we talked with the couples separately and together. Their views sometimes were the same and sometimes differed. Since we group their views here by couple, we had to give them one single perspective, however. We found that couples have arrived at a working consensus about the actions they will take as they approach 1997. This agreement is clearest on the decision whether to emigrate or to adapt to local life in Hong Kong.[3]

We consider it important to contextualize people's answers. We place them in their personal contexts as if we were doing a "sociology of the individual." We describe their circles of social relations. These include their close kin and friends they saw and to whom they looked for advice. These 30 respondent families identified 400 siblings, parents and children, whose location is an important part of our analysis.

We interviewed these folk yearly from 1991 through 1996. We talked with them, and joined in some of their activities in this naturalistic study. We transcribed the interviews, or recorded them from notes. The comments are close renditions of what they said, and hence we call them texts. In 1991 and 1992, these couples shared with us their views toward the transition. Our follow-up interviews, reported on here, aimed to match their later actions with earlier views. Indeed, we remain in touch with nearly all, including the emigrants. We plan to carry forward our talks to update their experiences in the aftermath of reversion to China.

Chinese Identities

We organize our texts into patterns of political attitudes. Their diverse views of Hong Kong reversion politics challenge a simplistic view of the identities constructed by Hong Kong people as they count down to 1997. Here, we organize them into four sets of political views:

1. Some are keen on reversion. Family centered, they see reversion as good for their family. We call these "Loyalists."
2. Some are more ambivalent, others cling to Hong Kong as the promised land. They especially enjoy the lifestyle. We call them "Hong Kong Locals."
3. The "Waverers" have changed their minds over the period we studied them, from antagonism to the HKSAR to resigned acceptance.
4. Finally, some see themselves as China's "Class Enemies." They hold fairly negative views toward reversion politics.

Loyalists

Six of the 30 respondent-couples are Loyalists. Loyalists are not anguished by the idea of returning to China.

Economy Versus Polity

Loyalists do not seek to return to the past. They are not well to do. First is their origin. The closing of the border in the early 1950s divided some working class families. Others later fled village poverty illegally and could not bring their families to Hong Kong. The three lower middle class couples lack cultural capital in Hong Kong. They came legally to Hong Kong to join family members, and left kin behind. But they could not reproduce their mainland cultural capital in Hong Kong and lost the solid position they had enjoyed in China. There are no upper middle class Loyalists.

Economic concerns dominate Loyalists' views. The past means hard times to them. They are grateful that the turn toward privatization in China has improved the position of those in their family left behind, whom they now no longer have to support. They expect that after reunification with Hong Kong, China will continue to progress to economic modernity. So should Hong Kong.

These Hong Kong folk profess continued confidence in the future HKSAR economy, because they do not cede much to the colonial state. Some credit local Chinese merchant families with Hong Kong's success; others credit Hong Kong's development to its standing as an "international city." Having taken "ownership" of Hong Kong's development prowess, they maintain that Hong Kong can continue without the British. More, they criticize the British for monopolizing profitable opportunities and distorting the economy. Transportation is often mentioned. The litany of complaints start with the double decker buses imported from England, going on to the MTR subway, and on to most recently, the new airport. Will Chinese politics disrupt the Hong Kong economy? The Loyalists expect there is no reason for China to upset the Hong Kong rice bowl.

This confidence stems also from their political experiences in China. These are not particularly negative. The family of only one of the six had owned property in the past, and had that property taken away. But his wife did not have that experience and her view has come to dominate in the couple's assessment of 1997. Three respondent-couples lived in China during the Cultural Revolution, but managed to miss its most demoralizing features.

Colonialism and Nationalism

The Loyalists voice attachment to China's culture. They feel Hong Kong rightly is politically part of China. In this power vacuum, it does not make sense to most to throw their weight on the side of the retreating colonial regime. However, they are not politically involved. Nor do they have a refugee or a sojourner mentality. Rather most express their belonging to Hong Kong, referring to their participation in the lifestyle that has emerged in Hong Kong. They believe the "one country, two systems" formula will protect their way of life in Hong Kong.

Underlying Social Bases to Political Themes: Family, Generation, and Social Networks

Loyalists were born in China and lived their formative years there.[4] They found themselves divided between China and Hong Kong when the border closed after 1950; the ways they were separated from their China kin differs by their ages. Two elderly men were caught on the Hong Kong side when the border closed. Two middle-aged couples came legally to Hong Kong later on to join family members. Two men dared flee China when they had only to "touch base" in Hong Kong to remain.

Because they emigrated late in their lifetimes, their ties to Chinese kin are ongoing and dense. They see these ties as important to them. They cross the border to see their China kin often, and hope they can have closer contact after reunification. They may give kin money, and their economic fates are intertwined with kin. Four of the six have shared an occupation with kin. In Hong Kong their economic way of life has been intertwined with the mainland economy.

The following table describes the whereabouts of 73 "kin units" of the Loyalist couples.[5] Although most of the Loyalists' kin units live in Hong Kong, a substantial proportion are in China. The Western nations claim few. As many live in other Asian communities (Taiwan, Indonesia, the Philippines) as in the West. That most have kin in Hong Kong or China helps explain the basis of their turnings toward China. With few kin living abroad at the time of our study, these folk have no plans to go West. Their attention is drawn to China. Indeed three of the six couples have recently bought new homes and moved part of their household to China.

Table 6.1

Location of Loyalist Kin Units
(six couples or 12 respondents, their parents, siblings and children)

	Number	Percentage
China	16	22
Hong Kong	40	55
The West	8	11
Other Asian Places	9	12
TOTAL	73	100

Loyalists include people in different age groups and with different patterns of movement to Hong Kong. But they share views toward economy and politics in the HKSAR future. Let us start with an elderly couple that lives in the traditional Hong Kong western district. The husband uses the abacus to render accounts in a firm trading in dried imported fungi and other foodstuffs from China and Japan. The wife is a homemaker, who cares for her new grandchild and does some putting out work.

The 1949 Chinese Communist Revolution divided his family, and for years the husband could only travel to visit his wife and two children a few times a year. After decades of effort, his wife and youngest daughter legally joined him in Hong Kong. The other married daughter and her family remain in China. They keep close contact, and the Hong Kong branch often sends money and help. Yet the husband is pleased that the kind of help he used to give them is no longer needed because China's economy has improved so much. Further, the daughter's family does not wish to move to Hong Kong now that they can get solid working class jobs (as driver, factory worker) suited to their skills in China. Such experientially based information gives him pride in China's accomplishments.

The husband does not worry that much will change to his family in Hong Kong and China after 1997. Despite his pride in China's improvements, he considers himself a "Hong Kong person." As do many southerners, he constructs a regional stereotype of northern Chinese as rude, country bumpkins. He mentions many examples of his identity with Hong Kong. For instance, he enjoys the same kinds of leisure as do others in Hong Kong. The couple joins tour groups to Asia and China. The husband notes that his reading patterns are typically those of Hong Kong. He reads through many newspapers daily. He responded to our queries about freedom of the media, "Like the newspapers, the quality of TV has been lowered. Of course it's related to 1997! It's essential for the Communist Party to control mass media. In the past they did so and will also do it in the future. Maybe not as tight as in China. Probably, media control will be as in Shenzhen, which anyway is becoming more open in recent years."

He qualifies to vote, but has never used the ballot. He anticipates he can survive the narrowing of political expression in the press. When asked about Governor Patten's moves to expand voting, he replied that the new policies are not useless, "just too theoretical." He views the British colonial establishment cynically, "It wrings money from the Hong Kong people."

Like other loyalists that see Hong Kong as a Chinese subculture, akin to Guangdong province, he believes the two territories are economically interdependent. Further, he feels that Hong Kong truly belongs to China. In his case, his Pacific rim trade in the wholesale of dried seafood serves as an example, and he concludes that the Hong Kong people need Chinese trade. "Hong Kong has to exist with China."

Proud of his roots in China, he sees reversion as historically inevitable. He stated he would never emigrate. "In each place, there will always be a time of adjustment. But you get used to it. The difference is "roots." Even if you have a good life abroad, your roots will always come back to China. We Chinese are traditional and like to help one another. China has a lot of troubles now, and we'll try to help one another and become even stronger." He was, in the end, Chinese.

Two middle-aged Loyalists from Fukian province in our sample arrived legally in the 1960s to reunite with elderly Hong Kong family members. They are not well to do in Hong Kong, although their family background was above average in China.

For instance, a Fukian couple were post-secondary graduates in Shenyang and were posted to Sichuan. They moved to Hong Kong to reunite with the husband's family. Hoping to better their living standards, they found their credentials are not recognized in Hong Kong. Without "cultural capital," they turned to working-class jobs.

Nevertheless, they felt attached to Hong Kong. The husband said he felt like a Hong Kong person, although his Cantonese accent might be hard to understand. "When you work in a place and get involved, you gradually get attached to life there. When I lived in Shenyang and Sichuan, I did not commit myself to life there, but I do in Hong Kong." He spoke emotionally about wanting to be regarded as a Hong Kong person, even though local Cantonese might argue against it.

China politics do not embitter them. No longer students during the Cultural Revolution, the couple did not participate in the Cultural Revolution. They simply felt that the Red Guards were impractical. From his safe Hong Kong perch, the husband interpreted the June 4 crackdown like the Cultural Revolution. He stated that while he did not like corruption he preferred milder ways of appeal, "Those naive students knew too little!" He considers himself a realist that pays more attention to his family's economic living than to politics or protest. The husband optimistically believed Hong Kong would remain autonomous, and Hong Kong's return to China would not seriously affect the future of Hong Kong. "Hong Kong, the source of wealth, will not be ill-treated by China, its master."

Their family bonds link them to other Fukian-originated kin in the Philippines or Taiwan. Few go directly to the West. The sister of the college graduate couple, a nurse, emigrated from Fukian to the Philippines and thence to the United States. But this path does not originate in Hong Kong and does not tempt our couple. Instead of going abroad, our contacts feel more comfortable returning to China. Another returned to his Fukian village to look for suitable work from kin when he quit his Hong Kong job.

Improving family economies by crossing the border is part of family plans. A young construction worker fled his impoverished Paoan village in a "snakeboat" a decade ago. Arriving in Hong Kong, he phoned his uncle who fetched him to safety. He then joined his older brother and older sister who already lived in the colony. His parents and five other siblings remained in China. Having fled China's poverty, our respondent greatly improved his earnings doing heavy construction work. "In fact, Father asked me to come to Hong Kong for my own benefit," he stressed. He finally could afford an arranged match with an Indonesian Chinese, who came to Hong Kong on a bridal tour. Now the two brothers live with their families in an apartment they bought together. They work in interior decoration and construction with their elder sister, her husband, and their uncle.

The pair of brothers visit their China kin several times a year, on the major Chinese holidays. They are familiar with conditions back home. Compared with the harsh life in China, our respondent was satisfied with Hong Kong life. They know that China's economic reforms have raised the living standard of his village. They expect reunification to bring the two parts of the family closer in many ways. But our respondent strongly feels that life in Hong Kong is much better, and is not willing to return to China. "Go back to live? What an idea!" he retorted rhetorically to our question.

While the lad may not welcome the return of Hong Kong to China, ("The best would be not to take back Hong Kong!"), he had great confidence in Hong Kong's future. "I don't believe that China will ruin Hong Kong because there's no point in doing so." Young and from a rural family, he had not experienced much of the Cultural Revolution, and had little information about past political events in China. Asked whether his parents told him about the Cultural Revolution, he responded forcefully, "It was China's policy! How could we dare to talk about it?" Nevertheless, he thought that what the communists had done on June 4 or during the Cultural Revolution would not happen again in Hong Kong. "According to my friends' opinions, there should be no great change after 1997."

The brothers were critical of the Hong Kong government's economic policy. They felt that the Hong Kong government looked after the rich, not people of their class. The elder brother complained, "Take hiring foreign workers. Just because they can speak a few English words, they were able to get a high paid job at the airport. And because we can't speak English, we end up with a low paid job."

Indifferent about the transition, they plan to treat July 1, 1997 as a holiday. "It has nothing to do with us. We work as usual. Maybe there will be a public holiday." Did they vote? The younger brother replied, "It doesn't make a difference to me. I told my wife to throw the form away. I don't know the candidates, how can I vote?' The elder brother had voted with faint enthusiasm. He spoke against the use of English in documents, "I did vote, but just blindly chose among the candidates. Most of the information and discussion was in English, and I don't understand any of it. If I could understand, why would I be doing hard work as a coolie, or as a construction worker? It's very simple, the more educated you are, the more pay you get." Their economic view dominated their politics.

Family economies, theirs and those of China kin, shape the terms through which Loyalists voice acceptance of reversion. While the economy does not solely define their views, it influences an approach to politics and nationalism in which reunification with China is inevitable, natural, and acceptable.

Hong Kong Locals

Nine couples are deeply Hong Kong based, and we call them "Hong Kong Locals." Locals expect China to continue to progress economically and politically, but have no personal connection to China. Nor do they express an affinity to the British. They are firmly attached to Hong Kong, yet accept the changeover without fanfare.

Economy Versus Polity

Their view toward the economy is rooted in their social and demographic characteristics, starting with social class. They were born to working and lower middle class families, who were not subject to political movements on the mainland. Most are fairly young. Brought up in Hong Kong, they are politically neutral. They own some property, which they got entirely from their own cultural capital in Hong Kong, struggling hard to finish school and secure a career. They feel part of Hong Kong's development.

Few are politically minded. They see Hong Kong as an economic colony, and expect it will continue as such. Two applied to emigrate, "as insurance" in case there is economic chaos. But few expect chaos, and they do not plan to leave. Reversion to China symbolizes the integration of the two economies. This integration may affect Hong Kong's economy in the short run, but is inevitable. China and Hong Kong cannot be unified overnight, and there will be turnings in the road. Wait and see is a common view. "Give the Chinese time, they have to learn how Hong Kong works."

Colonialism and Nationalism

Hong Kong Locals ally their future with the territory. They give voice to identity, nationalism, a search for roots, and anti-colonialism. They not only do not oppose reversion to China. They are glad that the British will pull out and leave Hong Kong for the Hong Kong people. Neutral, having accepted reversion to China as natural, they are proud of being Chinese.

They are closely attached to the local cultural lifestyle, which includes wide ranging personal expression. Trepidation about reversion mainly turns on fear of loss of this lifestyle.

Underlying Social Bases to Political Themes: Family, Generation, and Social Networks

Hong Kong Locals have most of their important kin in Hong Kong.[6] They no longer have close bonds to China. Few have kin abroad. Only 22% of the kin units applied to emigrate. And in no family in this group do both husband and wife have kin abroad. Thus, the emigrant kin do not form a dense overseas group that these couples wish to join. They are not torn in different geographical directions. To the contrary, their focus is on Hong Kong.

Table 6.2

Location of Hong Kong Locals' Kin Units
(eight couples or 16 respondents, their parents, siblings and children)

	Number	Percentage
China	4	4
Hong Kong	93	85
The West	8	8
Other Asian Places	4	4
TOTAL	109	100

This pattern includes a young lower-middle class couple that works in large Hong Kong bureaucracies. The wife is a member of the administrative civil service. Her husband, an engineer with a diploma, is employed in Cathay Pacific Airlines, and works on airport-related projects in China. Politically, husband and wife feel they do not take sides. Although both work for the British, they do not identify with the colonial order. They are proud to be Hong Kong Chinese and at the same time look forward to China's regaining sovereignty.

In a tentative emigration step, the wife applied for the United Kingdom Right of Abode. She later dropped the application as it appeared more trouble than it was worth, especially since she sensed she might be turned down. After her elder sister graduated from a marketing course in England and married a Hong Kong Chinese naturalized UK citizen, the couple saw even less reason to apply to emigrate. They reasoned if life in Hong Kong became too chaotic, the younger sister would return to England and would sponsor them. The couple did not expect this however, for they had faith in the Sino-British Joint Declaration. Family oriented, they are loath to separate from local kin, whom they visit weekly.

Neither concerns about the economy nor worry about law and order after 1997 propels them to leave Hong Kong. "I think the living standard will drop in the years to come. There won't be enough space for all the people who will flood into Hong Kong from China. So, if you're interested in changing your life, you should do it now, or it will be too late. That's why we've already bought our own apartment. On the other hand, the effect of 1997 will be minimal on the overall financial situation of the colony.

"The most important thing is to make the society a safe place. Politics, laws, and the public order are most important. If the SAR does not change the laws, our society won't be in trouble. In China, it's common that 'there's no law except for the officials.' If they say you make a mistake, even if you have proven yourself innocent, as long as the accuser is a high-ranking official you'll be found guilty. There's a lot of red tape, and black can even turn into white. It's different in Hong Kong where you have to go to court to prove that you are guilty. So, I worry about this part. I don't worry much about the economy. Maybe because I don't expect too much for myself, that's why the economy aspect doesn't seem a big problem. I think basic necessities like food and housing will not be affected at all."

She judges Governor Patten: "I don't have much of an opinion about him because I don't like politics. But I feel he's in a bit of a rush, and that can't benefit the Hong Kong people. He doesn't work for us, just thinks of himself. We all know who asked him to come here (the British)! But we can't blame him. Because a lot of Hong Kong people, including me, don't know whether democracy is good or bad." (Question: "Do you feel that legal reforms have been done in haste?") "Yes, so fast that I feel it's a bit unsafe." Further, she felt insecure that her fate depended on a few lower class voters that turned out. "Actually, few people voted. Take night watchmen. The Governor just goes and talks to these people, then they will vote for him. But what do they represent? Nothing compared to the rest who don't vote and who're the most influential in Hong Kong.

"I don't have any interest in politics, I wasn't the type who joined activities even when I was in school. So, nothing has really changed. My activity is just my family, and other things are minor. In Hong Kong, a lot of people are like me, they only care about their own business . . .

"At the time of June 4, I felt the Chinese government made a mistake. But looking back at it now, they must have their own reasons for doing it. There's no perfect government. A government can't please everybody!"

Her husband thought people should only vote if they were experts. He did not feel knowledgeable enough.

"I won't waste my time knowing in detail the election dates and the people involved, because I don't believe in what they say. That's why I decided not to concentrate on this election thing. Actually, the candidates have their good points. I think they are good people. But it is very difficult to tell who works hard and who doesn't. You can't do research on them. Like a salesman, there are good and bad things about a product, and it all depends on what the customer wants. . . . Hong Kong is just starting running elections, that's why not everybody spends time on it. Most of us don't have the time to play this 'game.' But even if I were to spend enough time, I don't think it would make a difference . . . Besides, you don't really know the candidate. Like for instance, in a certain district, if you feel that the candidate is not good, you can't even complain. The only thing you can do is not to vote for him, but instead vote for the other candidate. There's nothing you can really do about elections. So sometimes you can feel that it's just a waste of time.

Suppose I didn't vote for him, and he won! So for me, elections don't mean anything. As long as it doesn't affect me, then it is okay. But I won't waste my time. Whoever wins, I won't feel bad for the other party who lost. . . .

"It's just like horse racing. Some just bet for fun, while some really read and study it carefully before placing their bet. Elections also depend on the seriousness of the person voting. If I am going to spend a lot of time knowing the candidate, I might as well spend it on horses . . .

"As long as it doesn't affect the lifestyle of the people, who can continue to work and live, then who owns the place is not important."

Another engineer with a diploma, married to a nurse, similarly expressed alienation from local politics because of his lack of expertise. He, too, argued that since he could not spend time on the issue, it would be better if he left it to others that could. "I'm sorry that I'm not interested in politics," he apologized. "When I find things that I can't control, I get very lazy. Knowing the result is enough. I think one single vote is not important. In fact, all you can know about the candidates is what you get from their propaganda. It's not much. I may not vote for the right person. If I vote in a bad candidate, I'll make the situation even worse!"

A computer systems hardware consultant stressed the opportunities he could get by seizing the advantage in this uncertain time. He intended to marry a locally rooted woman and did not intend to emigrate. But he applied for Singapore residency as security. He argued, "In the long run, China will become more open, with the influx of outside knowledge and information. But in the short run, before reaching that stage, there may be fluctuation and bloodshed, similar to civil war. So insurance [his Singapore immigration papers] is necessary." He did not plan to emigrate, however. His papers were a fallback. "In a crisis, heroes have a good chance to show their abilities. There may be lots of opportunities after 1997. So when my brother (also an emigrant to Singapore) asked me if we could jointly buy a house in Singapore, I refused. I won't leave unless the situation worsens rapidly and is life threatening."

Yet another Hong Kong Local is a self employed car mechanic, who spent his youth in China. He owns his tools but rents a pair of small shacks where he does the repairs. The wife is a driver of a school van. With the two incomes, they live a modest but comfortable working class life. They have made a deposit on a new low cost apartment. The husband expressed pride in China's new strength and power to determine policy. He stressed that the British "did not belong" in Hong Kong. The return of Hong Kong to China after 1997 was at least better than "foreign rule" under Britain. It was better for "Chinese to rule over Chinese." He felt that the recent Policy Speech by Governor Patten was "useless," since China "should" take over Hong Kong The rule of British government in the past was only "so-so." In our talks, he mainly criticized, not praised, what the British had done through its monopoly over the colony's economic sector. "Voting is not useful because those who had been elected are wealthy people of status. Thus, lower class interests [like ours] will remain unattended," he argued. "Forced to choose between British and China's communist rule, I'd chose China because it has improved over the past." He believed that communist rule would not necessarily limit Hong Kong's freedom.

The wife believed in democratic opportunities and parted from her husband's optimism. She worried that without democracy, there would be corruption in Hong Kong. She thought that China would not act according to its signed agreement. "I agree with [Singapore leader] Lee Kwan Yew, that it is impossible for China, without democracy in its past history, to democratize." Asked about her opinion about June 4, she retorted, "no money, no opinion." She meant that it was useless for her to worry since without money, she must stay in Hong Kong. She had no plan to emigrate. Nevertheless, the couple acknowledged that they do not fear the rule of communist China after 1997. "We're not wealthy and will not become targets. We can survive if we're not outspoken."

Waverers

We term Waverers those families that had wanted to emigrate but were turned down by foreign communities. Over the course of our interviews. many changed their views from critical anxiety to "wait and see," and even on to acceptance of reversion to China. There are eight couples in this category.

Economy Versus Polity

Waverers are mostly working class. Their lack of resources made it hard for them to emigrate. Once rejected, they do not have the resources to reapply to other countries or for visas in other categories. They have not merely given up, however. They have reframed their views. Cynical and negative about China when we first met, they are now more optimistic. They had been outraged by the June 4 Tiananmen events. Since then, they now expect no immediate change in Hong Kong. They do not expect their children to suffer. However, they remain more negative than the Hong Kong Locals we met. Waverers distrust the Chinese system, and prefer what the British have done in the colony to what they see in China.

Colonialism and Nationalism

Waverers are pragmatists, not ideologues. They had enjoyed the Hong Kong way of life and saw it threatened by the new regime. They tried to leave for a more secure future, failed, and readjusted to a life in Hong Kong. They would accept this life because it promised enough comfort, not because they "belonged' to the new nation.

Family, Generation, and Social Networks

Waverers are enmeshed in networks that reach abroad. Although they were mainly born in Hong Kong, many of their kin live abroad, and others have applied to emigrate.[7] Forty percent of Waverers' siblings applied to emigrate to a Western nation or already live there. They recognize few mainland kin. That their circles include those that think of going abroad, or who have gone abroad figures in their attitudes toward 1997.

Table 6.3

Location of Waverers' Kin Units
(eight couples or 16 respondents, their parents, siblings, and children)

	Number	Percentage
China	11	1
Hong Kong	84	73
The West	24	21
Other Asian Places	6	5
TOTAL	115	100

As an example we introduce a prison guard, married to a homemaker, formerly a garment seamstress. Both were born in Hong Kong, and recognize no kin ties to China. They have no real attachment abroad either. The husband considers himself a Hong Kong person and expects that China will corrupt Hong Kong. He and his sister, also a prison guard, applied for the UK Right of Abode. She was accepted while he was not. He still wishes he could take his family out of Hong Kong.

The couple does not identify ideologically with China, and ethnic identification as Chinese does not bridge the credibility gap. "Although the Chinese shared the same race, people in Hong Kong have a different lifestyle." He referred to the social and economic systems, as well as freedom of speech. He lacked confidence in the commitments of the Chinese government in the Sino-British Joint Declaration. He argued, "Such promises are made by the leaders who are very old. They may not be still alive after 1997. When others come into power, they may say this promise was only made by previous leaders, and refuse to follow it." He wanted to take the family to the United Kingdom, "We're used to the UK system. We're not so secure with the communist system. But in the UK, there is freedom!"

On the other hand, he acknowledged, "Hong Kong will not become as bad as China. Firstly, Hong Kong people will still control the place, not people from China. If that were not the case, China could order big changes. Of course, there will be some changes, but they will take time. A major change will take maybe 10 years. Like now, there are already some changes. There's nothing you can do but just to abide by them. Eventually, you'll get used to it. A few years ago, I was a bit scared. But right now, it doesn't worry me anymore. Even if you go to another place, so what? You need to adjust again, start learning new things and meeting people."

He stressed the importance of maintaining law and order, perhaps because of his civil service job. Regarding June 4, "You cannot say that the students are completely wrong. They are partly wrong in a sense that they protested in a public place. Beijing is the capital of the country. If you protest there, you're committing an offense. That's why the government has to do something to make you realize that it is wrong. Of course, their method might be wrong, but they have to do it. They need to make it clear to everybody, or else nobody is going to listen to the government."

His wife also lacked confidence in the Chinese government. She disliked the working style of the Chinese bureaucrats, listing examples of corruption from mainland officials. Thus she was afraid that after 1997 Hong Kong officials would become as corrupt as those of China. Nevertheless, having no real choice, they adjusted to remaining in Hong Kong.

The bitter choice of the Waverers was sweetened by Hong Kong's prosperity for people of their class. They ended up reasoning that while they could not leave, at least they would be economically better off in Hong Kong.

Class Enemies of China

In sharp contrast, those opposed to reunification with China prefer life as it was. Many are political emigrants who fled China. They see themselves as China's Class Enemies. There are seven couples in this group.

Class Enemies have upper middle class backgrounds. Five of the seven are now upper middle class; the remaining two never regained their position after their families' property was confiscated in China. Class Enemies account for half the upper middle class in our sample. Their response is not panic and exit. Instead, they planned their escape for years. They organized for emigration well in advance of 1997

Economy Versus Polity

Class Enemies have deep misgivings about the Chinese political system. Political justice is salient to those four couples who had close family members that suffered politically in China; the collective memory of having lost family property in China fuels their anxiety about 1997.

Others have not experienced class-based discrimination in China. But their experiences as businessmen or professionals in China shakes their trust in China's ability to handle the delicately balanced Hong Kong economy. They attribute Hong Kong's economic development to the presence of the British colonial government and the absence of China's "rule of people, not of law."

Colonialism and Nationalism

Class Enemies did not express strong feelings of "belonging" to China simply because they were of the Chinese race. They spoke more in cosmopolitan terms. Since they were "Chinese", they did want to "help" China; however, they wished to help from a professional vantage point. Their criticism came when they could not do so. They felt China did not use their talents in the way they felt they should be used. They were most annoyed with China's bureaucrat-officials.

Family, Generation, and Social Networks

Class Enemies do not have ongoing dependency ties with China kin. Class Enemies were mainly born in Hong Kong.[8] Some were born in China of well-to-do parents, who fled after land reform when their property was taken away leaving behind kin in the rush to flee. They lack ongoing contact with their siblings on the mainland because of this politically caused rupture. Two couples come from a long line of Hong Kong kin. Their parents before them were born in Hong Kong as well.

Table 6.4

Location of Kin Units of Class Enemies
(seven couples or 14 respondents, their parents, siblings and children)

	Number	Percentage
China	5	5
Hong Kong	67	65
The West	28	27
Other Asian Places	3	3
TOTAL	103	100

Few still have kin in China. Those that do have broken with them years before. Loyalists who have part of their kin units in China want to help them, and favor family reunification. In contrast, the Class Enemies' decision to leave China for Hong Kong is not shaped by any need to help kin. They do not contribute to a common family economy with mainland kin. Indeed, for some the contrary is the case: China represents a place where ties to kin were rup-

tured. The absence of identification with mainland kin reinforces negative attitudes toward China.

Most have kin abroad in the Western nations that are the major destinations
for Hong Kong emigrant Chinese. They have close friends and classmates abroad
as well, with whom they keep in contact. They are part of a stratum that spans
the seas. They have more kin abroad than in China, and all have close kin that
applied to emigrate. Three of the four upper middle class couples that have
exited Hong Kong already have siblings or children abroad.

For instance, the parents of two couples fled when their property was appropriated, leaving behind several older siblings, the separation rupturing family
ties. They do not take China kin into account in their daily actions. On the other
hand, another couple increasingly comes into contact with their Chinese kin, and
increased contact moderates views.

Kin abroad, not those in China, most shape their opinions. These kin portray
life overseas. They provide information, and tend to reinforce negative views
about Chinese anti-democratic processes.

Many Class Enemies have applied to emigrate. Some have left. Those that
applied to emigrate express their lack of faith in the institutional protections in
the Joint Declaration in more extreme terms than those that have not applied.
Those with the strong negative political views have already exited. The greatest
misgivings about reunification lie in this group, and include concerns about
corruption.

Those that have applied to emigrate, but have not left, are mildly negative
about China's likely political acts in Hong Kong. However, they believe Chinese
political processes are improving. They tend to stress China's inability, not lack
of integrity. In this weak version of disaffection, they expect that the Joint
Declaration will be maintained. These mildly negative views do not propel
people outward.

The first two Class Enemies we meet here did not lose property, yet still feel
deep class-based disaffection from China, while the third lost property.

A manager emigrated on his retirement. He and his wife were born in Hong
Kong; their parents before them lived in Hong Kong most of their lives. Their
three children live abroad. The two eldest had gotten degrees in Toronto col-
leges, married and stayed on, and the parents joined them several years later.
They have other siblings abroad, but these ties are not economic and not dense.
They state their decision to emigrate was not due to reversion, but to bring the
family together, to help out their children as much as they can by being present.
As well, they prefer the Canadian lifestyle.

A businessman, who managed a van service that delivers Hong Kong publications to chain stores, derived all his funds from businesses based in Hong
Kong. He prefers retirement to starting a new career in China trade. He suspects
corruption in China would undercut earnings. He predicts that the PRC's assumption of political control in Hong Kong will introduce rampant corruption as

on the mainland. He also anticipates that China will take control of local institutions. From this view, the children will do better in Toronto than in Hong Kong. They are deeply suspicious of the Joint Declaration — "It's on paper only." The couple expresses no loyalty to China.

An administrator, keen to leave Hong Kong, increased contacts with his wife's kin in Canada. The family had no kin in China, nor did they lose property there. Rather, the husband's desire to emigrate was grounded in British-oriented cultural capital. From his position as a senior management staff in the real estate department of a major British firm, he saw the orderliness of British rule. He contrasted this with his view of "lawlessness" in China. He thought there would be no hope for his family in Hong Kong, he also sought to place his challenged son in a better life abroad. The family "landed" in Canada at considerable cost, and the husband has returned to Hong Kong to a new job to secure his family finances.

He placed a lot of importance on education. Having struggled through adult education class to get an MA. he felt that the Chinese government put too little effort on education. He thought that the education standard of the Chinese can be raised only after "the age-old rulers go." He had hoped to contribute what he learned to educate the Chinese people. "I have Chinese blood. I wish to help China modernize." He tried to give his expertise to China, but the experience of teaching in China disappointed him. "Several hundred [of us in Hong Kong] to educate several billion is just like a drop of water in the ocean!" "I love China but China doesn't love us [Hong Kong people]." Having had dealings with China, he found Chinese bureaucrats hard to work with. He feared the corruption he saw in China was already coming to Hong Kong. "We have increased our vigilance here, but we Hong Kong people have a double standard. When we go there, we pay. We give people gifts. Maybe we hire Chinese policemen to protect our buildings. If you build in Hong Kong, it's simple, you can get gas, water, light. Here, we have guards, or our own people. In China, it's hard. You have to visit the offices of gas, water, light one by one, go to the higher ups, give them gifts and only then can you get service." The raging debate on political reforms further confirmed to him that the "one country, two systems" proposal is insincere." He was disappointed at the comments of the Chinese officials which undermined Sino-British relations. He exclaimed, "Seven million people are under the control of such kind of people!"

"The future of Hong Kong and China is just like mixing lemon tea with water. Hong Kong will be worse off by sharing her benefits with China. China will be better because she gets the benefits of Hong Kong." He thought that there was too much uncertainty in Hong Kong's future. "No one wants to leave Hong Kong, but the environment forces us to."

The family waited until 1996 to sell their apartment, until then they lived as ordinary Hong Kong people. The only difference was that their passports enabled them to leave whenever necessary. The husband told us in 1995, "I'm not afraid. I have the British passport. I can leave at any time." He also said, "Emigration is the last resort." To him, holding a passport was like buying an insurance policy. "When you have bought the insurance policy, you put it aside. . . . When you need it, you take it out again." The family finally landed in Canada in early 1996.

The husband maintained that he emigrated for his son's sake. In 1993 he told us, "I am now 45 years old. In 1997, I'll be an old man. It doesn't mean much to me whether I stay in Hong Kong or not, but it's for the next generation." Although he believes that "he cannot become rich in a foreign country," he hopes that his son can "live in a liberal land."

A supermarket clerk, whose family lost its property in China, married a butcher in Hong Kong. The husband now works for the butcher shop owned by the wife's father. The wife recounted, "The Communist Party forced my father to give his land to the Party and distribute it to the poor. A few years later, there was another movement of workers dissatisfied with the employers. In 1958 everything was taken over by the state. My father owned a butcher shop, became afraid and fled to Hong Kong. He had suddenly changed from the employer to employee in a year. He started his pork business again in Hong Kong. After his business was stable, he applied for my mother and some of my siblings to Hong Kong and later the rest of us. So, my father hated the Communist Party. He seldom returned to China, but as for me, in these few years, the situation has changed. The Chinese government is not focusing on politics and has become more economic minded. If the open door policy can still continue, the situation will be better."

She joined the street demonstrations on June 4, 1989. "I am Chinese so I want to join these functions. Support the students! People in China cannot express their views and we in Hong Kong can. So I think we should make use of this opportunity." She was pessimistic about Hong Kong after 1997. She emphasized that China was backward and due to this, people had become selfish and money-oriented. She pointed out that the Chinese government's attack on Governor Patten's political reform proposal made Hong Kong unstable. She believed the Chinese government would threaten Hong Kong's economic interests in exchange for political gains. "Comparing Chinese rule with British rule, I'm satisfied with the British government rule."

Her husband, who had grown up in Hong Kong, did not share these views. He stressed that Governor Patten's political reform proposal, which he was not clear about, was only good on paper and had no practical value — "Useless!" It was also useless to worry, since he could control nothing. He had concluded there would not be much change after 1997, since Hong Kong plays an important role in helping China to build its economy. "The Chinese government does not want any changes in this goose that lays golden eggs."

Linkages Between Elements of the Patterns

Family background, where husband and wife were brought up, and the length of time they spent in Hong Kong, shape political views. The longer our respondents have lived in Hong Kong, the more they are "used to" Hong Kong life. They feel they would not be able to adjust to life under mainland rule.

Some expect the "one country, two systems" policy to be respected, whereas others do not. The ways they came to Hong Kong also affect views toward China. Those that have fled China's politics are more negative than those that fled China's poor economy.

Social class background shapes attitudes toward China. The four groupings based on views toward 1997 come close to class groupings. Those with upper middle class background are least eager to live under communist rule, owing to their earlier family experiences. Those with only labor to sell most welcome reversion (Wong and Salaff, 1996).

Nevertheless, because connections with kin also affect attitudes toward China, we do not term these patterned attitudes "class groupings." Attitudes are communicated. Those with ongoing relations with kin in China are most open to reversion. Those with no ongoing ties are neutral or negative. Those with kin in the Western nations are most pessimistic about 1997. Moreover, the density of group membership also affects whether people share attitudes. Close and reciprocal ties leads to shared attitudes. Distant and independent, loosely structured ties indicates less close adherence, less effect of others' ties.

These elements cohere. The working class and those in traditional lower middle class occupations are more likely to have fled China's poverty, and less likely to have fled China's politics. Without economic capital, they cannot expect to leave Hong Kong either. They tend to accept the future, in a neutral fashion.

In contrast, those with economic capital who invest in industries based mainly on the Hong Kong economy may distrust China's institutional framework. If they invest in enterprises that profit from the integrated Pacific Rim economies, they are more likely to see positive changes and be optimistic. If they work in firms that have had negative experiences negotiating with China, they will not see such changes and may wish to leave. Those with economic capital are also most likely to have had negative family histories with China and are those with most connection abroad. These connections are not necessarily with kin, but with coworkers or schoolmates (Salaff, Fong and Wong, 1996).

Conclusion

Analyzing the social basis of these patterns of views on Hong Kong's reversion to China, we find that regularities to the political views fit patterns in family experiences. Indeed, most opinions about 1997 were drawn from family experiences, rather than liberal politics. We thus stress that personal experiences shape political views on the reversion.

The data from in-depth interviews with 30 families in Hong Kong are thematic, and do not represent a public opinion poll. But our analysis of the themes suggest that measures of kinship contact — where kin live; reciprocity with kin — and the age at which the respondents came to Hong Kong contribute to the construction of views that others might view as political. These political views include attitudes toward a range of political issues and emigration behavior. It is true that as widely perceived, political attitudes affect views toward emigration and investment and even toward one's kin. Yet we find kinship and family histories affect political opinions.

Some people note the variability of identities of Chinese. Where assimilation is difficult, the Chinese adopt "intermediate identities." They stress different identities for different purposes (Gosling, 1983). The Hong Kong people we met drew upon a wide range of identities. In stressing their personal experiences with China and the West in their values and identity formation, our study has rooted these identities into the lived experience of these people. In this study, then, ideology is rooted in experience.

Just as past experiences and social status shape current views toward 1997, how will the coming years reshape popular views? As experiences change, so may their identifications mutate. Those, mainly in the affluent group, are most conflicted and frequently reevaluate their position. These have now turned their ambivalences to qualified support for the current regime. They could, if their family economy is challenged by economic downswings in Hong Kong, reassess and turn the other way. Having the social networks that extend out of Hong Kong, the affluent have more mixed input and can change their attitudes. The lower middle and working class may change their views as well. However, generally less conflicted than the affluent, the lower middle and working class would have to experience considerable disconfirming evidence to change their identifications (Salaff and Wong, 1995). Identities are dynamic and changeable, but they are nonetheless rooted in experiences, in socioeconomic structures, and in structured networks.

References

Boyd, Monica. 1989. "Family and Personal Networks in International Migration: Recent Developments and New Agendas." *International Migration Review*, xxiii no 3: 638–663.

Cheng, S.L. 1995. *Hong Kong on a Plate*. Hong Kong: Department of Sociology, University of Hong Kong. M.Phil.

Choi, Po-king. 1990. "Popular Culture." Pp. 537–63 in Richard Y.C. Wong and Joseph Y.S. Cheng, eds. *The Other Hong Kong Report, 1990*. Hong Kong: The Chinese University Press.

Deyo, Frederic C. 1990. *Beneath the Miracle: Labor Subordination in the New Asia Periphery.* Berkeley: University of California Press.

Fanon, Frantz. 1967. *Wretched of the Earth.* Harmondsworth: Penguin.

Freeman, Michael, 1996. Lecture on self determination, Hong Kong, School of Law, December, 1995.

Gosling, Peter L.A. 1983. "Changing Chinese Identities in Southeast Asia: An Introductory Review." pp. 1–14 in Peter L.A. Gosling and Linda Y.D. Lim, eds. *The Chinese in Southeast Asia.* Singapore: Maruzen Asia, Vol. 2.

Guldin, Gregory Eliyu. 1995. "Toward a Greater Guangdong: Hong Kong's Sociocultural Impact on the Pearl River Delta and Beyond." pp. 89–118 in Kwok and So, eds.

Guldin, Gregory Eliyu. 1980. "Multilineal Modernity: Ideologies of Modernization in Hong Kong." In *Proceedings of the 2nd International Symposium on Asian Studies,* Vol. I: 69–86.

Hong Kong Voices; Corporate Hong Kong: Beyond 1997, views of business executives, government leaders and journalists, published by The Global Group (St. Helena, Ca. 1996).

Isaacs, Harold. 1958. *Stratches on Our Minds: American Views of China and India* New York: John Day Co.

Kwok, Reginald Yin-wang and Alvin Y. So, eds. 1995. *Hong Kong-Guangdong Link: Partnership in Flux.* Hong Kong: Hong Kong University Press.

Lee Ming-kwan. 1995. "Community and Identity in Transition in Hong Kong." Pp. 119–132 in Kwok and So, eds.

Li, F.L.N., A.J. Jowett, A.M. Findlay, R. Skeldon. nd. "Discourse on Migration and Ethnic Identity: Interviews with Professionals in Hong Kong."

Li, F.L.N., A.J. Jowett, A.M. Findlay, R. Skeldon. 1994. "Talking Migration: An Interpretation of the Migration Intentions of Hong Kong Engineers and Doctors." Applied Population Research Unit Discussion Paper 94/1. University of Glasgow.

Madsen, Richard. 1995. *China and the American Dream.* Berkeley: University of California Press.

Massey, Douglas S. 1990. "Social Structure, Household Strategies and the Cumulative Causation of Migration," *Population Index* 56 (1): 3–26 Spring.

Ng Sek-hong and Cheng Soo-may. 1994. "The Affluent Migrants as a Class Phenomenon: The Hong Kong Case." pp. 171–204 in Lau Siu-kai, Lee Ming-kwan, Wan Po-san, Wong Siu-lun, eds. *Inequalities and Development: Social Stratification in Chinese Societies.* Hong Kong Institute of Asia Pacific Studies, the Chinese University of Hong Kong.

Said, Edward W. 1994. *Culture and Imperialism.* New York: Vintage Books.

Salaff, Janet W., Eric Fong, and Siu-lun Wong. 1996. "Using Social Networks to Emigrate from Hong Kong: How Present Directions Fortell the Future." Paper delivered at the Annual Meeting of the Association of Asian Studies, Hononlu, Hawaii.

Scott, Ian. 1989. *Political Change and the Crisis of Legitimacy in Hong Kong.* Hong Kong. Oxford University Press.

Scott, Ian. 1995. "Political Transformation in Hong Kong: From Colony to Colony." pp 189–223 in Kwok and So, eds.

Skeldon, Ronald. 1991. "Emigration, Immigration and Fertility Decline: Demographic Integration or Disintegration?" pp. 259–274. In Sung Yun-wing and Lee Ming-kwan, *The Other Hong Kong Report, 1991.* Hong Kong: The Chinese University Press.

So, Alvin Y. and Ludmilla Kwitko. 1992. "The Transformation of Urban Movements in Hong Kong, 1970–90" *Bulletin of Concerned Asian Scholars* 24.4: 32–44.

Tam, Maria. 1996. "Youth Culture in Hong Kong: Re-rooting of an Identity." Paper delivered at the 1996 Annual Meeting of the Association of Asian Studies, Honolulu, Hawaii.

Watson, J.L. 1975. *Emigration and the Chinese Lineage: The Mans in Hong Kong and London.* Berkeley: University of California Press.

Wong Siu-lun, 1995. "Political Attitudes and Identity." pp. 147–175 in Skeldon, ed. *Emigration from Hong Kong.* Hong Kong: Chinese University Press.

Wong, Siu-lun, and Janet Salaff. 1996."Network Capital." Typescript, accepting pending revisions to British Journal of Sociology.

Notes

1. Islands east of China, Senkaku gunto in Japanese. Territorial ownership of the islands, claimed by Japan during the war, has not been settled. China's unresolved bitterness over Japan's wartime aggression is reflected in the dispute over the island chain. The discovery that more Japanese have settled here has recently inflamed emotions in China, Hong Kong, Macau, and Taiwan.

2. The affluent group includes managers and professionals. The middle class consists mainly of white-collar workers There are petty bourgeois businessmen. Finally, the working class is composed of menial and seasonal workers. We classified married respondents' occupational class by the highest occupation of either spouse.

3. However, while 26 held the same views toward China, in four cases the husband and wife disagreed over their assessment of Chinese rule. We classified three of them by the more critical pattern. In one case the wife dominated their decision making and overrode the husband's and we classified the case by her views.

4. Nine of the 12 husbands and wives in this group were born in China.

5. Here and in later tables respondents' "kin units" refer to the respondents themselves, their children, brothers and sisters, and their parents. We include here only those still alive about whom they had information.

6. There are 17 individuals in this group, 6 born in China, 10 born in Hong Kong, 1 elsewhere.

7. Of the 16 in this pattern, only 1 is China born, 12 are born in Hong Kong, 1 elsewhere

8. Ten of the 14 husbands and wives in this group were born in Hong Kong; 3 were born in China; 1 elsewhere.

7

Hong Kong in Transition: Globalization Versus Nationalization

James T.H. Tang

Justifying the importance of international links to Hong Kong is a superfluous exercise. Hong Kong is an archetypal international city. Subscribing to the philosophy of free trade, the British colony practices economic liberalism and pursues a policy of openness. In recent years Hong Kong has been consistently ranked the most liberal economy in the world with virtually no barriers to trade and capital flow by the Heritage Foundation's *Index of Economic Freedom*.[1] What will happen to the international character of the Hong Kong Special Administrative Region (SAR) as China resumes sovereignty over the British colony?

Although Hong Kong is largely populated by Cantonese Chinese, the number of foreign citizens working in the territory has been increasing continuously while 1997 approaches. The foreign community in the territory at the end of February 1996 (excluding short term visitors and Hong Kong Chinese residents with foreign passports) reached almost 450,000 (see Table 7.1).[2] Hong Kong's international and cosmopolitan nature has always been a key feature of its economic success. The territory's extensive linkages and interactions with the outside world have long been a central dimension of its existence. The political transition of Hong Kong, however, has cast doubt on the continuation of its special international character.[3] Are Hong Kong's international links at risk?

There are people who believe that the territory can survive with its international character intact under the "one country, two systems" formula as promised by the Sino-British Joint Declaration in 1984. The commitment to maintain Hong Kong's existing system is further confirmed by the Beijing government

Table 7.1

Foreign Citizens in Hong Kong

Country	2/96	6/95	12/94	12/93	12/92	12/91
Philippines	139,300	137,000	115,500	99,200	83,800	72,000
USA	36,000	32,100	29,900	26,100	23,500	21,000
UK	34,500	24,800	23,700	20,300	18,400	16,000
Canada	29,000	26,900	24,700	20,400	17,500	15,000
Indonesia	25,900	22,800	19,700	14,700	11,000	—
Thailand	25,100	25,700	23,800	21,500	19,500	17,000
Japan	24,200	22,100	17,600	14,000	12,300	11,000
Australia	21,100	20,600	18,700	16,700	14,800	13,000
India	21,000	20,900	19,500	18,700	18,000	18,000
Malaysia	13,900	14,400	13,800	13,000	12,600	12,000

Source: Immigration Department, *South China Morning Post,* April, 8, 1996

with the promulgation of the Basic Law, a mini-constitution for the Hong Kong SAR. In fact, both the Joint Declaration and the Basic Law maintain that Hong Kong will be allowed to manage its own external economic and cultural relations. Although the Joint Declaration makes it very clear that foreign affairs are the responsibility of the Beijing government, it also suggests "representatives of the Hong Kong SAR may participate, as 'members of delegations of the Government of the People's Republic of China,' in diplomatic negotiations conducted by the Central Government which would affect the SAR."[4] Confirming the Sino-British agreement, the Basic Law also states that the SAR may use the name "Hong Kong, China" to maintain and develop relations, and conclude and implement agreements with foreign states and regions and relevant international organizations in the appropriate fields, including economic, trade, financial, monetary, shipping, communications, tourism, cultural, and sports fields.[5] It also specified that the Hong Kong SAR may send representatives to participate in international organizations or conferences in appropriate fields limited to states and affecting the region as members of delegations of the PRC, or may attend in such other capacity as may be permitted by the central government and the international organization or conference concerned, and may express their views, using the name "Hong Kong, China." Similarly, the SAR may, using the name "Hong Kong, China," participate in international organizations and conferences not limited to states. Not only did the Beijing government declare its willingness to give Hong Kong a free hand in managing its external economic and cultural affairs, it also declared its commitment to ensure that the SAR retain "its status in an appropriate capacity in international organizations."[6] In fact the SAR enjoys unparalleled latitude in conducting its own external relations compared to most sub-state units in the world. With extensive formal capacity as an international actor, and a well developed economy and efficient bureaucratic machinery, it has been argued that the SAR can perhaps qualify as a quasi-state.[7]

Despite the legal guarantee and promises made by the Beijing government, many observers are uncertain about the prospects of Hong Kong's international character. With the end of British rule, as one political observer noted, "Hong Kong will be left to face its future as a small, insignificant enclave within the vast mass of China's one billion people."[8] A number of people have also predicted the demise of the territory. *Fortune* magazine, for example, predicted the death of Hong Kong as an international city in a special issue on developments in the territory.[9] As the transformation of Hong Kong from a British colonial territory to a Chinese SAR takes place, the territory has become the focus of international attention. The Clinton administration, for example, has adopted a high profile approach toward developments in the territory in early 1997. Will tiny Hong Kong be absorbed into the gigantic China without trace? To what extent would international forces shape developments in the territory?

This chapter examines the character of Hong Kong's interactions with the global community through two competing perspectives on Hong Kong's transition: globalization and nationalization. At one end, as a major international city without strong political identities, Hong Kong is perhaps an ideal candidate as a global city. The globalization perspective views developments in the territory as part of the globalization process which is changing the world and will eventually change China. At the other end, the nationalization perspective sees the rise of China as part of the re-assertion of nationalism in the contemporary world. As China resumes sovereignty over Hong Kong, the territory will become part of a rising power seeking to restore its national dignity as a world power, and gradually it will be no more than an ordinary Chinese city with an interesting past.

Hong Kong and Emerging Globalism

Much has been said about global changes in the contemporary world. Globalization has increasing become an important theme in scholarly analysis on world politics in the 1990s.[10] According to this interpretation, the international system, as we know it, has been moved from the state-centric world to a far more complex and turbulent multi-centric world.[11] Indeed as one observer has noted, "the prime characteristic of this new political agenda is that it is global."[12]

A myriad number of organizations and institutions, in varying forms, including international organizations, multinational corporations, and non-governmental organizations (NGOs), have emerged as major actors in the international stage. Worldwide problems such as environmental protection, human rights, proliferation of arms, social development, and poverty have also captured transnational attention. Moreover, the globalization of economic activities, the information revolution and new technology are also weakening the traditional international order based on the concept of sovereignty. The transformation taking place, as popularized to some extent by Peter Drucker, is creating "the post-capitalist society" in which the nation state would have to compete and co-exist with transnational, regional, local, and even tribal, structures.[13] Key elements in the globalization process which have been identified included: the changing nature of economic interdependence, growing international communications, the movement of people around the globe, and the rise of international institutions and transnational social movements. Economic force is at the forefront of such a global transformation from a state-centric world to a more interdependent transnational and borderless world.[14]

In many ways world trade has played a central part in the deepening of economic interdependence. Although weaknesses of the world trade system centerd around the General Agreement on Tariff and Trade were revealed since the 1970s with the rise of international protectionist sentiments, the establishment of the World Trade Organization (WTO) represented the recognition of the importance of a liberal and multilateral global trade regime.[15] In 1995 the expansion of world trade reached a new height with over US$5000 billion.[16]

Hong Kong's developments do seem to fit into the globalization formula. If trade is a major force in globalization, Hong Kong is clearly very much at the forefront of the process. As the world eighth largest trader (the fourth if the European Union is counted as one), after the US, Germany, Japan, France, UK, Italy and Canada (Table 7.2A & B). Hong Kong trades with countries from all over the world. At the beginning of 1996, its major trading partners are China, the US, Japan, Taiwan, Singapore, and Germany (Table 7.3). In spite of international protectionism, the territory's trade expanded solidly in the 1990s. Since 1980, exports to the Asia-Pacific region as a whole has grown rapidly as a result of import liberalization in the region. Total exports to the Asia-Pacific region increased 18% to US$93 billion in 1995. Total exports (including re-exports) increased by more than 17% and total imports (including re-exports) increased by almost 12% in 1995 (Table 7.4).

That Hong Kong is linked to the globalization of the world is also reflected in its role as an international hub of various business activities, and as a major finance, communications, and transport center. As a source of business information and product sourcing as well as a financial center, it is a meeting place for businesses from around the world. The Hong Kong Trade Development Council (HKTDC), a semi-governmental organization in charge of trade promotion, outlines the territory's importance as a business center on a routine basis. The territory is a highly popular location for international conferences and trade fairs. According to the TDC over 300 international conventions and exhibitions are held in Hong Kong each year. The territory is to host the World Bank and International Monetary Fund (IMF) annual meetings in 1997.[17]

The territory's status as a leading international financial center is beyond

Table 7.2A

Leading Exporters and Importers in World Merchandise Trade, 1996 (billion dollars and percentage)

Rank	EXPORTERS	Value (f.o.b.)	Share in Value	Change	Rank	IMPORTERS	Value (c.i.f.)	Share in Value	Change
1	US	624.8	11.9	6.8	1	US	817.8	15.2	6.1
2	Germany	521.2	9.9	-0.3	2	Germany	456.3	8.5	-1.5
3	Japan	412.6	7.9	-6.9	3	Japan	349.6	6.5	4.1
4	France	290.3	5.5	1.3	4	U.K.	278.6	5.2	5.0
5	U.K.	259.1	4.9	7.0	5	France	275.3	5.1	-0.2
6	Italy	250.7	4.8	7.1	6	Italy	207.0	3.8	0.4
7	Canada	201.2	3.8	4.7	7	Hong Kong[c]	202.0	3.7	3.0
						-retained imports[b]	48.5	0.9	-7.0
8	Netherlands	197.1	3.8	0.9	8	Canada	175.0	3.2	3.9
9	Hong Kong[c]	180.9	3.4	4.0	9	Netherlands	174.1	3.2	-1.0
	- domestic exports	27.4	0.5	-8.4					
10	Belgium-Luxembourg	166.7	3.2	-1.8	10	Belgium-Luxembourg	154.6	2.9	-0.4
11	China	151.1	2.9	1.5	11	S. Korea	150.3	2.8	11.2
12	S. Korea	129.8	2.5	3.8	12	China	138.8	2.6	5.1
13	Singapore[c]	125.1	2.4	5.8	13	Singapore[c]	131.5	2.4	5.6
	- domestic exports	73.6	1.4	5.7		- retained imports[b]	79.9	1.5	5.4
14	Chinese Taipei	116.0	2.2	3.9	14	Spain	121.9	2.3	6.1
15	Spain	102.1	1.9	11.4	15	Chinese Taipei	102.5	1.9	-1.1
16	Mexico	95.9	1.8	20.6	16	Mexico	90.3	1.7	23.6
17	Sweden	84.2	1.6	5.8	17	Malaysia	78.6	1.5	1.0
18	Switzerland	80.0	1.5	-2.0	18	Switzerland	78.5	1.5	-2.1
19	Malaysia	78.4	1.5	5.8	19	Thailand	68.3	1.3	-3.5
20	Russia[a]	70.4	1.3	8.6	20	Austria	65.0	1.2	1.0

a Data exclude trade with the Baltic States and the CIS. Including trade with these states would lift Russian exports and imports to $89.6 billion and $64.3 billion respectively.
b Retained imports are defined as imports less re-exports.
c Includes significant re-exports or imports for re-export.
Source: World Trade Organization, Report on Trade Development, 1997.

Table 7.2B

Leading Exporters and Importers in World Merchandise Trade (Excluding European Union Intra-Trade), 1996 (billion dollars and percentage)

Rank	EXPORTERS	Value (f.o.b.)	Share in Value	Change
1	European Union (15)	800.0	20.2	6.5
2	United States	624.8	15.8	6.8
3	Japan	412.6	10.4	-6.9
4	Canada	201.2	5.1	4.7
5	Hong Kong[d]	180.9	4.6	4.0
	- domestic exports	27.4		
6	China	151.1	3.8	1.5
7	S. Korea	129.8	3.3	3.8
8	Singapore[d]	125.1	1.3	5.8
	- domestic exports	73.6	1.9	5.7
9	Chinese Taipei	116.0	2.9	3.9
10	Mexico	95.9	2.4	20.6
11	Switzerland	80.0	2.0	-2.0
12	Malaysia	78.4	2.0	5.8
13	Russia[a]	70.4	1.8	8.6
14	Australia	59.9	1.5	13.8
15	Saudi Arabia	56.3	1.4	13.9
16	Indonesia	54.8	1.4	-2.9
17	Thailand	49.9	1.3	9.8
18	Norway	48.7	1.2	16.8
19	Brazil	47.8	1.2	2.7
20	India	33.3	0.8	8.3

Rank	IMPORTERS	Value (c.i.f.)	Share in Value	Change
1	United States	817.8	20.0	6.1
2	European Union (15)	725.0	17.8	1.7
3	Japan	349.6	8.6	3.0
4	Hong Kong[d]	202.0	4.9	-7.0
	- retained imports[b]	48.5	1.2	
5	Canada	175.0	4.3	3.9
6	S. Korea	150.3	3.7	11.2
7	China	138.8	3.4	5.1
8	Singapore[d]	131.5	3.2	5.6
	- retained imports[b]	79.9	2.0	5.4
9	Chinese Taipei	102.5	2.5	-2.2
10	Mexico	90.3	2.2	23.6
11	Malaysia	78.6	1.9	1.0
12	Switzerland	78.5	1.9	-2.1
13	Thailand	68.3	1.7	-3.5
14	Australia	65.5	1.6	6.9
15	Brazil	57.5	1.1	6.9
16	Russia[a]	44.4	1.1	9.9
17	Indonesia	42.8	1.0	9.9
18	Turkey	42.0	1.0	4.5
19	Poland	38.3	0.9	17.6
20	India	37.5	0.9	26.0

a Data exclude trade with the Baltic States and the CIS. Including trade with these states would lift Russian exports and imports to $89.6 billion and $64.3 billion respectively.
b Retained imports are defined as imports less re-exports.
c Imports are valued f.o.b.
d Includes significant re-exports or imports for re-export.
Source: World Trade Organization, Report on Trade Development, 1997.

Table 7.3

Hong Kong's Trading Partners

Major Trading Partners (Jan 96)		Export Markets** (Jan 96)		Import Sources (Jan 96)	
China	(36.2%)	China	(35.6%)	China	(36.9%)
US	(12.8%)	US	(18.4%)	Japan	(12.8%)
Japan	(9.8%)	Japan	(6.5%)	Taiwan	(8.7%)
Taiwan	(5.8%)	Germany	(4.6%)	US	(7.7%)
Singapore	(4.2%)	UK	(3.1%)	Singapore	(5.4%)
Germany	(3.5%)	Singapore	(2.8%)	Korea	(4.6%)

Source: Hong Kong Trade Development Council, Trade Statistics, March 1996.

Table 7.4

Values of Hong Kong's Trade

Trade of Goods	1994		1995	
Total Exports (US$)	172.32 bn.	(+14.9%)	27.00 bn.	(+13.2%)
- Domestic Exports (US$)	29.70 bn.	(+ 4.3%)	4.25 bn.	(+ 0.7%)
- Re-exports (US$)	142.62 bn.	(+17.4%)	22.75 bn.	(+15.8%)
Imports (US$)	191.17 bn.	(+19.2%)	29.01 bn.	(+10.6%)
Total Trade (US$)	363.49 bn.	(+17.1%)	56.01 bn.	(+11.8%)
Trade Balance (US$)	-18.85 bn.		-2.01 bn.	

Source: Hong Kong Trade Development Council, Trade Statistics, March 1996.

dispute. The banking sector is like the who's who in world banking. Leading financial institutions from all over the world operate in Hong Kong. At the end of 1995, there were 537 authorized banks and related institutions (including representative offices) from over 40 countries in the territory, and 85 of them were among the world's largest 100 banks. The Hong Kong stock market is also highly international. At the end of 1995 the territory's stock market was the world's eighth largest and the second largest in Asia. There were over 500 companies (including 18 mainland China enterprises) listed on the local stock exchange, with a market capitalization over US$300 billion. About US$60 billion in over one thousand funds were managed in the territory in 1995. Hong Kong's foreign exchange market, linked to major overseas centers such as London and New York, was the fifth largest in the world. The government possessed the world's seventh largest foreign currency holding, with the Exchange Fund totalled US$57.2 billion at the end of 1995 — on a per capita basis at US$9,370, it is the second highest in the world, after Singapore. The gold bullion market was the world's third largest after London and New York.[18]

As a key transport and communications center for the Asia-Pacific region, Hong Kong has the world's busiest container port. In 1995 the a total cargo throughput of the port reached 12.5 million TEUs. The number of container throughput is expected to increase to 31 million TEUs in year 2006. Hong Kong also has the world's second busiest airport in terms of tonnage handled (with a total international air-freight volume of 1.46 million tonnes in 1995). In terms of passenger throughput, the Kai Tak airport was the fourth busiest international airport in the world in 1994, after London-Heathrow, Frankfurt, and Paris-Charles De Gaulle. Over half of the passenger traffic was generated by overseas visitors.[19]

The 1997 issue does not seem to have affected Hong Kong's international economic position. Business interests from all parts of the world have not been diminished by the prospect of the territory's political transition. A 1995 government survey covering 8,956 overseas companies in Hong Kong confirmed Hong Kong's status as a major commercial hub and the regional base for firms from different parts of the world. Of the 3,431 responses, 782 companies identified themselves as regional headquarters and 1,286 identified themselves as regional offices. Among these companies, almost 200 were American firms, followed by Japan (116), the UK (94), and China (71).[20] If the rise of the role of multinational corporations and the changing power structure between firms and the state is a key element in the restructuring of the global order, Hong Kong is well placed to serve as a base for the development of such structures.

Hong Kong also remains a favorable business center for overseas investors. In a business confidence survey conducted by the American Chamber of Commerce among its member companies in Hong Kong. A overwhelming number of respondents believed that the business climate in Hong Kong over the next five years would be "very favorable" or "favorable," and many expected to either maintain or expand their investment in the territory. Investment from abroad continued at a solid rate throughout the first half of the 1990s. At the end of 1994 accumulated overseas investment in the manufacturing sector totalled US$5.64 billion, up 8% from 1993. Companies from major industrialized countries — Japan taking the lead, closely followed by the US — continued to invest heavily in the territory. This trend is also observable in the non-manufacturing sector as the territory's economic structures shifted to a more service-oriented direction. Accumulated overseas investment in the non-manufacturing sector at the end of 1994 amounted to US$88 billion, an increase of 8% from 1993. The largest investor was the UK, accounting for almost 30%, followed by Japan at 20%, mainland China with 19%, and the US at 11%. Banks and related companies constituted the largest share of investment, with about half of the total investment in the non-manufacturing sector.[21]

Another globalizing trend which is observable in the Hong Kong economy is the growing importance of its service sector. An indication of its shift from the labor intensive mode of production to a more knowledge-base mode of productivity. The contribution of the service industry to the economy of Hong Kong rose from just above 67% to 83% between 1984 and 1994. Hong Kong has also become the world's eighth largest exporter and eleventh largest importer of services (Tables 7.5, 7.6, 7.7). In fact the Hong Kong government felt so strongly about the importance of the service industry that it developed a new strategy to promote the service sector.[22]

Table 7.5

Contribution of Services to the Hong Kong Economy

	1984	1994	1995
Contribution to GDP (%)	67.3	83.0	n.a.
Value added/gross output (%)	57.9	57.8*	n.a.
Exports of services/GDP (%)	22.0	24.0	26.2
Trade in services/trade in goods (%)	20.2	15.9	16.0
Trade in services/total trade in goods & services (%)	16.8	13.8	13.8

* 1993 figure

Source: Estimates of GDP 1961 to 1995, Quarterly Estimates of GDP; compiled by the Trade Development Council, *Trade Statistics*, March 1996.

Table 7.6

Hong Kong's Trade Balance

Trade of Services	1994		1995	
Exports (US$)	31.27 bn.	(+13.1%)	37.31 bn.	(+19.3%)
Imports (US$)	18.26 bn.	(+15.8%)	21.11 bn.	(+15.6%)
Total Trade (US$)	49.54 bn.	(+14.1%)	58.42 bn.	(+17.9%)
Trade Balance (US$)	13.00 bn.		16.20 bn.	

Source: Hong Kong Trade Development Council, *Trade Statistics,* March 1996.

If the globalization of Hong Kong is measured by its involvement in international institutions, the territory has performed well too. Although Hong Kong's status as a non-sovereign actor has limited its international capacity, the territory has always enjoyed a high degree of autonomy in its external relations, and participated actively in international institutions.[23] The territory's multilateral

Table 7.7

Leading Exporters and Importers of World Trade in Commercial Services, 1995 (billion dollars and percentage)

Rank	EXPORTERS	Value (f.o.b.)	Share in Value	Change	Rank	IMPORTERS	Value (c.i.f.)	Share in Value	Change
1	United States	189.5	16.2	8	1	Germany	130	10.7	20
2	France	96.0	8.2	8	2	United States	128.3	10.5	7
3	Germany	79.5	6.8	25	3	Japan	121.6	10.0	15
4	United Kingdom	69.4	5.9	13	4	France	76.9	6.3	11
5	Italy	64.7	5.5	17	5	Italy	62.9	5.2	17
6	Japan	63.9	5.4	13	6	United Kingdom	5.8	4.7	10
7	Netherlands	47.2	4.0	12	7	Netherlands	45.3	3.7	11
8	Spain	39.6	3.4	17	8	Belgium-Luxembourg[a]	33.7	2.8	...
9	Hong Kong	36.1	3.1	16	9	Canada	29.3	2.4	4
10	Belgium-Luxembourg[a]	35.3	3.0	...	10	S. Korea	27.5	2.3	36
11	Austria[b]	31.5	2.7	...	11	China	24.6	2.0	57
12	Singapore	29.3	2.5	26	12	Chinese Taipei	23.8	2.0	13
13	Switzerland	26.1	2.2	14	13	Austria[b]	23.1	1.9	...
14	Korea, Rep. of	25.1	2.1	33	14	Spain	21.6	1.8	17
15	Canada	21.2	1.8	10	15	Hong Kong	21.2	1.7	17
16	China	18.4	1.6	14	16	Russia	20.2	1.7	31
17	Chinese Taipei	15.6	1.3	15	17	Thailand	18.6	1.5	22
18	Sweden	15.2	1.3	13	18	Australia	17.2	1.4	12
19	Australia	15.1	1.3	13	19	Sweden	17.1	1.4	17
20	Thailand	14.7	1.2	28	20	Singapore	16.5	1.4	23

a Not comparable to previous years due to change in methodology.
b Estimate.
Source: World Trade Organization, *Report on Trade Development*, 1997.

and bilateral international legal and institutional links are extensive. Under the umbrella of the United Kingdom, more than 200 multilateral international treaties are applicable to Hong Kong. Many of these treaties, covering international civil aviation, merchant shipping, private international law, international arbitration and customs co-operation are critical to Hong Kong's position as an international commercial center.

Considering Hong Kong's size and population, its participation in both non-governmental (NGOs) and inter-governmental (IGOs) international organizations is indeed impressive. In 1993 the respective international organization memberships of Hong Kong, the PRC, and Taiwan were: 932 (NGOS 921;IGOs 11), 947(NGOs 900; IGOs 47), and 741 (NGOs 733; IGOs 8). In fact the headquarters of 62 international organizations were in Hong Kong. The territory was also the fourth preferred headquarters/main offices for regional organizations in Asia, with 77 principal secretariats of such organizations choosing to locate themselves in the territory.[24]

The British and Chinese governments have agreed in principle, on the continued application of some 175 treaties. By early 1997, the two sides agreed that Hong Kong would continue to participate in 32 international organizations after 1997, including the General Agreement on Tariff and Trade (GATT) which has been replaced by the World Trade Organization, the Asian Development Bank, the World Health Organization, the Customs Cooperation Council, the International Maritime Organisation, and the World Intellectual Property Organization, International Textiles and Clothing Bureau, the International Civil Aviation Organizations, and the United Nations Conference on Trade and Development. In fact, Hong Kong's continued participation in organizations such as the Asia-Pacific Economic Cooperation forum and various OECD committees do not even require Sino-British agreement.[25]

The two governments also reached agreements on Hong Kong's bilateral legal links with other countries in areas such as investment promotion and protection, extraditions, legal assistance, and transfer of prisoners. By early 1996, Hong Kong has signed investment promotion and protection agreements with 11 countries (The Netherlands, Sweden, Denmark, Switzerland, Australia, New Zealand, Germany, Italy, France, Canada, Belgium, and Austria). It has also signed Surrender of Fugitive Offender Agreements with eight countries, and air services agreements with 18 countries. Mechanism to assure the international community that these multilateral agreements to Hong Kong would continued to apply to the territory is being discussed. The British and Chinese governments are to present separate notes to the United Nations Secretary-General and to the depositaries of the relevant agreements. A comprehensive framework of bilateral agreements is also expected to be in place by July 1, 1997.[26]

From the globalization perspective, Hong Kong is very much part of the globalizing process — a major international city in a world without boundaries. If the world is being globalized, Hong Kong will surely find a place in the emergent order as a global city and an agent in bring about the new changes toward the new global order. Hong Kong's future is therefore closely linked with external forces. Such a view, however, is problematic. Globalism in the Hong Kong context seems to be of a particular kind. Transnational social movements, for example, has not taken root in the territory. Commercialism in Hong Kong is such that many would argue that the people of Hong Kong view the territory's external links primarily through an instrumental perspective. The extent to which people in Hong Kong have developed a global outlook is therefore still questionable. The Hong Kong polity, as a dependent British territory, has long been characterized as an administrative state, its style of politics described as "administrative absorption of politics."[27]

Transnational forces and economic interdependence, important as they are, have been defined and discussed within the context of the state system. Sovereignty states are very much still the core of world politics. While many countries express support for the territory's continuing existence as a separate unit of China, they see the changing status of the territory primarily as China's internal issue. It is true that there are strong international concerns about developments in Hong Kong and many countries have openly stated their support for the continuing development of Hong Kong as a major international city. The US Congress, for example, has passed the 1992 US-Hong Kong Policy Act to monitor developments in the territory. The US government has also expressed concerns over political developments in the territory.[28] Some, like Australia, Canada, and Singapore have opened their doors to Hong Kong immigrants, but their capacities to intervene in developments within the jurisdiction of another sovereign state are obviously limited. Moreover, many countries consider their ties with China far more important than their links with Hong Kong.[29] It is perhaps not surprising that countries with large economic stakes in Hong Kong are more concerned with developments in the territory. In fact bilateral difficulties between China and other countries such as the human rights issue in Sino-American relations may easily affect Hong Kong's own economic links with these countries.

As Hong Kong's new political master, China's policy toward the territory is therefore the most critical factor in determining its future. In fact the transfer of sovereignty in Hong Kong may provide the answer to its search for an identity. As the territory becomes a Special Administrative Region of the PRC, it is almost certain that Chinese nationalism will become a major force in shaping its developments. In the economic sphere, the Hong Kong economy has almost completely integrated with mainland China. Paradoxically, the globalization of the Hong Kong's economy is conducted through its deepening links with mainland China. In the political sphere, the Beijing government has opposed plans for a faster pace of democratization in the territory. The Chinese leadership seemed determined to incorporate Hong Kong into the Chinese system through a process of nationalization.

Hong Kong and Chinese Nationalism

The decolonization of Hong Kong is very much about the assertion of Chinese sovereignty. It symbolises the triumph of Chinese nationalism over Western colonialism. The return of the territory to Chinese sovereignty is to end one and a half centuries of Chinese humiliation in Western hands. As a historian has noted, "An important and even dominant feature of Chinese national identity has been a preoccupation with creating and maintaining a strong centralized state".[30] With the rise of the country's economic power, the Chinese state has entered its most assertive phase since the beginning of the twentieth century. Seen from this perspective the incorporation of Hong Kong into mainland China under the "one country, two systems" formula is therefore only the beginning of a longer and gradual process of the nationalization of Hong Kong by China. A senior official responsible for China's Hong Kong policy, for example has suggested that educationists in the territory should promote patriotism among the children in Hong Kong.[31]

The nationalization perspective has been manifested in the three aspects: first, China's uncompromising assertion of sovereignty in Hong Kong; second, the economic integration between Hong Kong and mainland China, and third, the dominance of China in Hong Kong's political agenda.

For the Chinese leaders, sovereignty is central to the question of Hong Kong. In September 1987 when Deng Xiaoping met British Prime Minister Margaret Thatcher to discuss the Hong Kong question, the Chinese leader addressed three issues: sovereignty, the administering of Hong Kong after 1997, and appropriate discussions between Britain and China to avoid major disturbances. On the question of sovereignty, Deng stated bluntly that "China has no room for manoeuvre. . . If China failed to recover Hong Kong in 1997, when the People's Republic will have been established for 48 years", he explained, "no Chinese leaders or government would be able to justify themselves for that failure before the Chinese people or before the people of the world." Deng linked Hong Kong's future with the future of China, and the legitimacy of the Chinese regime by asserting that if the government could not recover Hong Kong by 1997, it would lose the trust of the people and would have no alternative but to step down.[32]

Deng Xiaoping's uncompromising stance on the sovereignty question is clearly linked to the leadership's Chinese nationalism. In fact the Chinese communist movement has been interpreted as a nationalist movement, and part of a lengthy process in China's search for national dignity.[33] The impact of Western humiliation of China was so strong that the core of the Chinese communist leaders' nation-building agenda has always been state-building. A study of China's behavior as a revolutionary power during the formative years of the People's Republic, for example, identified its primary concern to survive and consolidate as a state, and its aspiration to register and confirm China's place in the world.[34] The recovery of Hong Kong is an important step toward the fulfilment of that aspiration. Nationalism is a powerful force which has shaped the attitude of the Chinese leadership toward Hong Kong. The Chinese leadership clearly feels strongly about the reunification of China. The tense military situation over the Taiwan Strait during the March 1996 presidential elections in Taiwan is an indication of Beijing's sentiments. Chinese leaders were prepared to ignore external opinion when they considered that reunification was at risk.

The identify of the Hong Kong people, however, is rather complex. Many Hong Kong Chinese identify themselves as Hong Kong people (Xianggang ren). In a 1985 survey conducted by two Hong Kong scholars,[35] almost 60% of the respondents selected their primary identity as Hong Kong people (Xianggang ren), and just slightly more than 36% selected Chinese. But their Hong Kong identify is closely associated with the ethno-cultural dimension of being Chinese. Many who identified themselves as Hong Kong people were proud to be Chinese. Over 60% agreed or strongly agreed that the Chinese culture was the finest culture on earth, and almost 79% felt proud to be Chinese. While their identity with the People's Republic of China was significantly weaker, there is clearly a solid basis for the assertion of Chinese nationalism in the territory.

The economic interdependence of Hong Kong and mainland China is deepening as 1997 approaches. This economic relationship has been described by a leading business group in the territory as a symbiosis and "the single most important feature of Hong Kong's economic future."[36] As often noted, Hong Kong serves as China's window to the world. More than half of China's exports are re-exported through Hong Kong. Out of Hong Kong's total re-exports in 1995, almost 90% were either originated from or destined for China. But the territory is more than an entrepot to China, excluding re-exports, Hong Kong was still China's second largest trading partner, accounted for 16% of the country's total trade in 1995. Hong Kong also contributes to about one-third of China's foreign exchange earnings annually. Among the 245,400 foreign funded projects in China by the end of September 1995, about 60% are tied to Hong Kong investors. Between 1979 and 1994, Hong Kong investments accounted for 64% of the total foreign direct investment contracted in China.[37]

But the Hong Kong-China economic links are by no means one-way traffic. China is one of the leading investors in Hong Kong. At end of 1994, there were almost 2000 mainland Chinese enterprises registered in Hong Kong, with total assets valued at over US$42 billion.[38] In the field of finance, 18 Chinese banks are operating in the territory. The Bank of China and its sister banks constitute the second largest banking group in the territory, after Hongkong Bank. From May 1994 the Bank of China have also become a bank-note issuing bank of Hong Kong dollar banknotes. The Industrial and Commercial Bank of China, the Agricultural Bank of China, and the People's Bank of Construction of China have all opened branches in Hong Kong.

The increase in China-Hong Kong trade and re-export through the territory clearly reflects the degree of mutual reliance between the two economies. More significantly, it reveals the re-structuring which has taken place in the local economy. The growth in re-exports is largely the result of Hong Kong's outward processing activities in neighbouring Guangdong. By the mid 1990s over one-third of Hong Kong's re-exports were destined for China, and over half of the re-exports were of China origin. About 70% of Hong Kong's domestic exports and just under half of its re-exports to China were related to outward processing. Over 200,000 joint ventures with Hong Kong interests operated in China, and a majority of Hong Kong manufacturers had production facilities in Guangdong. The northward shift of production activities of Hong Kong industries has resulted in the integration of the two economies. Southern China has been effectively turned into the manufacturing base for Hong Kong industries, and the territory has become the marketing pad as well as the source of financial resources and investments for its hinterland.[39] Paradoxically, the Hong Kong economy is increasingly reaching to global economy via China.

Politically, the Beijing government is becoming increasingly assertive. Following the breaking down of Sino-British talks over political reform introduced by Hong Kong Governor Chris Patten in 1992, the Chinese government decided to set up the so-called "second stove," their own arrangements for the political structure of the Special Administrative Region. To accomplish this goal, the Beijing government developed a two-prong political strategy. On the one hand it rejected in total the political and constitutional changes introduced by Chris Patten. The Chinese refused to recognize the Legislative Council which was elected by the people of Hong Kong in 1995. They regarded it as an advisory body formed by the British government unilaterally without consultations with the Chinese. It also sought to isolate the Democratic Party which is under the leadership of Martin Lee and Sezto Wah, both are pro-democracy activists who had supported the 1989 pro-democracy movement in China. On the other hand, they put forward plans for a different set of political arrangements in post-1997 Hong Kong, including a provisional legislature. One of the first steps the Chinese side took was to cultivate political support from the Hong Kong community by appointing a large number of Hong Kong Affairs Advisers from the business circle, the professionals, unionists and other fields. More importantly, the Chinese government set up new institutional mechanism for arranging the changeover of sovereignty. Hence the creation of the SAR Preliminary Working Committee in 1993 which was not provided for in the Basic Law.[40] Although there were concern in Hong Kong about the legality of such an institution, it seemed clear that as the incoming political master, China can exercise considerable political influence in Hong Kong. The setting up of the SAR Preparatory Committee (with 54 mainland and 96 Hong Kong members all appointed by Beijing) in 1996 and the public rebuke of a Hong Kong member,[41] who voted against the setting up of a SAR provisional legislature, demonstrated that the Chinese government was not only able to influence events in the territory, it had no hesitation in exercising that influence. The 60-member SAR provisional legislature was also set up in December 1996. While 33 serving 1995 elected Legislative Councillors were "elected" to become members of the SAR provisional legislature by a Selection Committee, members of the most popular political party in Hong Kong — the Democratic Party — and most leading democrats boycotted and thus were not represented in this new body.

In addition to adopting an uncompromising attitude toward the introduction of Patten's democratic reform package, the Chinese government is also highly sensitive of external intervention in the Hong Kong question. Senior Chinese officials had repeatedly denounced what they described as Patten's efforts in "internationalizing" the question of Hong Kong and "foreign interference" of Hong Kong affairs. In fact the Basic Law specifically requires the SAR to enact laws to "prohibit any act of treason, secession, sedition, subversion against the Central People's Government, or theft of state secrets, to prohibit foreign political organizations or bodies from conducting political activities in the Region, and to prohibit political organizations or bodies of the Region from establishing ties with foreign political organizations or bodies."[42] In April 1997, the Chief Executive-designate introduced the notion of "national security" in a consultation document on civil liberties and social order. It proposed that the SAR government could refuse the registration of a society or reject application for demonstrations on the ground of national security. The proposal also suggested that political groups in Hong Kong can neither accept financial contributions from an alien or from a foreign organization nor have a connection with a foreign political organization.[43] Hong Kong's reunification with China can therefore be seen as a nationalization process.

The nationalization perspective, like the globalization perspective, however, is not without limitations. Nationalism has remained a powerful force in Chinese politics at the same time when transnational forces are making a significant impact on China's international behaviour. In asserting importance of sovereignty in China's conduct of foreign affairs, the Chinese leaders have to recognize the constraints imposed on their capacity to a act within the context of interdependence. The opening up the Chinese economy to the outside world means a significant degree of accommodation and acceptance of external standards. The notion of sovereignty has to be changed, even though this is not necessarily acknowledged.

In fact, developments in Hong Kong have also influenced the mainland. As China's window to the world, information, technology, western political and social attitudes found their ways through the territory. The impact of the Hong Kong presence on the mainland (estimated at about one thousand) and frequent visits by residents from both sides are difficult to measure, but the Hong Kong economic model has clearly inspired changes on the mainland. The Chinese economy has been described as Hongkongization.[44] In fact the rise of the so-called Greater China phenomenon demonstrates how the periphery is changing the core,[45] giving rise to a coast identity.[46]

Associated with Hong Kong's growing influence in neighbouring coastal China is the broader process of regionalization. Hong Kong's links with the rest of the Asia-Pacific have become far more significant in recent years. The territory's trade within the Asia-Pacific region has grown rapidly in the past two decades. Its role as the key communication center in the region will soon bee further strengthen by the installation of high-speed optic-fiber transmission systems linking Hong Kong with Guangdong and neighboring economies. Hong Kong is also serving as the hub of satellite links in the region.

Conclusion: Globalism Versus Nationalism

The two perspectives of globalization and nationalization are developed from different assumptions: the former assumes that powerful transnational forces are reducing the capacity of states to such an extent that the new world order will see the blurring of political boundaries and new actors are to replace or compete with states in a much more powerful manner. The later assumes that there are no alternative to the state system as yet, and nationalism will continue to dominate world politics and remain a critical force in shaping the behaviour of individual states.

Both perspectives offer useful insights in understanding the internationalization of Hong Kong. In approaching the question of Hong Kong's involvement with the world from a broader angle, the globalization perspective concentrates on the territory's extensive external links and reliance on the global economy and its role as a center of transnational activities. It serves to demonstrate the importance of external forces in the development of the territory. It will be a major folly to overlook the impact of global transformation on the territory's development. From a narrower angle, the nationalization perspective focuses on China's importance in determining Hong Kong's future and the Chineseness of the Hong Kong community. This perspective places emphasis on the continuing relevance of the state and the centrality of sovereignty in the contemporary world. It brings us down to earth by highlighting the power of nationalism and the pivotal role China plays in determining the future of the territory.

In examining two different ways of understanding Hong Kong's interactions with the global community, this overview points to limitations of both processes in analysing Hong Kong's changing interactions with the outside world. Hong Kong's colonial status and rampant commercialism generated complexities in the political psyche and cultural identity of the population which may in turn create barriers to the city's global character. The global perspective also fails to accommodate the China factor which clearly dominates current debates on Hong Kong's development. By placing too much emphasis on the importance of the China factor, the narrower nationalization view may have under-estimated the transformation of the Chinese polity and the impact of global forces on the perceptions and behavior of China's leaders. It also fails to note that the nationalization of Hong Kong is a two-way process of mutual influence.

In assessing the Hong Kong's international linkages, this essay supports arguments that while globalization has been associated with powerful economic forces, it should not be understood simply in economic terms, but a more comprehensive economic political, social, and ideological phenomenon "which carries with it unanticipated often contradictory and polarizing consequences."[47] Similarly the nationalization process should not be understood simply as a political force, but a far more complex phenomenon involving political, economic, social and cultural factors. The two processes are not necessarily mutually exclusive.

The Hong Kong question has emerged as a major issue in the international arena. Western leaders including US President Bill Clinton publicly expressed concern over the territory's future. President Clinton also met the leader of Hong Kong's Democratic Party, Martin Lee who has been denounced by the Beijing officials as seeking "the internationalization of Hong Kong" and "to invite foreign interference in the affairs of Hong Kong."[48] Maintaining its multiple international linkages is critical, if the Hong Kong SAR is to survive as an international city and commercial center in the region. But the reunification process is imposing major constraints on the territory. The balancing act of maintaining its openness on the one hand, and demonstrating its patriotic credentials to the Beijing government on the other is a delicate task. Ultimately, the SAR's international character may be determined by the globalization and nationalization processes which are shaping developments not only in Hong Kong, but also in mainland China.

Notes

1. In 1997, for example, with the exception of taxation (rated at 1.5), Hong Kong was rated 1 in all the categories (trade, taxation, foreign investment rights, banking, property regulation). The top 15 economies were: Hong Kong (1); Singapore (2), Bahrain (3); New Zealand (4); Switzerland (5); United States (6); U.K. (7); Taiwan (8); Bahamas (9) Netherlands (10); Canada (11); Czech Republic (12); Denmark (13); Japan (14); Luxembourg (15)

2. Immigration Department figures. See *South China Morning Post*, April 8, 1996.

3. For more detailed discussions see David Clarke, "A High Degree of Autonomy under the Basic Law", in Kathleen Cheek-Milby and Miron Mushkat, eds., *Hong Kong: The Challenge of Transformation* (Hong Kong: Centre of Asian Studies, University of Hong Kong, 1989); Michael Davis, *Constitutional Confrontation in Hong Kong* (London: Macmillan, 1989), chapter 5; see also Gerard Postiglione and James T H Tang, eds., *Hong Kong's Reunion with China: The Global Dimensions* (New York: M.E. Sharpe, forthcoming, 1997)

4. Joint Declaration of the Government of the United Kingdom of Great Britain and Northern Ireland and the Government of the People's Republic of China on the Question of Hong Kong (December 19, 1984), annex IX.

5. The Basic Law of the Hong Kong Special Administrative Region of the Peopleís Republic of China (April 4, 1990), article 151.

6. See annex of the Sino-British Joint Declaration and Chapter 7 of the Basic Law.

7. James T H Tang, "Hong Kong's International Status," *Pacific Review*, Vol. 6 No. 3, 1993, pp. 205–215.

8. Norman Miners, *The Government and Politics of Hong Kong* (Hong Kong: Oxford University Press, 5th ed., 1991), p. 244

9. Louis Kraar, "The Death of Hong Kong", *Fortune*, June 26, 1995, pp. 42–52.

10. See, for example, Ernst-Otto Czempiel and James N. Rosenau, *Global Changes and Theoretical Challenges: Approaches to World Politics for the 1990s* (Massachusetts: Lexington, 1989), Evan Luard, *The Globalization of Politics: The Changed Focus of Political Action in the Modern World* (London: Macmillan, 1990), Ernst-Otto Czempiel and James N. Rosenau, *Governance Without Government: Order and Change in World Politics* (Cambridge: Cambridge University Press, 1992), Matthew Horsman and Andrew Marshall, *After the Nation-State: Citizen, Tribalism and the New World Disorder* (London: Harper Collins, 1994), Linda Basch, Nina Glick Schiller, and Christina Szanton Blanc, *Nations Unbound: Transnational Projects, Postcolonial Predicaments, and Deterritorialized Nation-States* (Langhorne, Pa: Gordon and Breach, 1994), Geraint Parry, "Political life in an interdependence world", in *Politics in an Interdependent World: Essays Presented to Ghita Ionescu* (Aldershot: Edward Elgar, 1994).

11. James Rosenau, *Turbulence in World Politics: A Theory of Change and Continuity* (Princeton, NJ: Princeton University Press, 1990).

12. Geraint Parry, "Political life in an interdependence world", in *Politics in an Interdependent World: Essays Presented to Ghita Ionescu* (Aldershot: Edward Elgar, 1994), p. 1.

13. Peter F. Drucker, *Post-Capitalist Society* (New York: Harper Business, 1994), p. 4.

14. Kenichi Ohmae, *Borderless World: Power and Strategy in the Interlinked Economy* (New York: Harper Collins, 1990).

15. For an account of the problems of the world trading system from a free trade perspective prior to the establishment of the WTO see Jagdish Bhagwati, *The World Trading System at Risk* (Princeton: Princeton University Press, 1991)

16. WTO figures 1996.

17 The statistical information on the territory's importance as a major business center is obtained from Hong Kong Trade Development Council, *Economic and Trade Information on Hong Kong,* March 1, 1996.

18. TDC figures. See also *Annual Report on Hong Kong 1995 to Parliament,* presented by the Secretary of State for Foreign and Commonwealth Affairs, March 1996, pp. 13–15.

19. TDC and Hong Kong Airport Authority figures.

20. TDC and Hong Kong government figures.

21. TDC and government figures.

22. See *The Services Sector: Support and Promotion,* presented as an addendum in the Financial Secretary's 1996–97 Budget.

23. James T H Tang, "Hong Kong's International Status", *Pacific Review*, Vol. 6 No. 3, 1993, pp. 205–215

24. *Yearbook of International Organizations,* 1993/1994 (Munchen: K.G. Saur, 1993)

25. See Notes for the Legislative Council presented to the Constitutional Affairs Panel: *Joint Liaison Group: Achievements in the Past Ten Years,* November 1995. Hong Kong's participation in multilateral agreements and international organizations is also recorded in the government's annual report. The US State Department's annual report on Hong Kong also contains similar information.

26. Information from Hong Kong government. See also "Hong Kong's International

Rights and Obligations", speech by the Chief Secretary, Mrs Anson Chan, at the LawAsia Business Law, Conference, Thursday, March 28, 1996

27. Ambrose Y.C. King, "The administrative absorption of politics in Hong Kong", *Asian Survey*, Vol. 15, 1975.

28. See for example the 1997 US State Department Report on Hong Kong as required by the US-Hong Kong Policy Act. State Department, March 31, 1997. See also, James T.H. Tang, "Hong Kong in US-China Relations", forthcoming, *Journal of Contemporary China Studies.*

29. One account of the attitudes and policies of major countries in the world is in Gerald Segal, *The Fate of Hong Kong* (London: Simon & Schuster, 1993). See also Kim Richard Nossal, "Playing the international card: the view from Australia, Canada, and the United States", in Gerard Postiglione and James T H Tang, eds., *Hong Kong's Reunion with China: The Global Dimensions* (New York: M.E. Sharpe, forthcoming, 1997)

30. Michael Hunt, "Chinese national identity and the strong state: The Late Qing-Republican Crisis", in Lowell Dittmer and Samuel Kim, eds., *China's Quest for National Identity* (Ithaca: Cornell University Press, 1993)

31. See different views on the subject reported in "Panic Over Patriotism Push," *South China Morning Post,* April 7, 1996.

32. Deng Xiaoping's talk with British Prime Minister Margaret Thatcher, September 1982, *Deng Xiaoping on the Question of Hong Kong* (Hong Kong: New Horizon Press, 1993), pp. 1–2

33. A useful interpretive analysis of the nature of the Chinese communist revolution is: Lucien Bianco, *Origins of the Chinese Revolution, 1915–1949* (Stanford: Stanford University Press, 1971)

34. James T.H. Tang, *Britain's Encounter with Revolutionary China, 1949–1954* (London: Macmillan, 1992) p. 200

35. Lau Siu-kai and Kuan Hsin Chi, *The Ethos of the Hong Kong Chinese* (Hong Kong: Chinese University Press, 1988), p. 178–186

36. *Hong Kong 21: A Ten Year Vision and Agenda for Hong Kong's Economy,* a report presented by the Business and Professionals Federation of Hong Kong with the assistance of Booz Allen and Hamilton, May 1993.

37. TDC figures.

38. Hong Kong Trade Development Council, *Economic and Trade Information on Hong Kong,* 1 March 1996.

39. See Reginald Yin-Wing Kwok and Alvin Y. So, eds, *The Hong Kong-Guangdong Link: Partnership in Flux.* (Armonk, New York: M. E. Sharpe, 1995)

40. A useful account of the Chinese government's reaction to the Patten reform package and subsequent to set up a new set of political arrangements in Hong Kong is: Lo Chi-kin, "From 'Through Train' to 'Second Stove'" in Joseph Y S Cheng and Sonny Lo, eds., *From Colony to SAR: Hong Kong's Challenges Ahead* (Hong Kong: Chinese University Press, 1995), pp. 25–37.

41. Frederick Fung, chairman of the Association for the Promotion of Democracy and People's Livelihood, a pro-democracy party acceptable to Chinese government.

42. Article 23, Basic Law of Hong Kong SAR.

43. Civil Liberties and Social Order Consultation Document, Chief Executive's Office, Hong Kong Special Administrative Region, the People's Republic of China, April 1997.

44. A solid analysis of the China-Hong Kong economic links is in Yun-wing Sung, *The China-Hong Kong Connection* (Cambridge: Cambridge University Press, 1991)

45. See the special issue on Greater China, *The China Quarterly,* no. 136, December 1993.

46. Lynn White and Li Cheng, "China's Coast Identities: Regional, National and Global" in Lowell Dittmer and Samuel Kim, eds., *China's Quest for National Identity* (Ithaca: Cornell University Press, 1993)

47. Claire Turenne Sjolander, "The rhetoric of globalization: what's in a wor(l)d?", *International Journal*, Vol. LI, Autumn 1996, p. 604.

48. For President Clinton, Vice-President Gore, and Secretary of State Madeleine Albright's meeting with Lee in Washington on April 19 & 16, 1997, see *South China Morning Post*, April 19 & 16, 1997. For the PRC official condemnation of Lee, see *Sing Tao Daily*, April 16, 1997.

Bibliography

Adams, J.S. "Interview with Sir Percy Cradock," *Asian Affairs: Journal of the Royal Society for Asian Affairs* 26, 1995, p. 9.

Basch, Linda, Schiller, Nina Glick and Blanc, Christina Szanton. *Nations Unbound: Transnational Projects, Postcolonial Predicaments, and Deterritorialized Nation-States.* Langhorne, Pa: Gordon and Breach, 1994.

Bennett, Lance. "Toward a Theory of Press-State Relations in the United States," *Journal of Communication* 40, 2, 1990, pp. 103–125.

Berlin, Isaiah. *Four Essays on Liberty.* Oxford: Oxford University Press, 1969.

Bhagwati, Jagdish. *The World Trading System at Risk.* Princeton: Princeton University Press, 1991.

Bian, Yanjie. "Guanxi and the Allocation of Urban Jobs in China," *The China Quarterly*, 140, December 1994, pp. 991–998.

Bianco, L. *Origins of the Chinese Revolution, 1915–1949.* Stanford, Calif.: Stanford University Press, 1971.

Blyth, Sally and Wotherspoon, Ian. *Hong Kong Remembers.* Hong Kong: Oxford University Press, 1996.

Boyd, Monica. "Family and Personal Networks in International Migration: Recent Developments and New Agendas," *International Migration Review* 33.3, 1989, pp. 638–663.

Burns, John P. "Administrative Reform in a Changing Political Environment: The Case of Hong Kong," *Public Administration and Development* 14, 1994, pp. 241–252.

———. "Hong Kong in 1992: The Struggle for Authority," *Asian Survey* 33, January 1993, pp. 22–31.

———. "Hong Kong in 1993: The Struggle for Authority Intensifies," *Asian Survey* 34, 1994, pp. 55–63.

Bynes, Andrew and Chan, Johannes, eds. *Public Law and Human Rights: A Hong Kong Sourcebook.* Hong Kong: Butterworths, 1993.

Caporaso, James A. and Levine, David P. *Theories of Political Economy.* New York: Cambridge University Press, 1992.

Chan, Johannes. "Representation in Dispute," *China Rights Forum,* Winter 1996, pp. 5–6.

Chan, Joseph Man and Lee, Chin-Chuan. *Mass Media and Political Transition: The Hong Kong Press in China's Orbit.* New York: Guilford Press, 1991.

———., Lee, Paul Siu-nam and Lee, Chin-Chuan. *Hong Kong Journalists in Transition.* Hong Kong: Hong Kong Center of Asia-Pacific Studies, The Chinese University of Hong Kong, 1996.

Chan, Ming K. "All in the Family: The Hong Kong-Guangdang Link in Historical Perspective," in *The Hong Kong-Guangdong Link: Partnership in Flux,* eds. Reginald Y. Kwok and Alvin Y. So. Armonk, New York: M.E. Sharpe, 1995, pp. 31–63.

———. "Decolonization without Democracy: The Birth of Pluralistic Politics in Hong Kong," in *The Politics of Democratization: Generalizing East Asian Experiences.* ed. Edward Friedman. Boulder: Westview Press, 1994, pp. 161–181.

———. "Democracy Derailed: Realpolitik in the Making of the Hong Kong Basic Law, 1985–90," in *The Hong Kong Basic Law: Blueprint for 'Stability and Prosperity' under Chinese Sovereignty?* eds. Ming K. Chan and David Clark. Armonk, New York: M.E. Sharpe, 1991.

———. *Global Dimensions of Hong Kong's Transition Toward 1997.* Milwaukee: University of Wisconsin-Marquetee University Center for International Studies Occasional Paper #95–03, June 1995.

———, ed. *Precarious Balance: Hong Kong Between China and Britain, 1842–1992.* Armonk, New York, M.E. Sharpe, 1994.

———. "The 1991 Elections in Hong Kong: Democratization in the shadow of Tiananmen," in *China in Transition: Economic Political and Social Developments,* ed. George T. Yu. Lanham: University Press of America, 1993, pp. 229–250.

———. "Under China's Shadow: Realpolitik of Hong Kong Labour Unionism Toward 1997," in *Politics and Society in Hong Kong Towards 1997,* ed. Charles Burton. Toronto: University of Toronto-York University Joint Centre for Asia Pacific Studies, 1992.

———. and Clarks, David, eds. *The Hong Kong Basic Law: Blueprint for "Stability and Prosperity" Under Chinese Sovereignty?* Armonk, New York: M. E. Sharpe, 1991.

————. and Lau, Tuen-yu. "Dilemma of the Communist Press in a Pluralistic Society: Hong Kong in the Transition to Chinese Sovereignty, 1988–1989," *Asian Survey* 30, 1990, pp. 731–747.

Chen, Albert H. Y. "Questions of Law and Order," *South China Morning Post*, January 30, 1997, p. 17.

Chen, Jiakang. "Louis Cha on Yu Pun-hoi," *Eastweek*, (Note 77) 1995.

Cheng, Joseph Y. S. "Sino-British Negotiations and Problems of the British Administration," Paper presented to the Conference on Hong Kong and its Pearl River Delta Hinterland: Links to China, Links to the World, at the University of British Columbia, Vancouver, May 1995,

————. and Lo, Sonny S. H., eds. *From Colony to SAR: Hong Kong's Challenges Ahead.* Hong Kong: Chinese University Press, 1995.

Cheng, S.L. *"Hong Kong on a Plate"* M. Phil thesis, Department of Sociology, University of Hong Kong, 1995.

Cheung, A.B.L. "The Civil Service," in *The Other Hong Kong Report 1991*, eds. Sung Yun-wing and Lee Ming-kwan. Hong Kong: Chinese University Press, 1991.

Ching, Frank. "Implementation of the Sino-British Joint Declaration," in *The Other Hong Kong Report 1992*, eds. Joseph Y.S. Cheng and Paul C. K. Kwong. Hong Kong: Chinese University Press, 1992.

————. "Politics, Politicians and Political Parties," in *The Other Hong Kong Report 1993*, eds. Po-King Choi and Lok-sang Ho. Hong Kong: The Chinese University Press, 1993, pp. 23–37.

————. "Time for Hong Kong Conciliation," *Far Eastern Economic Review*, January 19, 1995, p. 29.

————. "Toward Colonial Sunset: The Wilson Regime, 1987–92," in *Precarious Balance: Hong Kong Between China and Britain, 1842–1992*, ed. Ming K. Chan. Armonk, New York: ME Sharpe, 1994, pp. 189–191.

Choi, Po-king. "Popular Culture," in *The Other Hong Kong Report, 1990*, eds. Richard Y.C. Wong and Joseph Y.S. Cheng. Hong Kong: The Chinese University Press, 1990.

Chomsky, Noam. *Necessary Illusions*. Boston: South End Press, 1989.

Chull, Shin Doh. "On the Third Wave of Democratization: A Synthesis of Recent Theory and Research," *World Politics* 47, 1994, pp. 135–170.

Chung, Robert Ting-yiu, ed. *Pop Press*. Hong Kong: Social Science Research Centre, University of Hong Kong 3, 3, November 1996.

————. "Public Opinion," in *The Other Hong Kong Report 1993*, eds. Donald H. McMillen and Si-Wai Man. Hong Kong: The Chinese University Press, 1994, pp. 103–123.

Civil Service Branch, Hong Kong Government. *Human Resource Management*. Hong Kong: Government Printer, 1995.

Clark, David J. "A High Degree of Autonomy under the Basic Law," in *Hong Kong: The Challenge of Transformation*, eds. Kathleen Cheek-Milby and

Miron Mushkat. Hong Kong: Centre of Asian Studies, University of Hong Kong, 1989.

Cohen, Stanley and Young, Jock, eds. *The Manufacture of News*. Beverly Hills, Ca: Sage, 1981.

Conner, Alison W. "Final Appeal Court Proposal Stirs Controversy in Hong Kong," *East Asian Executive Reports*, November 1991.

Cottrell, Robert. *The End of Hong Kong: The Secret Diplomacy of Imperial Retreat*. London: John Murray, 1993.

Cradock, Percy. *Experiences of China*. London: John Murray, 1994.

Czempiel, Ernst-Otto, and Rosenau, James N. *Governance without Government: Order and Change in World Politics*. Cambridge: Cambridge University Press, 1992.

Czempiel, Ernst-Otto and Rosenau, James N. *Global Changes and Theoretical Challenges: Approaches to World Politics for the 1990s*. Massachusetts: Lexington, 1989.

Dahlgren, Peter. *Television and the Public Space*. London: Sage, 1995.

Davis, Michael. *Constitutional Confrontation in Hong Kong*. London: Macmillan, 1989.

Davies, Simon T. "Hong Kong Broadcasting," in *The Other Hong Kong Report 1993*, eds. Po-King Choi and Lik-sang Ho. Hong Kong: Chinese University Press, 1993.

de Mesquita, Bruce Buneo, Newman, David and Rabushka, Alvin. *Red Flag Over Hong Kong*. Chatham, New Jersey: Chatham House Publishers, 1996.

DeGolyer, Michael. "Politics, Politicians, and Political Parties," in *The Other Hong Kong Report 1993*, eds. Donald H. McMillen and Si-Wai Man. Hong Kong: The Chinese University Press, pp. 75–101.

——— and Scott, Janet Lee. "The Myth of Political Apathy in Hong Kong," *The Annuals of the American Academy of Political Science,* Vol. 547. *The Future of Hong Kong*, September 1996, pp. 68–78.

Deng Xiaoping. *Deng Xiaoping on the Question of Hong Kong*. Hong Kong: New Horizon Press, 1993.

Deyo, Frederic C. *Beneath the Miracle: Labor Subordination in the New Asia Periphery*. Berkeley: University of California Press, 1990.

Dittmer, Lowell. "The Politics of Publicity in Reform China," in *China's Media, Media's China*, ed. Chin-Chuan Lee. Boulder: Westview Press, 1994.

Donohue, George A., Tichenor, Phillip and Olien, Clarice. "A Guard Dog Perspective on the Role of Media," *Journal of Communication* 45, 2, 1995, pp. 115–132.

Donsbach, Wolfang and Klcft, Bettina. "Subjective Objectivity. How Journalists in Four Countries Define a Key Term of their Profession," *Gazette* 51, 1993, pp. 53–83.

Dreier, Peter. "The Position of the Press in the U.S. Power Structure," *Social Forces* 29, 1982, pp. 298–310.

Drucker, Peter F. *Post-Capitalist Society.* New York: Harper Business, 1994.

Dykes, Philip. "The Hong Kong Bill of Rights 1991: Its Origin, Content and Impact," in *The Hong Kong Bill of Rights: A Comparative Approach,* eds. Johannes Chan and Yash Ghai. Hong Kong: Butterworths, 1993, pp. 40–41.

Economist Intelligence Unit, *Country Report: Hong Kong, Macau.* London: Economic Intelligence Unit, 1994.

Elliot, Dorinda. "Betrayed?" *Newsweek,* May 13, 1996. pp. 37–38.

Entman, Robert M. *Democracy without Citizens: Media and the Decay of American Politics.* New York: Oxford University Press, 1989.

Fan Zhongliu. "A Rugged Road for the Democratic Party After 1997," *Hong Kong Economic Journal,* January 10, 1997, p. 23.

Fanon, Frantz. *Wretched of the Earth.* Harmondsworth: Penguin, 1967.

Fishman, Mark. *Manufacturing the News.* Austin: University of Texas Press, 1980.

Forney, Matt. "Coming to Get You," *Far Eastern Economic Review,* October 31, 1996.

Freeman, Michael. *Lecture on Self Determination.* Faculty of Law, University of Hong Kong, December 1995.

Frieberg, J. W. *The French Press: Class, State and Ideology.* New York: Praeger, 1981.

Fung, Anthony and Lee, Chin-Chuan. "Hong Kong's Changing Media Ownership: Uncertainty and Dilemma," *Gazette* 53, 1994, pp. 127–133.

Gans, Herbert. *Deciding What's News.* New York: Pantheon, 1979.

Gargan, Edward. "New Jitters from Hong Kong: In Economics, as in Politics, China Exerts Control," *New York Times,* May 18, 1996, pp. 17–18.

Ghai, Yash. "Back to Basics: The Provisional Legislature and the Basic Law," *Hong Kong Law Journal 25,* 1995, pp. 6–7.

———. "The Bill of Rights and the Basic Law: Inconsistent or Complementary?" in *Hong Kong's Bill of Rights: 1991–1994 and Beyond,* eds. George Edwards and Andrew Byrnes. Hong Kong: University of Hong Kong, Faculty of Law, 1995, pp. 53–67.

Gilley, Bruce. "Shoe-In's Challenge," *Far Eastern Economic Review,* November 28, 1996, p. 24.

Gitlin, Todd. *The Whole World is Watching.* Berkeley: University of California Press, 1980.

Gold, Thomas. "Go with Your Feelings: Hong Kong and Taiwan Popular Culture in Greater China," *The China Quarterly* 136, 1993. pp. 907–925.

Goldstein, Carl. "Hong Kong Past and Future," text of speech given at St. Johns University, Minnesota, May 1, 1996.

Gosling, Peter L.A. "Changing Chinese Identities in Southeast Asia: An Introductory Review," in *The Chinese in Southeast Asia,* eds. Peter L.A. Gosling and Linca Y.D. Lim. Singapore: Maruzen Asia, Vol. 2, 1983, pp. 1–14.

Government Information Services. *Hong Kong 1995.* Hong Kong: Government Printer, 1995.

————. *Hong Kong 1996*. Hong Kong: Government Printer, 1996.

Guldin, Gregory Eliyu. "Multilineal Modernity: Ideologies of Modernization in Hong Kong," *Proceedings of the 2nd International Symposium on Asian Studies*, 1980, Vol. 1, pp. 69–86.

————. "Toward A Greater Guangdong: Hong Kong's Sociocultural Impact on the Pearl River Delta and Beyond," in *The Hong Kong-Guangdong Link: Partnership in Flux*, eds. Reginald Yin-wang Kwok and Alvin Y. So. Armonk, New York: M.E. Sharpe, 1995.

Hallin, Daniel. *The 'Uncensored' War*. New York: Oxford University Press, 1986.

Harding, Harry. "The Concept of Greater China: Themes, Variations and Reservations," *The China Quarterly* 136, 1993, pp. 660–686.

Harris, Peter. *Hong Kong: A Study in Bureaucratic Politics*. Hong Kong: Heinemann Asia, 1978.

Herman, Edward and Chomsky, Noam. *Manufacturing Consent*. New York: Pantheon, 1988.

Ho, Leung-mou. "China News in the Hong Kong Press," M. Phil thesis, Chinese University of Hong Kong, 1996.

Hong Kong Journalists Association. "China's Challenge: Freedom of Expression in Hong Kong," Annual report, 1996.

Hong Kong Voices. *Corporate Hong Kong: Beyond 1997, Views of Business Executives, Government Leaders and Journalists*. St. Helena, Ca: The Global Group, 1996.

Horsman, Matthew and Marshall, Andrew. *After the Nation-State: Citizen, Tribalism and the New World Disorder*. London: Harper Collins, 1994.

House of Commons, Foreign Affairs Committee. *Relations Between the United Kingdom and China in the Period up to and Beyond 1997*. London: Her Majesty's Stationery Office, March 23, 1994.

Hu Sheng. *Imperialism and Chinese Politics*. Beijing: Foreign Language Press, 1953.

Huang, Wenfang. "To Secure the Confidence of Hong Kong People," *Ming Pao*, May 2, 1995.

Hunt, Michael. "Chinese National Identity and the Strong State: The Late Qing-Republican Crisis", in *China's Quest for National Identity*, eds. Lowell Dittmer and Samuel Kim. Ithaca: Cornell University Press, 1993.

Huntington, Samuel. *The Third Wave: Democratization in Late Twentieth Century*. Norman: University of Oklahoma Press, 1991.

Isaacs, Harold. *Stretches on Our Minds: American Views of China and India*. New York: John Day Co., 1958.

Jayawickrama, Nihal. "'One Country, Two Systems' and the Law: Illusion or Reality," in *One Culture, Many Systems*, eds. Donald H. McMillen and Michael E. DeGolyer. Hong Kong: The Chinese University Press, 1993, pp. 46–47.

————. "Public Law," in *The Law In Hong Kong, 1969–1989*, ed. Raymond Wacks. Hong Kong: Oxford University Press, 1990, pp. 107–108.

————. "The Bill of Rights," in *Human Rights in Hong Kong*, ed. Raymond Wacks. Hong Kong: Oxford University Press, 1992, pp. 65–71.

Ji Wen. "Hong Kong Media," *Nineties Monthly*, February 1995, pp. 94–95.

Journalist. "From a Cold-War Outpost to a Bridge for Mutual Flow Across the Strait," *Open*, May 1995, pp. 42–43.

Ju, Zhong. "Assumptions Behind Commentaries on Taiwan," *Hong Kong Economic Journal*, July 13–14, 1995.

————. "Listen to the Voices of People on Taiwan," *Hong Kong Economic Journal*, June 20–21, 1995.

Kairys, David. "Freedom of Speech," in *The Politics of Law: A Progressive View*, ed. David Kairys. New York: Pantheon, 1982.

King, Ambrose Y. C. "Administrative Absorption of Politics: Emphasis on the Grass Roots Level," *Asian Survey* 15, 1975, pp. 422–439.

————. "The Hong Kong Talks and Hong Kong Politics," in *Hong Kong: A Chinese and International Concern*, eds. Jurgen Domes and Yu-ming Shaw. Boulder: Westview Press, 1988.

Kocher, R. "Bloodhounds or Missionaries: Role Definitions of German and British Journalists," *European Journal of Communication* 1, 1986, pp. 46–65.

Kraar, Louis. "The Death of Hong Kong", *Fortune*, June 26, 1995, pp. 42–52.

Kuan, Hsin-Chi. "Power Dependence and Democratic Transition: The Case of Hong Kong," *The China Quarterly* 128, 1991, pp. 775–793.

Kwok, Reginald Yin-wang and So, Alvin Y., eds. *Hong Kong-Guangdong Link: Partnership in Flux.* Armonk, New York: M.E. Sharpe, 1995.

Kwong, Kevin. "High Price for Telling the Truth," *South China Morning Post* (Int. Weekly), February 17, 1996, p. 11.

Lai, Tse han, Myers, Ramon and Wou, Wei. *A Tragic Beginning: The Taiwan Uprising of February 28, 1947.* Stanford: Stanford University Press, 1991.

Lam, Jermain T.M. "Chris Patten's Constitutional Reform Package: Implications for Hong Kong's Political Transition," *Issues and Studies* 29, 7, 1993, pp. 55–72.

————. "Failure of Sino-British Talks over Hong Kong: Consequences and Implications," *Issues and Studies* 30, 1994, pp. 95–115.

————. "From a Submissive to an Adversarial Legislature: The Changing Role of the Hong Kong Legislative Council in the Political Transition," *Asian Profile* 22, 1994, pp. 21–32.

————. "The Last Legislative Council Election in Hong Kong: Implications and Consequences," *Issues and Studies* 31, 12, 1995, pp. 68–82.

————. and Lee, Jane C.Y. *The Political Culture of the Voters in Hong Kong: Part Two, A Study of the Geographical Constituencies of the Legislative Council.* Hong Kong: City Polytechnic of Hong Kong, 1992.

Lam, Kam. "Finding Legal Reason Difficult to Follow," *South China Morning Post*, December 19, 1996, p. 18.

Lang, Kurt and Lang, Gladys. *Batting for Public Opinion.* New York: Columbia University Press, 1981.

Lau, Siu-kai, "Hong Kong's Path of Democratization," *Asiatische Studien Etudes Asiatiques* 49, 1995, pp. 71–90.

————. "Hong Kong People's View of the Government," *Wide Angle*, 238, 1992.

————. "HongKongese or Chinese: The Problem of Identity on the Eve of Resumption of Chinese Sovereignty over Hong Kong," unpublished paper, 1996.

————. *Society and Politics in Hong Kong*. Hong Kong: Chinese University Press, 1982.

———— and Kuan, Hsin-chi. *The Ethos of the Hong Kong Chinese*. Hong Kong: Chinese University Press, 1988.

Law, Connie. "Beijing asks for information on who is staying after '97," *South China Morning Post*, December 10, 1995.

Law, Stephen Shing-yan. "The Constitutionality of the Provisional Legislature," *Hong Kong Law Journal* 26, 1996, pp. 153–54.

Lee, Chin-Chuan. "Ambiguities and Contradictions: Issues in China's Changing Political Communication," in *China's Media, Media's China*, ed. Chin-Chuan Lee. Boulder: Westview Press, 1994.

————. "Conglomeration, Professionalism, and Strategic Rituals: The Hong Kong Press and Political Transition," in *Power, Money, and Media: Communication Patterns in Greater China*, ed. Chin-Chuan Lee (in preparation).

————. "Partisan Press Coverage of Government News in Hong Kong," *Journalism Quarterly* 62, 1985, pp. 770–776.

————. "Sparking a Fire: The Press and the Ferment of Democratic Change in Taiwan," *Journalism Monographs*, No. 138, 1993.

———— and Chan, Joseph Man. "Government Management of the Press in Hong Kong," *Gazette* 46, 1990, pp. 125–139.

———— and Chan, Joseph Man. "The Hong Kong Press in China's Orbit: Thunder of Tiananmen," in *Voices of China: The Interplay of Politics and Journalism*, ed. Chin-Chuan Lee. New York: Guilford Press, 1990.

Lee, Jane C.Y. "Campaigning Themes of the Candidates in the 1991 Legislative Council Election," in *Hong Kong Tried Democracy: The 1991 Elections in Hong Kong*, eds. Lau, Siu-Kai and Kin-Shuen Louie. Hong Kong: Hong Kong Institute of Asia-Pacific Studies, The Chinese University of Hong Kong, 1993.

————. "The Emergence of Party Politics in Hong Kong, 1982–92," in *25 Years of Social and Economic Development in Hong Kong*, eds. Benjamin K.P. Leung and Teresa Y.C. Wong. Hong Kong: Centre of Asian Studies, the University of Hong Kong, 1994.

————. "Political Accountability of Senior Civil Servants in Hong Kong: A Study of the Bureaucrat-Politician Relationship," Paper prepared for the International Conference on the Quest for Excellence: Public Administration in the Nineties, City Polytechnic of Hong Kong, February 26, 1994.

———. and Cheung, Anthony B.L. eds. *Public Sector Reform in Hong Kong: Key Concepts, Program-to-Date and Future Directions.* Hong Kong: Chinese University Press, 1995.

Lee, Lai To. *The Reunification of China: PRC-Taiwan Relations in Flux.* New York: Praeger, 1991.

Lee, Ming-kwan. "Community and Identity in Transition in Hong Kong," in *The Hong Kong-Guangdong Link: Partnership in Flux,* eds. Reginald Y. Kwok and Alvin Y. So. Armonk, New York: M.E. Sharpe, 1995, pp. 119–132.

———. "Issue-Positions in the 1991 Legislative Council Election," in *Hong Kong Tried Democracy: The 1991 Elections in Hong Kong,* eds. Siu-kai Lau and Kin-Shuen Louie. Hong Kong: Hong Kong Institute of Asia-Pacific Studies, The Chinese University of Hong Kong, 1993.

Leung, K.K. "The Basic Law and the Problem of Political Transition," in *The Other Hong Kong Report 1995,* eds. Stephen Y.L. Cheung and Stephen M.H. Sze. Hong Kong: Chinese University Press, 1995, pp. 33–49.

Leung, Sai-wing. "The 'China Factor' in the 1991 Legislative Council Election," in *Hong Kong Tried Democracy: The 1991 Elections in Hong Kong,* eds. Siu-kai Lau and Kin-shuen Louie, Hong Kong: Hong Kong Institute of Asia-Pacific Studies, The Chinese University of Hong Kong,1993.

Li, Fln, Jowett, A.J., Findlay, A.M., Skeldon, Ronald. "Talking Migration: An Interpretation of the Migration Intentions of Hong Kong Engineers and Doctors," *Applied Population Research Unit Discussion Paper,* no. 1. University of Glasgow, 1994.

Li, Gladys. "Argument Leads Back to Same Absurd Result" (Letter to the Editor), *South China Morning Post,* November 7, 1996, p. 18.

———. "Must Find Legal and Constitutional Solution" (Letter to the Editor), *South China Morning Post,* August 21, 1996, p. 14.

Li, Pang-kwong. "Elections, Politicians, and Electoral Politics," in *The Other Hong Kong Report 1995,* eds. Stephen Y.L. Cheung and Stephen M.H. Sze. Hong Kong: The Chinese University Press, 1995, pp. 51–65.

Li, Ruhai and Zhu, Qingfang. *Zhongguo gongwuyuan guanlixue [Chinese civil servant management]* Beijing: Falu chubanshe, 1993.

Liang, Yu-ying. "Beijing Set on Establishing a Provisional Legislature in Hong Kong," *Issues and Studies* 31, 1, 1995, pp. 101–102.

———. "Preparatory Committee Established for Hong Kong SAR," *Issues and Studies* 32, 1, 1996, pp. 122–124.

Liao, Gailong. "The '1980 Reform' Program in China, Part IV," in *Policy Conflicts in Post-Mao China: A Documentary Survey with Analysis,* eds. John P. Burns and Stanley Rosen. Armonk, New York: M.E. Sharpe, 1986, pp. 87–102.

Lin, You-lan. *History of the Hong Kong Press.* Taipei: World, 1997.

Lo, Chi-kin. "Constitution and Administration," in *The Other Hong Kong Report 1995.* Stephen Y.L. Cheung and Stephen M.H. Sze, eds. Hong Kong: The Chinese University Press, 1995, pp. 1–12.

Lo, Shiu-hing. *Political Development in Macau.* Hong Kong: Chinese University Press, 1995.

———. "The Problem of Perception and Sino-British Relations Over Hong Kong," *Contemporary Southeast Asia* 13, 1991, pp. 200–219.

———. "The Politics of Cooptation in Hong Kong: A Study of the Basic Law Drafting Process," *Asian Journal of Public Administration* 14, 1992, pp. 3–24.

——— and McMillen, Donald Hugh, "A Profile of the 'Pro-China Hong Kong Elites': Images and Perceptions," *Issues and Studies* 31, 6, 1995, pp. 98–127.

Loh, Christine. "Chance to Discuss the Basic Problems," *South China Morning Post* (Int. Weekly), June 24, 1995, p. 10.

———. "Keeping Up the Fight," *South China Morning Post*, December 7, 1996, p. 19.

Luard, Evan. *The Globalization of Politics: The Changed Focus of Political Action in the Modern World.* London: Macmillan, 1990.

Lui, Ta-lok. "Two Logics of Community Politics: Residents' Organizations and the 1991 Election," in *Hong Kong Tried Democracy: The 1991 Elections in Hong Kong*, eds. Siu-kai Lau and Kin-shuen Louie. Hong Kong: Hong Kong Institute of Asia-Pacific Studies, The Chinese University of Hong Kong, 1993.

Lui, Terry. "Changing Civil Servants' Values," in *The Hong Kong Civil Service: Personnel Policies and Practices*, eds. Ian Scott and John P. Burns. Hong Kong: Oxford University Press, 1988, pp. 139–140.

Luk, Bernard. "Reactions to Patten's Constitutional Proposals," *Canada and Hong Kong Update* 8, 1992.

Ma, Josephine. "Bankruptcy Law in Doubt," *South China Morning Post*, February 12, 1996.

Madsen, Richard. *China and the American Dream.* Berkeley: University of California Press, 1995.

Man, Cheuk-fei. "How Did Xinhua Launch its Propaganda Work Through the Leftist Newspapers (1949–1982)?" *Hong Kong Economic Journal Monthly*, 226, January 1996, pp. 10–17.

Manoff, Robert K. and Schudson, Michael, eds. *Reading the News.* New York: Pantheon, 1986.

Massey, Douglas S. "Social Structure, Household Strategies and the Cumulative Causation of Migration," *Population Index 56*, 1, Spring 1990, pp. 3–26.

Maxwell, Neville. "Britain Backs Off," *Far Eastern Economic Review*, November 9, 1995.

McManus, John H. *Market-driven Journalism.* Thousand Oaks, Ca: Sage, 1994.

Miners, Norman. *The Government and Politics of Hong Kong.* Hong Kong: Oxford University Press, 5th ed., 1991.

———. "Constitution and Administration," in *The Other Hong Kong Report 1993*, eds. Po-King Choi and Lok-sang Ho. Hong Kong: The Chinese University Press, 1993, pp. 1–37.

————. "The Transformation of the Hong Kong Legislative Council 1970–1994: From Consensus to Confrontation," *The Asian Journal of Public Administration* 16, 1994, pp. 224–248.

Ministry of Personnel. *Provisional Regulations on Civil Servants.* Beijing: Ministry of Personnel, 1993.

Mitchell, Robert E. "How Hong Kong Newspapers Have Responded to 15 Years of Rapid Social Change," *Asian Survey* 9, 1969, pp. 673–678.

Mueller, Richards W. "America's Long-term Interest in Hong Kong," *The Annals of the American Academy of Political and Social Science*, 547, September 1996, pp. 144–152.

Mushkat, Roda. *One Country, Two International Legal Personalities: The Case of Hong Kong.* Hong Kong: Hong Kong University Press, 1997.

Nee, Victor. "Peasant Entrepreneurship and the Politics of Regulation in China," in *Remaking the Economic Institutions of Socialism: China and Eastern Europe*, eds. Victor Nee and David Stark. Stanford: Stanford University Press, 1989, pp. 169–207.

Ng, Catherine. "Plea for Neutral Civil Service" *South China Morning Post*, April 1, 1996.

Ng, Sek-hong and Cheng, Soo-may. "The Affluent Migrants as a Class Phenomenon: The Hong Kong Case," in *Inequalities and Development: Social Stratification in Chinese Societies*, eds. Siu-kai Lau, Ming-kwan Lee, Po-san Wan and Siu-lun Wong. Hong Kong Institute of Asia Pacific Studies, Chinese University of Hong Kong, 1994. pp. 171–204

No, Kwai-yan. "Britain Warned It Must Give Archives to China," *South China Morning Post*, December 9, 1995.

Nossal, Kim Richard. "Playing the International Card: The Wiew from Australia, Canada, and the United States," in *Hong Kong's Reunion with China: the Global Dimensions*, eds. Gerard Postiglione and James T. H. Tang. Armonk, New York: M.E. Sharpe, forthcoming, 1997.

O' Brien, Kevin. "Agents and Remonstrators: Role Accumulation by Chinese People's Congress Deputies," *The China Quarterly* 138, June 1995, pp. 359–380.

O'Donnell, Guillermo A. *Modernization and Bureaucratic-Authoritarianism.* Berkeley: Institute of International Studies, University of California, 1973.

Okensberg, Michel, Sullivan, Lawrence, and Lambert, Marc, eds. *Beijing Spring, 1989, Confrontation and Conflict: The Basic Documents.* Armonk, New York: M.E. Sharpe, 1990.

Parry, Geraint. "Political Life in an Interdependence World," in *Politics in an Interdependent World: Essays Presented to Ghita Ionescu.* Aldershot: Edward Elgar, 1994.

Patten, Christopher. "Governor Patten's Policy Speech to Legco," *Canada and Hong Kong Update* 8, 1992.

————. *Our Next Five Years: The Agenda for Hong Kong* (Address by Governor Chris Patten to the opening session of the Legislative Council on October 7, 1992) Hong Kong: Government Printer, 1992.

Patterson, Thomas E. and Donsbach, Wolfgang. "Press-Party Parallelism: A Cross-National Comparison," presented at the International Communication Association conference, Washington, D.C., May 28, 1993.

Pepper, Suzanne. "Hong Kong in 1994: Democracy, Human Rights, and the Post-Colonial Political Order," *Asian Survey* 35, 1, January 1995, pp. 48–60.

Pool, Ithiel de sola. *Prestige Papers*. Stanford: Stanford University Press, 1952.

Postiglione, Gerard and Tang, James T. H., eds., *Hong Kong's Reunion with China: The Global Dimensions*. Armonk, New York: M.E. Sharpe, forthcoming, 1997.

Qi, Xin (Lee Yee). "To the Granddaddy Up there, Yours Little Servant Confesses a Mistake," *Hong Kong Economic Journal*, October 18, 1993.

Roberti, Mark. *The Fall of Hong Kong: China's Triumph & British's Betrayal*. New York: John Wiley & Sons, revised edition, 1996.

————. *The Fall of Hong Kong*. New York: John Wiley & Sons, 1994.

Rosenau, James. *Turbulence in World Politics: A Theory of Change and Continuity*. Princeton, NJ: Princeton University Press, 1990.

Said, Edward W. *Covering Islam*. New York: Pantheon, 1981.

————. *Culture and Imperialism*. New York: Vintage Books, 1994.

Salaff, Janet W., Fong, Eric, and Wong, Siu-lun. "Using Social Networks to Emigrate from Hong Kong: How Present Directions Fortell the Future," Paper delivered at the Annual Meeting of the Association of Asian Studies, Hononlu, Hawaii, 1996.

Schlesinger, Peter. *Putting 'Reality' Together*. Beverly Hills, Ca: Sage, 1978.

Schudson, Michael. *Discovering the News*. New York: Basic, 1978.

Scott, Ian. "An Overview of the Hong Kong Legislative Council Elections of 1991," in *Votes Without Power: The Hong Kong Legislative Council Elections*, eds. Rowena Kwok, Joan Leung and Ian Scott. Hong Kong: Hong Kong University Press, 1992.

————. "Party Politics and Elections in Transitional Hong Kong," *Asian Journal of Political Science*, 4, 1, June 1996.

————. *Political Change and the Crisis of Legitimacy in Hong Kong*. Hong Kong: Oxford University Press, 1989.

————. "Political Transformation in Hong Kong: From Colony to Colony," in *The Hong Kong-Guangdong Link: Partnership in Flux*, eds. Reginald Y. Kwok and Alvin Y. So. Armonk, New York: M.E. Sharpe, 1995, pp. 189–223.

———— and Burns, John P., eds. *The Hong Kong Civil Service and Its Future*. Hong Kong: Oxford University Press, 1988.

———— and Burns, John P., eds. *The Hong Kong Civil Service: Personnel Policies and Practices*. Hong Kong: Oxford University Press, 1984.

Segal, Gerald. *The Fate of Hong Kong*. London: Simon & Schuster, 1993.

Seymour-Ure, Collin. *The Political Impact of Mass Media.* Beverly Hills, Ca: Sage, 1974.

Shu, Yufei. "The Hong Kong Times's Quarrel in Taipei," *Nineties Monthly,* March 1985.

Sing, Ming. "The Democracy Movement in Hong Kong, 1986–1990," D.Phil. thesis, University of Oxford, 1993.

Sjolander, Claire Turenne. "The rhetoric of globalization: what's in a wor(l)d?" *International Journal,* 51 Autumn 1996.

Skeldon, Ronald. "Emigration and the Future of Hong Kong," *Pacific Affairs* 63, 1990–91, pp. 500–523.

———. "Emigration, Immigration and Fertility Decline: Demographic Integration or Disintegration?" *The Other Hong Kong Report,* ed. Sung Yun-wing and Lee Ming-kwan. Hong Kong: The Chinese University Press, 1991, pp. 259–274.

———, ed. *Reluctant Exiles? Migration from Hong Kong and the New Overseas China.* Armonk, New York: M.E. Sharpe, 1994.

So, Alvin Y. "Western Sociological Theories and Hong Kong's New Middle Class," in *Discovery of the Middle Classes in East Asia,* ed. Michael Hsin-huang Hsiao. Taipei: Institute of Ethnology, Academia Sinica, 1993, pp. 219–245.

———. and Kwitko, Ludmilla. "The Transformation of Urban Movements in Hong Kong, 1970–90," *Bulletin of Concerned Asian Scholars* 24, 4, 1992, pp. 32–44.

So, Clement, Y. K. "Pre-1997 Hong Kong Press: Cut-throat Competition and the Changing Journalistic Paradigm," in *The Other Hong Kong Report 1996,* eds. Mee Kau Nyaw and Si-ming Li. Hong Kong: Chinese University Press, 1996.

———, Lee, Chin-Chuan and Fung, Anthony. "How Do Media Workers View Press Credibility?" *Ming Pao,* December 5, 1996, p. c5.

Song, Lingqi. "The Infighting between the two Leftist Papers," *Open,* May 1995, pp. 74–75.

Staniland, Martin. *What Is Political Economy?* New Haven: Yale University Press, 1985.

Suine, Karen. "The Political Role of Mass Media in Scandinavia," *Legislative Studies Quarterly* 12, 1987, pp. 395–415.

Sung, Yun-wing. *The China-Hong Kong Connection.* Cambridge: Cambridge University Press, 1991.

Sum, Ngai-ling. "More than a 'War of Words': Identity, Politics and the Struggle for Dominance During the Recent 'Political Reform' Period in Hong Kong," *Economy and Society* 24, 1995, pp. 67–100.

Tam, Camoes C.K. *Disputes Concerning Macau's Sovereignty Between China and Portugal (1553–1993).* Taipei: Yung-yeh Publishers, 1994.

Tam, Maria. "Youth Culture in Hong Kong: Re-rooting of an Identity," Paper delivered at the 1996 Annual Meeting of the Association of Asian Studies, Honolulu, Hawaii, 1996.

———. "Youth in Hong Kong: Re-Rooting of an Identity," Paper presented at the Annual Meeting of the Association for Asian Studies, Honolulu, April 1996, p. 9.

Tang, James T. H. *Britain's Encounter with Revolutionary China, 1949–1954.* London: Macmillan, 1992.

———. "Hong Kong's International Status", *Pacific Review* 6, 3, 1993, pp. 205–215.

———. and Ching, Frank. "The MacLehose-Youde Years: Balancing The "Three Legged Stool", 1971–86," in *Precarious Balance: Hong Kong Between China and Britain, 1842–1992*, ed. Ming K. Chan. Armonk, New York: M.E. Sharpe, 1994, pp. 149–172.

Tang, Stephen Lung-wai. "Political Markets, Competition, and the Return to Monopoly: Evolution amidst a Historical Tragedy," in *Hong Kong Tried Democracy: The 1991 Elections in Hong Kong*, eds. Siu-kai Lau and Kin-shuen Louie. Hong Kong: Hong Kong Institute of Asia-Pacific Studies, The Chinese University of Hong Kong, 1993.

Tien, Hung-mao & Chu, Yun-han, eds. *Yi jiu jiu qi quodu yu taigang quanxi (The 1997 Transition and Taiwan-Hong Kong Relations).* Taipei: Yeqiang chubanshe, 1996.

Tse, Patricia Wen-sei. "The Impact of 1997 on Political Apathy in Hong Kong," *Political Quarterly* 1995, pp. 210–220.

Tu, Weiming. "Cultural China: The Periphery as the Center," *Daedalus* 120, 2, 1991, pp. 1–32.

Tuchman, Gaye. *Making News.* New York: Free Press, 1978.

Walden, John. "Implementation of the Sino-British Joint Declaration," in *The Other Hong Kong Report 1993*, eds. Po-king Choi and Lok-sang Ho. Hong Kong: Chinese University Press, 1993.

Wallen, David and Manuel, Gren. "Patten Attacks Handover Tycoons," *South China Morning Post*, February 9, 1996.

Wang, Enbao. *Hong Kong, 1997.* Boulder: Lynne Rienner, 1995.

Watson, James L. *Emigration and the the Chinese Lineage: The Mans in Hong Kong and London.* Berkeley: University of California Press, 1975.

Weaver, David and Willhoit, G. Cleveland. *The American Journalist in the 1990s.* Mahwah, N.J.: Lawrence Erlbaum, 1996.

Wei Min, ed. *Taigang guanxi: jizhi ji fazhan (Taiwan-Hong Kong Relations: Mechanism and Development)* Taipei: Yeqiang chubanshe, 1996.

Weng, Byron S.J. "Mainland China, Taiwan and Hong Kong As International Actors," in *Hong Kong's Reunion with China: Global Dimensions*, eds. James Tang and Gerry Postiglione. Armonk, New York: M.E. Sharpe, 1997.

Wesley-Smith, Peter. *An Introduction to the Hong Kong Legal System.* Hong Kong: Oxford University Press, 1993.

————. *Constitutional and Administrative Law in Hong Kong.* Hong Kong: Longman Asia Limited, 1994.

————. "Judges and the Through Train," *Hong Kong Law Journal* 25, 1995.

White, Lynn T. III. "All the News: Structure and Politics in Shanghai's Reform Media," in *Voices of China: The Interplay of Politics and Journalism,* ed. Chin-Chuan Lee. New York: Guilford Press, 1990.

————. and Li Cheng. "China's Coast Identities: Regional, National and Global," in *China's Quest for National Identity,* eds. Lowell Dittmer and Samuel Kim. Ithaca: Cornell University Press, 1993.

Williams, Raymond. *Marxism and Literature.* New York: Oxford University Press, 1977.

Wong, Siu-lun. "Business and Politics in Hong Kong During the Transition," in *25 Years of Social and Economic Development in Hong Kong,* eds. Benjamin K.P. Leung and Teresa Y.C. Wong. Hong Kong: Centre of Asian Studies, University of Hong Kong, 1994, pp. 217–235.

and Salaff, Janet, "Network Capital," Typescript, 1996, accepting pending revisions to *British Journal of Sociology.*

————. "Political Attitudes and Identity," in *Emigration from Hong Kong,* ed. Ronald Skeldon. Hong Kong: Chinese University Press, 1995, pp. 147–175

Wu Jianfan. "Several Issues Concerning the Relationship between the Central Government of the People's Republic of China and the Hong Kong Special Administrative Region," *Journal of Chinese Law* 2, 1988, pp. 67–69.

Xiao Weiyun. "A Study of the Political System of the Hong Kong Special Administrative Region Under the Basic Law," *Journal of Chinese Law* 2, 1988, pp. 111–12.

Xu Jiatun. *Hong Kong Memoirs.* Hong Kong: United Daily News. 2-vols, 1994.

Yahuda, Michael. *Hong Kong: China's Challenge.* London: Routledge, 1996.

Yoon, Youngchul. "Political Transition and Press Ideology in South Korea, 1980–1989," Ph.D. dissertation, University of Minnesota, 1989.

Yu, Jinglu. "The Structure and Function of Chinese Television, 1979–1989," in *Voices of China: The Interplay of Politics and Journalism,* eds. Chin-Chuan Lee. New York: Guilford Press, 1990.

Zhang, Jiefeng, et al. *Bubian, Wushi Nian? Zhongyinggang Jiaoli Jibenfa [No Change, Fifty Years? China, Britain, and Hong Kong Wrestle with the Basic Law]* Hong Kong: Langchao Chubanse, 1991.

Zhang, Shengru. "Hu Xian (Sally Aw): The Tigress Who Inherits her Father's Fortune," *Next Magazine,* 257, Feb. 10, 1995, pp. 86–90.

————. "The Rise and Fall of Hu Xian," *Next Magazine,* 259, Feb. 24, 1995, pp. 102–108.

————. "The Tigress Who Turned the Paper Profitable," *Next Magazine,* 258, Feb. 17, 1995, pp. 98–104.

Index